CHINESE COMMUNISM IN 1927
CITY VS COUNTRYSIDE

CHINESE COMMUNISM IN 1927

CITY VS COUNTRYSIDE

HSIAO TSO-LIANG

The Chinese University of Hong Kong

Hong Kong

Printed in Hong Kong
By Caslon Printers

To

My Family

PREFACE

This book is the result of a research venture on the narrow subject of the Chinese Communist rural and urban revolutions in late 1927 with particular reference to their relations with Moscow. As the broad lines of Comintern policy have emerged from an examination of the complicated events of the few months under study, it has turned out that those lines of policy represent a revolutionary pattern not only for China but for the whole underdeveloped world as well. In a real sense, the questions at issue in the present study are questions of world history, not just questions of the history of the Chinese Communist movement. These questions are still disturbing the world today.

From the viewpoint of the history of either Chinese or international Communism, this volume is only a preliminary and incomplete study of a vast subject which is a challenge to modern scholarship. My efforts would not be in vain if this work would induce other scholars to bring out deeper and more comprehensive studies of the field. History is a science if materials are studied exhaustively. Different historians using the same materials should reach basically the same conclusions regarding the same questions.

In order to understand the background of the events in China during the latter months of 1927, a chapter on the Comintern impact is placed at the beginning of the text. A part of the preliminary work of this chapter was started in Taipei intermittently in 1962-63 and was improved in seminar discussions with my students in The American University in Washington, D.C., in 1964-65, from whom I learned a good deal. The first draft of my survey of a major part of the Comintern statements cited in this chapter was prepared at Columbia University under the sponsorship of its East Asian Institute during February-June 1965. This draft was subsequently revised several times in the United States and was reorganized with some new material and insight in Taipei in 1969.

Chapters II-V, like the repeated revisions of Chapter I, were prepared first under the joint sponsorship of the Institute for Sino-Soviet Studies of The George Washington University and the Far Eastern and Russian Institute of the University of Washington from July 1965 to August 1967, and then under the sole sponsorship of the former with assistance from The American University and the Hoover Institution of Stanford University from September 1967 through August 1968. Chapter V was recast and the conclusion, chronology and bibliography were prepared in Taipei from September 1968 to August 1969.

This study is, as a rule, based on documents. Where documents are lacking, major events like the Hai-feng Soviet are merely mentioned. The documents cited in this work were mainly drawn from the Bureau of Investigation holdings and the Ch'en Ch'eng collection in Taipei and from the Hoover Institution and Library and the Library of Congress in the United States. A small part of them was gathered from Columbia University and Japan. Some materials were obtained in the United States and Japan at the expense of the Institute for Sino-Soviet Studies of The George Washington University.

I am indebted to Professors Franz H. Michael, Hellmut Wilhelm, C. Martin Wilbur, George E. Taylor, Kurt London, Michael Lindsay, and Dr. Glenn Campbell for helping me with financial arrangements at different stages to keep my research going on for a number of years. I am also grateful to Professor Kung-chuan Hsiao for his helpful advice and suggestions. The greatest credit is due to Professor Franz H. Michael for his enthusiastic and patient support without which the main body of this work would have been impossible.

Messrs. Yü Ching-tang, Chi Yuan-p'u and Ni Pao-kwen helped me gather material for this volume in Taipei in 1957-58 when I started my long-range research project under the support of the Asia Foundation. Mr. Daniel H. Bay gave me information leading to the discovery of the materials on the Canton Commune in the Hoover Institution and Library. Other friends and scholars who assisted me in collecting data for this study include Lothar Metzl, Y. J. Chih, Ishikawa Tadao, David Tseng, T. I. Dow, Robert L.

Vandegrift, Joseph Heinlein, Tien-wei Wu, Charles W. Pugh, Chun-hsi Wu and Bruce Esposito.

Of course, thanks are due to all those with whom I discussed questions for the benefit of this volume.

I am also indebted to the editor of *The China Quarterly* for permission to utilize my articles published in its issues No. 30, April-June 1967, and No. 33, January-March 1968.

This volume was prepared with the help of my family from the beginning. This was particularly true of the final phase of my work in 1968-69 when all my sources of income and research facilities were cut off in Taipei.

Needless to say, I alone am responsible for all the statements and interpretations in this work.

HSIAO TSO-LIANG

Hong Kong
October 1969

CONTENTS

Preface vii

Chapter I   The Comintern Impact 1

Chapter II   The Land Revolution 39

Chapter III From Nanchang to Swatow 81

Chapter IV   Socialist Deviation and Insurrectionary Tactics 105

Chapter V   The Canton Commune 135

Conclusion 157

Chronology 167

Bibliography 173

Glossary 189

Index 193

MAPS

1. Projected Insurrection Areas in Hunan and Hupeh   57

2. Scenes of Autumn Harvest Uprisings   75

3. The Exodus from Nanchang   99

Maps by: Mr. Too See Lou

CHAPTER I

THE COMINTERN IMPACT

1. Revolutionary Pattern for the East

From the very beginning the Comintern approach to the revolution in the East was different from that in the West. In the West the revolution was one of the industrial proletariat against the bourgeoisie[1] with the rural toilers as the auxiliary revolutionary force.[2] In the East, where there was almost no industrial proletariat on the whole[3] or the industrial proletariat was just beginning to grow up in some relatively advanced lands,[4] the Comintern supported the native bourgeoisie temporarily and the peasantry permanently in its grand strategy against capitalist imperialism and feudal survivals represented chiefly by landlords.[5] While the Comintern support for the bourgeoisie in the precapitalist countries of the East should not hinder the Communist work of organizing and training the masses,[6] the Comintern support for the peasantry was so complete that it was believed that "in such countries, the Communist Party is not able to attain success unless it supports the peasants".[7]

The question of the emerging proletariat in the relatively advanced lands in the East was, indeed, raised in the Comintern in order to be tested in the light of practical experience.[8] But

---

[1] Lenin, *Selected Works*, Vol. 10, New York, International Publishers Co., Inc., 1943, pp. 26, 27, 28.
[2] Ibid., pp. 216 ff..
[3] Ibid., p. 242.
[4] *The Second Congress of the Communist International*, as Reported and Interpreted by the Official Newspapers of Soviet Russia, Washington, Government Printing Office, 1920, pp. 42, 43, 135; hereinafter cited as *The Second Congress*. M. N. Roy, "Supplementary Theses on the National and Colonial Questions", submitted to the Second Comintern Congress, as printed in *Blueprint for World Conquest*, as outlined by the Communist International, with an introduction by William H. Chamberlain, Washington and Chicago, Human Events, Inc., 1946, p. 128.
[5] Lenin, *Selected Works*, Vol. 10, pp. 236, 239-240, 240-241.
[6] Ibid., p. 41.
[7] *The Second Congress*, p. 38.
[8] *M. N. Roy's Memoirs*, Bombay, Allied Publishers, 1964, pp. 379-380.

the proletarian revolution which characterized the Communist revolution in the West would be out of the question in the precapitalist countries of the East.

It will be recalled that when the Comintern was formed under Lenin's leadership in 1919 as a general staff for world revolution, it focused its attention on the postwar revolutionary unrest in the West. But the Communist-led revolts in Central Europe soon collapsed one after another. At the Second Comintern Congress held in July-August 1920, Lenin decided to expand his revolutionary strategy to include the East where a powerful national liberation movement had been under way.

In his Preliminary Draft of Theses on the National and Colonial Questions submitted to the Second Comintern Congress, Lenin distinguished between the oppressing and oppressed nations. The characteristic feature of imperialism, he said, was the division of the world into a handful of imperialist powers and a much larger number of oppressed nations containing about 70 per cent of the entire population of the world. These oppressed nations were either outright colonies or "outlying colonial states" such as Persia, Turkey and China which were bound by treaties after military defeats.[9] Lenin thought that this unfair division of the nations would open up an important new field of work for the Communists in the fight against world capitalism which should be overthrown not only in the home countries but also in the colonial world from which it drew its resources. Consequently, he decided to utilize the national liberation movement in the colonial and backward nations to further the cause of world revolution.[10]

But the fact was that the national liberation movement in the colonial and backward nations was actually led by the bourgeoisie which is ordinarily the enemy of Communism. Can the Communists support their enemy as a political expedient? This question is most difficult to answer. It is to be expected that ordinary Communists would answer in the negative, for they can not afford to defeat their own purposes by lending support to their enemy. But Lenin was different. Being a realistic politician and revolutionary leader, he had the eye to see and the hand to execute what seemed to be the only practical way to challenge world capitalism

---

[9] Lenin, *Selected Works*, Vol. 10, pp. 239-240.
[10] *M. N. Roy's Memoirs*, p. 378.

in the circumstances—giving active support to the national liberation movement going on under the leadership of the native bourgeoisie in the colonial and backward nations. Accordingly, Lenin included a paragraph in his theses to the effect that all Communists must support the bourgeois-democratic liberation movement in the backward nations and that the support should come, first of all, from the workers of the lands on which the backward nations depended as colonies or in the financial sphere.[11]

It is not surprising that Lenin's proposal for support for the bourgeoisie met with resistance. He disclosed that this proposal gave rise to some disagreement in the Commission on the National and Colonial Questions set up by the Second Comintern Congress for panel discussion.[12] M. N. Roy, the Indian representative, went so far as to demand the elimination of the above-mentioned paragraph from Lenin's theses.[13] He pointed out that there were two different movements in the dependent countries, which grew farther apart from each other every day. One was the bourgeois-democratic nationalist movement aimed at political independence under the bourgeois order. The other was the mass struggle of peasants and workers for their liberation from exploitation. As the former movement sought control of the latter, the Communists should resist such control and help develop the class consciousness of the working masses. However, Roy conceded that since the overthrow of foreign capitalism was the first step in the revolution in the colonies, it would be helpful to make use of the cooperation of the bourgeois national-revolutionary elements.[14]

After heated discussions in the Commission, it was conceded that there were different kinds of bourgeois-democratic movements in the oppressed nations. On the one hand, some bourgeois democrats adopted reformist tactics and collaborated with both the ruling class at home and the exploiting nations abroad. On the other, there were liberation movements which were really revolutionary. It was these liberation movements that the Communists should support.[15] In consequence, the Commission decided that

[11] Lenin, *Selected Works*, Vol. 10, p. 236.
[12] Ibid., p. 240.
[13] *The Second Congress*, p. 43, cited from *Petrograd Pravda*, July 29, 1920.
[14] M. N. Roy, "Supplementary Theses on the National and Colonial Questions", as printed in *Blueprint for World Conquest*, p. 129.
[15] *The Second Congress*, p. 38, cited from *Petrograd Pravda*, July 28, 1920.

the bourgeois-democratic movement in the backward countries should be supported but that the term "bourgeois-democratic" should be changed to "national-revolutionary".[16]

The meaning of such a change of terminology, according to Lenin, was that the Communists should support the bourgeois liberation movements in the colonial countries only when these movements would not hinder the Communist work of training and organizing the peasants and the general exploited masses in a revolutionary spirit.[17] As a result, the following two major points were inserted in Lenin's theses: (1) the Comintern must support the revolutionary movements in the colonial and backward countries only on the condition that the various elements of future proletarian parties be grouped together and trained for the task of fighting the bourgeois-democratic tendencies in their own countries; and (2) the Comintern must establish temporary relationships and alliances with the bourgeois-democracy of colonial and backward countries, but must not merge with it.[18]

Thus, Lenin advocated not only revolution from above in the form of temporary undertakings with the bourgeoisie, but also revolution from below by means of Communist work against the bourgeoisie.

It is interesting to note that Lenin's apparently contradictory strategy of supporting and opposing the native bourgeoisie in the backward nations was accompanied by his equally contradictory policy of developing and curbing capitalism there. To the mind of a free man, Communism and capitalism can not co-exist in the same place at the same time. Communists are no longer Communists if they support capitalism. But the Communist way of dialectical thinking is allegedly different. Some Kremlin officials believed that only an economically developed country, led by a strong national bourgeoisie, could resist foreign imperialism. To them, a strong bourgeoisie meant a victory over feudal remnants and absolutism. It also meant the development of the productive

---

[16] Lenin, *Selected Works*, Vol. 10, p. 40.

[17] Ibid., p. 41.

[18] Ibid., pp. 236-237; for an interesting account of the question of the bourgeoisie in the Second Comintern Congress, see Allen S. Whiting, *Soviet Policies in China 1917-1924*, New York, Columbia University Press, first published 1954, second printing, 1957, pp. 49-54.

forces within the country, which would finally lead to class struggle and the establishment of a Communist regime.[19]

Is, then, the capitalist stage in the development of national economy inevitable for the Eastern countries? Lenin said no. He advanced the theory that with the assistance of the proletariat of the advanced lands, the backward countries could pass to the soviet system and then, after the lapse of a definite stage of development, to Communism without passing through the capitalist stage of development.[20]

According to D. Z. Manuilsky, a Ukrainian member of the Comintern leadership, the Second Comintern Congress was faced with two problems relating to the East, namely, (1) to what extent the Comintern could make use of the national movements in the fight against imperialism, and (2) to what extent the oppressed nations could bypass the stage of capitalist development. As it was impossible to work out details at the time, they would have to be spelled out by subsequent decisions on the basis of practical experience.[21]

Despite its importance to the national liberation movement, however, the bourgeoisie can merely be a temporary ally. In order to deal a deadly blow to the ancient regime, the Comintern had to find another class of people in the colonial and semi-colonial world who would really provide a colossal reservoir of revolutionary energy on a permanent basis. It is well known that Lenin found a great revolutionary force in the peasantry of Russia in 1905. It was natural for him to think of the peasant masses of the backward nations which were yet more agricultural in nature than were those of Russia in 1905. Indeed, Lenin was so much impressed by the teeming and powerful peasants in the backward nations that he doubted that proletarian parties, if ever they could be organized there, could pursue Communist tactics and policies "without

---

[19] Politicus, "We and the East", dated 1923, as printed in Xenia J. Eudin and Robert C. North, *Soviet Russia and the East 1920-1927, a Documentary Survey*, Stanford, Stanford University Press, 1957, p. 195, hereinafter cited as Eudin and North.

[20] Lenin, *Selected Works*, Vol. 10, p. 243.

[21] D. Z. Manuilsky, "The Importance of the National Problem in the Oppressed Countries", a statement at the Fifth Comintern Congress, June 1, 1924, as printed in Eudin and North, p. 326.

having definite relations with the peasant movement and without effectively supporting it".[22]

Then the question arises as to whether Communist policies can be carried out among the peasants in the precapitalist countries. Lenin answered in the affirmative. He cited the experience of the Russian Communists in former tsarist colonies and backward nations like Turkestan to show that Communist tactics and policies could be applied to precapitalist countries where "there is almost no industrial proletariat". It was the consensus of opinion that the Comintern must proceed on the assumption that the peasant soviets, the soviets of the exploited, were "applicable not only to capitalist countries but also to the countries of precapitalist conditions".[23]   Accordingly, Lenin advocated carrying on propaganda in favor of the idea of peasants' soviets and toilers' soviets in the backward and colonial nations and striving to create soviets of the toiling people as far as possible.[24]

Against the above background, Lenin's theses contain the following points regarding the peasant movement in the backward countries: (1) to support the peasant movement against the landlords, large landownership, and all feudal survivals; (2) to give the peasant movement the most revolutionary character by organizing the peasants and all the exploited into soviets as far as possible; and (3) to establish the closest possible union between the Communist proletariat of Western Europe and the revolutionary peasant movement of the Eastern countries.[25]

Here it is important to notice the striking contrast between the urban and the rural policies in the Eastern countries proposed by Lenin and adopted by the Second Comintern Congress.   While the Comintern supported the bourgeoisie in the city, it combated the landlords and all feudal survivals in the countryside.   Interestingly, the urban policy met with strong resistance in the conference room whereas the rural policy was passed with a remarkable measure of agreement.   Roy, who challenged Lenin's support for the bourgeoisie, endorsed his position on the peasant question.   In India, Roy said, the only slogan that would interest the greatest part of

---

22 Lenin, *Selected Works,* Vol. 10, pp. 240-241.
23 Ibid., pp. 241-242.
24 Ibid., p. 242.
25 Ibid., p. 236.

the population was: "The land to the land-tiller".[26] In the East on the whole, as he interpreted the theses of the Second Comintern Congress, the peasants represented a powerful revolutionary factor and were destined to play a role of paramount importance.[27]

Another interesting question facing the Second Comintern Congress was the role of the workers in the revolution in the Eastern countries. There is no doubt that Roy placed greater emphasis on the workers than Lenin did. Lenin stood for peasants' and toilers' soviets but he did not define the word "toilers". By contrast, Roy advocated peasants' and workers' soviets, viewed from the angle of the precapitalist countries like China and India.[28] As Roy's theses are supplementary rather than alternative in nature,[29] he supplied what fell short in Lenin's theses.

However, it must be remembered that to Roy, the workers in the Eastern countries were still young and weak at the time. He declared that a proletarian class, in the strict sense of the word, could not come into existence there until recently.[30] Accordingly, he took the position that in its first stages the revolution in the colonies would not be a Communist revolution but must be carried on with a program which would include many petty bourgeois reforms, such as the division of land, etc.[31]

What is, then, a Communist or proletarian revolution? Does the formation of peasants' and workers' soviets, as advocated by Roy, mean a Communist revolution? The answer is in the negative. This is evident from Lenin's statement, cited previously, that the backward nations could pass to the soviet system and then, after the lapse of a definite stage of development, to Communism. In order to understand this question properly, it is necessary, first of all, to grasp Lenin's revolutionary theory, which was behind the

---

[26] *The Second Congress,* p. 43, cited from *Petrograd Pravda,* July 29, 1920.

[27] M. N. Roy, "For a Better Understanding of the National Movements in Colonial and Semi-colonial Countries", a statement at the Fifth Comintern Congress, June 1, 1924, as printed in Eudin and North, p. 329.

[28] M. N. Roy, "Supplementary Theses on the National and Colonial Questions", as printed in *Blueprint for World Conquest,* pp. 126, 131.

[29] *M. N. Roy's Memoirs,* p. 380.

[30] M. N. Roy, "Supplementary Theses on the National and Colonial Questions", as printed in *Blueprint for World Conquest,* p. 128.

[31] Ibid., p. 130.

whole program of the Second Comintern Congress for the revolution in the East.

It will be recalled that Lenin divided revolution into two stages, namely, the bourgeois democratic revolution and the socialist revolution.[32] The former is also known as democratic revolution and the latter as proletarian-socialist or proletarian revolution.[33] It was Lenin's position that the proletariat must complete the democratic revolution by allying itself with the peasantry and accomplish the socialist revolution by allying itself with the semi-proletariat.[34] Thus, the democratic revolution is a proletarian-peasant revolution marked by the partnership of the peasantry while the socialist revolution is another name for the proletarian revolution. Indeed, the peasantry makes so much difference between the two kinds of revolution that Stalin pointed out that Lenin discerned the bourgeois democratic revolution with the agrarian movement as the principal axis and the October revolution with the capture of power by the proletariat as the principal axis.[35] It is common knowledge that the Russian revolution of 1905 has gone down in history as a bourgeois-democratic revolution while the October revolution of 1917 as a proletarian-socialist revolution.

If the peasantry was an important factor in the Russian revolution of 1905, it must have been more so in the revolution in the more backward countries in the East where by far the greatest part of the

32 Lenin, "The April (1917) Theses", printed in his *Collected Works*, Vol. 24, Moscow, Progress Publishers, 1964, pp. 42-106.

33 For the term "proletarian-socialist revolution" or "proletarian revolution", see Stalin's 1912 pamphlet *Marxism and the National Question* as cited by Mao Tse-tung in his essay "On New Democracy" printed in his *Selected Works*, Chinese edition, Vol. 2, p. 663, Peking, People's Publishing House, 1965, English edition, Vol. 3, p. 114, New York, International Publishers, 1954; Stalin's statement at the Tenth Session of the Eighth Plenum of the ECCI, May 14, 1927, as printed in Eudin and North, p. 369; Neumann's statement at the Sixth Comintern Congress, as printed in *International Press Correspondence*, (hereinafter referred to as *Inprecor.*) Vol. 8, No. 76, October 30, 1928, p. 1417; Mao Tse-tung, "On New Democracy", section 4, as printed in his *Selected Works*, Chinese edition, vol. 2, pp. 659-665, English edition, Vol. 3, pp. 109-115.

34 Lenin, "Two Tactics", printed in his *Collected Works*, Vol. 9, Moscow, Foreign Languages Publishing House, 1962, p. 100.

35 Stalin, "The International Situation", a speech delivered at the Plenum of the Soviet Communist Party, August 1, 1927, *Communist International*, October 15, 1927, p. 297, and, in extract form, in Stalin, *Marxism and the National and Colonial Questions*, New York, International Publishers, n. d., p. 323, and in Eudin and North, p. 377.

population was the peasantry. Accordingly, when Lenin made up his mind to utilize the national liberation movement of the East for the cause of world revolution in the Second Comintern Congress, he decided that "there is not the slightest doubt that every nationalist movement can only be a bourgeois-democratic movement, for the bulk of the population in the backward countries are peasants who represent bourgeois-capitalist relations". [36] This decision of Lenin was significant in that it determined the character of the national liberation movement in the colonial and semi-colonial world as bourgeois-democratic. In other words, the national liberation movement could not be a proletarian revolution. Though Lenin included the socialist stage in the revolution in the Eastern countries, this would be a remote possibility which would not arise until the completion of the national liberation movement.

It should, however, be noted that under Leninism-Stalinism the bourgeois-democratic revolution in an imperialist country is different from that in a backward and oppressed country. Stalin pointed out that the Russian revolution of 1905 was directed against the bourgeoisie because the bourgeoisie of an imperialist country was always counterrevolutionary. But the national bourgeoisie in a colonial and dependent country, he said, was different: it might support the revolutionary movement of its country against foreign imperialism at certain stages. That was why Lenin, who opposed the bourgeoisie in Russia, permitted temporary undertakings and alliances with the bourgeoisie in China, despite the fact that the revolutions in both countries were bourgeois-democratic revolutions.[37]

2. The Democratic United Front

The bourgeois-democratic revolution program, proposed by Lenin and adopted by the Second Comintern Congress for the Eastern countries, was not immediately introduced to the Chinese Communists. When the twelve bourgeois intellectuals including Mao Tse-tung met in Shanghai in July 1921 and formed what was supposed to be a proletarian party, they drew up a socialist rather than a bourgeois-democratic program according to their limited

[36] Lenin, *Selected Works*, Vol. 10, pp. 240-241.
[37] Stalin, "The International Situation ', August 1, 1927, op. cit.

book knowledge. Specifically, they advocated overthrowing the capitalist class, establishing proletarian dictatorship, abolishing private ownership of capital, and confiscating all production means such as machines, land, buildings, semi-manufactured products, etc.[38] Without proper training and indoctrination, they seemed to be laboring under the oversimplified notion, generally held by laymen, that Communism means the confiscation by the proletariat of the property of all capitalists for common ownership.

Under the sponsorship of the Comintern, the First Congress of the Toilers of the Far East was preliminarily opened at Irkutsk in November 1921 and formally held at Moscow and then Petrograd from January to February 1922. It was this congress which pressed the concept of the two-stage revolution, democratic and socialist, upon the representatives from the Far East and which was eventually instrumental in converting the Chinese Communists to the cause of democratic revolution. Safarov, chief of the Comintern Eastern Department, told the congress that in colonial and semi-colonial countries the first phase of the revolutionary movement must inevitably be a national democratic movement but not a struggle for the proletarian revolution. He said that if the Communists raised the slogans of democratic revolution such as land nationalization, democratic government, etc., it would show that they were ready to cooperate with all the nationalist democratic organizations.[39] According to Ch'en Tu-hsiu, chief of the CCP, the First Congress of the Toilers of the Far East decided that the struggle for the democratic revolution must be carried on in the colonial nations of the East and that the peasants' soviets were to be organized in the course of the revolution. In consequence, he stated, the Second Congress of the CCP, held in July 1922, adopted the policy of the united front of democratic revolution.[40] Chang Kuo-t'ao, who represented the CCP at the congress, recalls that the congress determined the anti-imperialist character of the

---

[38] Ch'en Kung-po, *The Communist Movement in China*, edited by C. Martin Wilbur, reproduced for private distribution by the East Asian Institute of Columbia University, September 1960, p. 106, hereinafter cited as Ch'en Kung-po.

[39] Safarov, "The Interrelation between the National Revolutionary Movement and the Revolutionary Proletarian Movement", a statement at the Tenth Session of the First Congress of the Toilers of the Far East, January 27, 1922, as printed in Eudin and North, pp. 227-228.

[40] Ch'en Tu-hsiu, "Letter to All Comrades of the Party", December 10, 1929.

Chinese revolution and gave birth to the notion of an anti-imperialist united front in China. After his return to China, he states, he reported the congress's ideas of anti-imperialism and of a united front to that end to the party leadership with the consequence that they were adopted and embodied in the CCP's Statement on the Current Situation of June and the Manifesto of its Second Congress of July.[41]

The most important thing in the Manifesto of the CCP Second Congress is the theory of the two-stage revolution, bourgeois-democratic and socialist. The proletariat and the impoverished peasantry, the Manifesto of the Second Congress of the CCP says, should support the democratic revolution which is directed against imperialism and feudalism. After the success of the democratic revolution, it is stated, the proletariat will have to combat the bourgeoisie which will challenge the proletariat. The Manifesto then outlines the socialist program in favor of the abolition of private property. In the present stage, however, the Manifesto provides for a democratic united front of workers, impoverished peasants and the petty bourgeoisie with the removal of warlords and imperialism as the most important item of a political program. The political program makes no provision for the confiscation of the property of capitalists. The workers are ensured of the eight-hour working day and the right to strike, which were the outstanding features of Comintern policy in Chinese cities at the time. For the benefit of the peasantry only rent ceilings are promised.[42]

Thus, the political program of the democratic united front forms a striking contrast to the platform of the First Congress of the CCP. It simply does not look like Communism in the proper sense of the word. Yet it stands out in Chinese Communist annals as marking the beginning of the very long period of democratic revolution.

---

[41] Chang Kuo-t'ao, "My Memoirs", *Ming Pao Monthly*, Hong Kong, No. 8, August 1966, p. 74; Ho Kan-chih, *History of the Modern Chinese Revolution*, Hong Kong, San-lien Bookstore, 1958, p. 40, hereinafter cited as Ho Kan-Chih; Ch'en Kung-po, op. cit., pp. 31, 32, 92.

[42] A text of "the Manifesto of the Second Congress of the CCP", taken from *Red Documents*, is printed in Wang Chien-min, *Draft History of the Chinese Communist Party*, Vol. I, Taipei, Taiwan, 1965, pp. 68-77; an English version of the Manifesto appears in Ch'en Kung-po, op. cit., pp. 111-123, but should be consulted with caution.

It is interesting to note that the national bourgeoisie was not originally made a member of the democratic united front. But the CCP Second Congress saw fit to seek a temporary union with the Nationalists who were considered to represent the bourgeoisie.[43] Subsequently, the national bourgeoisie was recognised as a member of the democratic united front.[44]

Under the bourgeois-democratic program of the CCP Second Congress, the workers were protected by a set of regulations governing the labor union movement.[45] It must be remembered that the labor union movement was the distinguishing feature of Chinese Communism in the first seven years.

As for the peasantry, it was indeed recognised as the greatest factor in the Chinese Communist movement in theory. But in practice, as described previously, it was promised no more than rent ceilings to be fixed in the days to come. This promise seems far too moderate in view of the fact that the idea of democratic revolution which, according to Lenin, should be based on the peasantry, was being made into a political program for the first time in China. No wonder that Pavel Mif, a prominent Comintern official, charged that the political program as well as other resolutions of the CCP Second Congress showed that the Chinese Party did not properly understand the importance of the peasant problem and the necessity of the fight for leadership over the peasant masses.[46]

It was natural that Moscow could not look on the Chinese situation with indifference. In May 1923 the ECCI issued a directive to the Third Congress of the CCP to be held the next month, emphasizing that the *peasant problem* became the central point of the entire policy of the CCP. The directive sets forth a whole list of specific contents of the agrarian revolution as slogans for propaganda and for action. At the head of the list is the confiscation without compensation of the land of landlords, monasteries and churches for redistribution to the peasants. Then follows the

---

43 Ch'en Kung-po, pp. 126-128.

44 Ho Kan-chih, p. 41.

45 Ch'en Kung-po, pp. 130-134.

46 Pavel Mif, *Heroic China: Fifteen Years of the Communist Party of China,* Chinese version, 1936, p. 27, English version, New York, Workers Library Publishers, 1937, p. 19.

abolition of such malpractices as exorbitant rents, the existing system of taxation, the "squeeze", the customs barriers between provinces, the tax-farmers, and the bureaucratic rule. Last in order comes the creation of the peasant self-governing agencies in charge of the confiscation of land, etc. The ECCI pointed out that the revolution would succeed only if the basic masses of the population—the small peasants—could be drawn into the movement.[47]

This Comintern instruction regarding the agrarian revolution in China was clear and definite. Viewed from the Comintern side, it served to fill a great gap in the bourgeois-democratic program of the Second Congress of the CCP. However, Pavel Mif charged that this Comintern instruction was not reflected in the decisions of the Third Congress of the CCP, an instruction which placed emphasis on the importance of a solution of the peasant problem in China and on the fundamental slogans of agrarian revolution such as the confiscation of the landlord's land for the benefit of the peasantry without compensation. He regretted that the CCP Third Congress failed to take the fundamental demands of the peasant masses into account.[48]

Mao Tse-tung, who insisted on his "correct views" in the CCP Third Congress and was elected a member of the Central Committee,[49] looked upon the businessmen rather than peasants as the most important class in the national revolution at the time.[50] In this matter, he was apparently under the influence of the Comintern's bourgeois-democratic program for China. But his understanding of the program was far too inadequate: he overstressed the role of the bourgeoisie which was merely a temporary ally, but underestimated the strength of the peasantry which was a permanent

---

47 "The ECCI's Directive of Policy to the Third Congress of the Chinese Communist Party, May 1923", as printed in Eudin and North, pp. 344-345; Pavel Mif, *Heroic China: Fifteen Years of the Communist Party of China,* Chinese version, p. 32, English version, p. 23.

48 Pavel Mif, op. cit., Chinese version, p. 32, English version, pp. 22-23.

49 Ho Kan-chih, p. 53.

50 [Mao] Tse-tung, "The Peking Coup and the Businessmen", *Guide Weekly,* combined issue of Nos. 31, 32, July 11, 1923, pp. 233-34. One Communist source attributes the formulation of the resolutions of the CCP Third Congress to Mao and Ch'ü Ch'iu-pai, see C. Martin Wilbur and Julie Lien-ying How, *Documents on Communism, Nationalism, and Soviet Advisers in China, 1918-1927,* New York, Columbia University Press, 1956, p. 86.

force of revolution. It took the party chief Ch'en Tu-hsiu to get the credit for publishing the first article on the peasant question on July 1, 1923, recognising the importance of winning over and organising the peasants in the Chinese revolution.[51]

Why, then, did the CCP Third Congress reject the Comintern instruction regarding the agrarian revolution? Possibly the Chinese Communists shared the Trotskyite view that there was no feudal exploitation in China and that therefore an agrarian revolution was not called for. It is also possible that since the party members totalled only a few hundred at the time and almost all of them lived in the cities, they had no way to reach the vast masses of the peasantry.[52] Whatever the reasons, the fact was that the Chinese Communists did not inject the land question into their deliberations and decisions on the peasant question until the CCP Fifth Congress of 1927 under the Comintern impact.

On the Comintern side, however, it was also doubtful that an immediate agrarian revolution was really contemplated. It seemed clear that Moscow gave priority to the formation of a united front with the KMT at the time and that the agrarian revolution would come next on the Communist program of action. This can be seen from the ECCI directive of May 1923 which begins by stating that "the national revolution in China and the creation of an anti-imperialist front will necessarily be followed by an agrarian revolution of the peasantry against the remnants of feudalism". [53] Pavel Mif charged that the CCP Fourth Congress of January 1925 placed on record that the stage of the united national liberation

---

51 Ch'en Tu-hsiu, "The Question of the Chinese Peasantry", *Vanguard* (*Chien Feng*), No. 1, July 1, 1923.

52 According to Ho Kan-chih, the CCP First Congress of 1921 was attended by 12 delegates representing a total of 57 party members, the Second Congress of 1922 attended by 12 delegates representing 123 members, and the Third Congress attended by 30 delegates representing 432 members (See Ho Kan-chih, op. cit., pp. 37, 40, 49).

53 "The ECCI's Directive of Policy to the Third Congress of the Chinese Communist Party, May 1923", as printed in Eudin and North, p. 344. The word "followed" is given as "accompanied" in Pavel Mif's afore-cited book, Chinese version, p. 32, English version, p. 23. But Mif testified that the Comintern foresaw that the first stage of the revolution, in which the movement was directed mainly against imperialism and was supported by the national bourgeoisie, would inevitably be superseded by a second stage in which the bourgeoisie would desert the revolution and the main content of the revolution would become the agrarian revolution. (See Mif's book, Chinese version, p. 56, English version, p. 41.)

front would be immediately followed by the stage of the proletarian socialist revolution, thus leaving out the agrarian revolution.[54]

As a matter of fact, Moscow was bent on forging a KMT-CCP alliance in its grand strategy against imperialism in the early twenties. In January 1923 the Comintern instructed the Chinese Communists to join the KMT but not merge with it.[55] In June the Third Congress of the CCP resolved that the Communists should join the KMT while the Communist Party was to preserve its complete organizational and political independence. The CCP undertook to convert the KMT into a really broad, mass, and revolutionary organization.[56] In January 1924 the Kuomintang formally admitted the Communists into its ranks, thereby completing the procedure for the Comintern strategy of forging a temporary alliance with the bourgeoisie in China.

It is common knowledge that Trotsky objected to collaboration with the bourgeoisie and, for that matter, the Kuomintang.

But the Comintern support for the bourgeoisie was on a temporary basis. As described previously, that support must not stand in the way of the Communist work of organizing and training the toiling masses in a revolutionary spirit. Thus, the Communist movement in China, as elsewhere, was designed by the Comintern to be a mass movement. It could not depart from the mass line. But the Chinese Communists in the first years of the movement were all white-collar intellectuals who learned Communism from books and who seldom stooped to mingle with the masses. Hence, when Ch'en Tu-hsiu led the Chinese delegation to the Fourth Comintern Congress toward the end of 1922, Karl Radek, a leading Comintern official, chided the Chinese comrades for locking themselves up in their studies and studying Marx and Lenin as they had studied Confucius. He exclaimed: "Get out of the Confucian study room of Communism, and go to the masses and coolies, and also to the peasant masses".[57]

---

54 Pavel Mif, op. cit., Chinese version, pp. 33-34, English version, p. 24.
55 "Resolution of the ECCI on the Expected Attitude of the Chinese Communist Party Toward the Kuomintang, January 12, 1923", as printed in Eudin and North, pp. 343-344.
56 Pavel Mif, op. cit., Chinese version, p. 31, English version, p. 22; C. Martin Wilbur and Julie Lien-ying How, op. cit., pp. 66-67.
57 *Fourth Congress of the Communist International*, Abridged Report of Minutes held at Petrograd and Moscow, November 7—December 3, 1922, published by the Communist Party of Great Britain, pp. 222-223.

The CCP's mass work made rapid progress in the succeeding years. In 1923 one of the reasons behind the Comintern effort to create the KMT-CCP entente was that the working class was weak and was not yet differentiated as an independent social force.[58]   In 1925, however, the strike wave demonstrated to Moscow that the Chinese proletariat had become an active revolutionary force against imperialism. When the Sixth Enlarged Plenum of the ECCI met at Moscow in February-March 1926, it looked upon the Chinese strikes as having revealed such a degree of revolutionary energy and organization as could not have been suspected to exist one or two years before.[59]

The rapid growth of the political power of the Chinese proletariat posed the question of the seizure of the revolutionary leadership.[60]   This question was nothing new. It emerged from M. N. Roy's proposal for support for the workers in the revolution in the Eastern countries.[61]   It was brought home to the CCP in the Comintern directive of May 1923.[62] But it was not until after the 1925 strike wave that this question assumed serious dimensions. The point is that the bourgeois-democratic revolution can develop in two different directions: the classical bourgeois revolution of the 19th-century type and the socialist revolution of the Soviet type. To make sure that the bourgeois-democratic revolution will grow into the socialist revolution, the leadership of the revolution must belong to the proletariat.[63]

Stalin pointed out that there were two paths for the development of the Chinese revolution: either the national bourgeoisie smashed the proletariat and established the rule of capitalism, or the proletariat pushed aside the national bourgeoisie and consolidated its hegemony in order to secure the complete victory of the bourgeois-

---

[58] "Resolution of the ECCI on the Expected Attitude of the Chinese Communist Party Toward the Kuomintang, January 12, 1923", as printed in Eudin and North, p. 344.

[59] "Theses on the Trade Union Movement in the East", adopted at the Sixth Enlarged Plenum of the ECCI, February 17—March 15, 1927, as printed in Eudin and North, p. 325.

[60] Ibid.

[61] M. N. Roy, "Supplementary Theses on the National and Colonial Questions", as printed in Blueprint for World Conquest, p. 130.

[62] Eudin and North, p. 345.

[63] Ch'en Po-ta, Stalin and the Chinese Revolution, Peking, People's Publishing House, 1952, p. 23; M. N. Roy's Mission to China, pp. 133, 135.

democratic revolution and then gradually convert it into a socialist revolution.[64] He thought that the capitalist bourgeoisie in China was extremely weak, much weaker than the Russian bourgeoisie in 1905, so that the initiator and guide of the Chinese revolution, the leader of the Chinese peasantry, must inevitably be the Chinese proletariat which was better organized and more active than the Chinese bourgeoisie.[65]

It seems superfluous to explain that the proletarian hegemony or leadership does not mean the proletarian revolution or dictatorship which belongs to the socialist stage of the revolution. It means what Stalin called "the hegemony of the proletariat in the bourgeois-democratic revolution".[66] The Eighth Plenum of the ECCI of May 1927 placed on record that the Chinese revolution could not develop further or achieve victory unless the working class became the leader of the whole of the democratic revolution.[67]

Largely under the impact of the 1925 strike wave, Mao Tse-tung declared on February 1, 1926 that the industrial proletariat was the main force or main army of the revolution while the poor peasantry and the agricultural proletariat could offer no more than "a brave striving" (yung-kan fen-tou).[68] In contrast, the Sixth Plenum of

---

[64] J. Stalin, "Questions of the Chinese Revolution: Theses for Propagandists", Approved by the CC, CPSU (B), April 21, 1927, as printed in *Stalin's Works*, Vol. 9, p. 225.

[65] Stalin's Speech delivered at the Seventh Enlarged Plenum of the ECCI, November 30, 1926, as printed in Eudin and North, pp. 350, 353.

[66] J. Stalin, "Questions of the Chinese Revolution: Theses for Propagandists", Approved by the CC, CPSU (B), April 21, 1927, as printed in *Stalin's Works*, Vol. 9, p. 225. According to M. N. Roy, the proletariat exercises hegemony but not leadership. This can be seen from his article "The Significance of the Fifth Congress of the CCP", May 13, 1927, published in *The Guide Weekly* (*Hsiang-tao chou-pao*), No. 195, p. 2119; but the whole paragraph in which this question of hegemony or leadership is discussed does not appear in the English version of this article as printed in *M. N. Roy's Mission to China*, p. 280. The Chinese Communists do not make a distinction between these two words but call them *ling tao* alike. In English-language Communist literature, the two words seem to be used interchangeably in most cases. For an interesting discussion of this question, see Charles B. McLane, *Soviet Policy and the Chinese Communists, 1931-1946*, New York, Columbia University Press, 1958, p. 24.

[67] "Resolution on the Chinese Question", adopted by the Eighth Plenum of the ECCI, May 8-30, 1927, section 4, as printed in Eudin and North, p. 372.

[68] Mao Tse-tung, "An Analysis of the Various Classes in Chinese Society", published in *The Chinese Peasantry*, a Monthly Magazine, No. 2, February 1, 1926. The English version of an extract of the article appears in Stuart R. Schram, *The Political Thought of Mao Tse-tung*, New York, Washington and London, Frederick A. Praeger, Inc., 1963, 5th printing 1967, pp. 143-147.

the ECCI, held during February 17-March 15, 1926, also saw the Chinese proletariat becoming the lever, the main force of the revolution,[69] but set itself against the tendency to skip over the democratic stage straight to the proletarian dictatorship, forgetting the most important and decisive factor of all—the peasantry. It was stressed that the fundamental problem of the Chinese national liberation movement was the peasant problem.[70]

It should be remembered that Mao Tse-tung is not of peasant origin in the proper sense of the term.[71] As described previously, he was one of the twelve bourgeois intellectuals who attended the First Congress of the CCP. During his school days he respected the intellectuals as the only clean persons in the world and looked down upon the workers and peasants as dirty.[72] He testified that he became a Marxist in 1920.[73] That means that he had not yet become a Leninist. He spent the first five years of his Communist life in organizing students and workers but not peasants, basically in Hunan. It was not until 1925 that he began to work among the peasants there for a while.[74]

It is thus apparent that Mao did not take an interest in the peasantry as a political force until about two years after the 1923 Comintern instruction regarding the agrarian revolution in China. As a matter of fact, he developed his interest in the peasant work during his tenure of office as director of the KMT Peasant Movement Training Institute at Canton in 1925-26. Graduates of that institute, who were natives of Hunan, began to be sent back to that

---

[69] "Theses on the Trade Union Movement in the Colonial and Semi-colonial Countries", adopted by the Sixth Enlarged Session of the ECCI, February 17—March 15, 1926, as printed in Eudin and North, p. 325.

[70] "Resolution on the Chinese Question", adopted by the Sixth Enlarged Session of the ECCI, *Inprecor.*, Vol. 6, No. 40, pp. 648-49, and Eudin and North, p. 349.

[71] For an interesting discussion of this question, see Karl Wittfogel, *A Short History of Chinese Communism*, an unpublished manuscript on file in the Far Eastern and Russian Institute of the University of Washington, 1956, section VA1.

[72] Mao Tse-tung, "Talks at the Yenan Forum on Art and Literature", May 1942, *Mao's Selected Works*, Chinese edition, Vol. 3, Peking, People's Publishing House, 1957, p. 853, English edition, Vol. 4, New York, International Publishers, 1956, p. 67; Stuart R. Schram, *The Political Thought of Mao Tse-tung*, p. 225.

[73] Edgar Snow, *Red Star Over China*, pp. 155-56.

[74] Ho Kan-chih, pp. 39, 45; Edgar Snow, pp. 158, 159-160.

province to organise peasants toward the end of 1925.[75] On the basis of his own experience and the work of those graduates, Mao published on January 1, 1926, what appeared to be his first article on the peasant question entitled "An Analysis of the Various Peasant Classes and Their Attitudes Toward the Revolution". In this article he stood for organization of the peasants ranging from owner-peasants to farm hands to the exclusion of landlords and idler-proletarians, i.e., soldiers, bandits, robbers, thieves, beggars and prostitutes. He advocated using the method of struggle to ask the landlord class to make economic and political concessions. Only in extreme cases like the most oppressive and reactionary village bosses and gentry in Hai-feng, etc., did he favor knocking them down completely. As for the idler-proletariat, he wanted to win it over to the side of the revolution.[76] To the mind of Mao, the idler-proletariat was one of the four kinds of people whom he lumped under the term "proletariat", the other three being the industrial proletariat, the urban coolie, and the agricultural proletariat.[77]

It should not be forgotten that in 1925, the year before the publication of the above-cited article of Mao, Stalin made the important statement that the national question was, in essence, a peasant question. In introducing this statement, Stalin pointed out that the peasant question was the basis, the quintessence, of the national question, that the peasantry constituted the main army of the national movement, and that there was no powerful national movement without the peasant army, nor could there be.[78] Mao might not read this statement of Stalin at the time, but he was exceedingly fond of reciting it over and over again years afterward.[79]

---

[75] Ho Kan-chih, p. 89.

[76] This article of Mao appears in *The Chinese Peasantry*, No. 1, January 1, 1926, pp. 13-20. It was probably this article which, Mao claims, was rejected by Ch'en Tu-hsiu, leading to a mounting struggle between them regarding agrarian policy until the climax in 1927 (Edgar Snow, *Red Star Over China*, pp. 160-162). But there is no evidence in support of his claim. For the English version of an extract of this article, see Stuart R. Schram, *The Political Thought of Mao Tse-tung*, pp. 172-177.

[77] Mao Tse-tung, "An Analysis of the Various Classes in Chinese Society", as printed in *The Chinese Peasantry*, No. 2, February 1, 1926, op. cit.

[78] Stalin, "Concerning the National Question in Yugoslavia", *Stalin's Works*, Vol. 7, Moscow, Foreign Languages Publishing House, 1954, pp. 71-72.

[79] Ch'en Po-ta, *Stalin and the Chinese Revolution*, Peking, People's Publishing House, 1952, p. 16.

As will be seen later, the influence of this statement on Mao's thinking was far-reaching.

By 1926 the agrarian revolution which had been postponed for the sake of the national united front could no longer be leashed. The Northern Expedition for which the KMT-CCP peasant organizers had paved the way carried the peasant movement wholesale into the Yangtse valley in the latter months of 1926. Stalin was so much impressed with this powerful peasant upheaval that he personally thought that instead of the two-stage revolution propounded by Lenin, there should be three stages in the Chinese revolution, namely, the national united front with the bourgeoisie in the Canton period, the bourgeois-democratic revolution starting with the agrarian movement growing into a mighty peasant revolution after the national troops reached the Yangtse River, and the soviet period in the future.[80]   But the Seventh Plenum of the ECCI, held in November-December 1926, went a step further. It put on record the diagnosis that the Chinese revolution continued to be a bourgeois-democratic revolution but would inevitably outstrip the narrow boundary of bourgeois democracy and enter into the stage of transition to non-capitalist (socialist) development. To that end, railways and waterways should be nationalized, large-scale enterprises, mines, and banks having the character of foreign concessions should be confiscated, and land nationalization would come about eventually.[81]

According to M. N. Roy, who participated in the drafting of the Seventh ECCI Plenum's resolution on the Chinese question, the Comintern did not mean to realize socialism in China at once. The Chinese revolution was intended to be a development toward socialism, not through capitalism, but through a non-capitalist development. In this period of non-capitalist development, the complete abolition of private property was out of the question. He said that only one class—the proletariat—favored abolition of private property. Since the Chinese revolution in its present

[80] Stalin, "The International Situation", a speech before the Soviet Communist Party, August 1, 1927, op. cit.

[81] "Resolution on the Chinese Question", adopted by the Seventh Plenum of the ECCI, November 1926, sections 3, 6; *M. N. Roy's Mission to China*, p. 231.   It should be noted that the Third Congress of the CCP adopted the policy of nationalizing the large enterprises in 1923 (See C. Martin Wilbur and Julie Lien-ying How, op. cit., p. 67).

stage was waged by a coalition of classes, the proletariat could not put forward a program for the immediate abolition of private property.[82]

The above-mentioned coalition of classes, as enunciated by the Seventh Plenum of the ECCI, consisted of the proletariat, the peasantry and the urban petty bourgeoisie, to the exclusion of the majority of the capitalist bourgeoisie.[83]

Above all, the Seventh ECCI Plenum proclaimed the agrarian question to be the "central question" of the Chinese revolution at the time. Whichever class could give a radical answer to this question, it was stated, would be the leader of the revolution. At the present stage, it was pointed out, the proletariat was the only class that was in a position to carry on a radical agrarian policy in China. If the proletariat did not put forward a radical agrarian program, it would fail to attract the peasantry into the revolution and would lose its hegemony in the national liberation movement. Then, the bourgeoisie would regain the leadership of the revolution.[84]

Does the agrarian revolution conflict with the national united front? On October 29, 1926, Moscow sent a telegram to the Communists at Shanghai, telling them to suspend agrarian revolution until the capture of that city in order to avoid alienating the landowning officers of the revolutionary army.[85] Finding the telegram to be a mistake, Stalin disclosed that it was canceled a few weeks later.[86] He straightened out this question on November 30 when he addressed the Chinese Commission of the Seventh ECCI Plenum to the effect that the sooner and more solidly the Chinese peasantry was drawn into the revolution, the stronger and more powerful

---

82 M. N. Roy, "The National Revolution and Socialism", a speech at the CCP Fifth Congress, as printed in *M. N. Roy's Mission to China*, p. 231.
83 "Resolution on the Chinese Question", adopted by the Seventh Plenum of the ECCI, section 2; *M. N. Roy's Mission to China*, p. 135.
84 "Resolution on the Chinese Question", adopted by the Seventh Plenum of the ECCI, November 1926, section 4; *M. N. Roy's Mission to China*, pp. 137-138.
85 Leon Trotsky, *The Stalin School of Falsification*, New York, Pioneer Publishers, 1937, pp. 165, 173; Joseph Stalin, *Marxism and the National and Colonial Question*, New York, International Publishers, n. d., translated from a Russian edition of 1934, p. 239.
86 Joseph Stalin, *Marxism and the National and Colonial Question*, p. 237.

would be the anti-imperialist front.[87]   Accordingly, the Seventh
ECCI Plenum dismissed as baseless the fear that the aggravation
of the class struggle would weaken the united front against imperialism.   It took the position that national liberation should be
identified with agrarian revolution.[88]

The Seventh Plenum of the ECCI approached the Chinese
agrarian question from two interrelated aspects: the peasantry and
the land.   Regarding the former, the Comintern ordered the arming
of the poor and middle peasants for the first time in China.   Regarding the latter, only the land of counterrevolutionaries rather than
of landlords as such was subject to confiscation.[89]

In attempting to coordinate with the Northern Expedition, the
CCP adopted a resolution on the peasant movement in July 1926.[90]
Meanwhile, Mao Tse-tung was appointed chairman of the Peasant
Movement Committee of the CCP leadership at Shanghai.[91]   In
January 1927 he was sent to his native province of Hunan to investigate the work of peasant unions in five counties.   He drafted
his report in February and submitted it to the Central Committee
in March.[92]   The central idea of this report was the borrowing of
Lenin's tripartite classification of the peasantry into rich peasants,
middle peasants and poor peasants, with the poor peasants as the
revolutionary vanguard.[93]   The bourgeois-democratic revolution,
as prescribed by Lenin and the Comintern, could not be otherwise.
The arbitrary thing was that Mao gave 70 per cent of the credit
for the democratic revolution to the peasants while allotting 30

[87] Stalin, "The Prospects of the Revolution in China", speech delivered at
the Chinese Commission of the Seventh Plenum of the ECCI, November
30, 1926, printed in *Stalin's Works*, Vol. 8, Moscow, Foreign Languages
Publishing House, 1954, p. 382; Eudin and North, p. 353.
[88] "Resolution on the Chinese Question", adopted by the Seventh Plenum
of the ECCI, section 4, as printed in *M. N. Roy's Mission to China*, p. 138.
[89] Ibid., p. 139.
[90] C. Martin Wilbur and Julie Lien-ying How, op. cit., pp. 296-302.
[91] Ho Kan-chih, p. 89.
[92] *The Guide Weekly*, No. 191, March 12, 1927, pp. 2061-66; *Mao's Selected
Works*, Vol 1, Chinese edition, Peking, People's Publishing Co., 1953, pp.
13-46, English edition, New York, International Publishers, 1954, pp. 21-59.
[93] Lenin, "Preliminary Draft of Theses on the Agrarian Question", prepared
for the Second Comintern Congress, printed in his *Selected Works*, Vol. 10,
pp. 218-230; "Theses on the Peasant Question", adopted by the Enlarged
ECCI Meeting, April 1925, *Inprecor.*, Vol. 5, No. 47, June 4, 1925;
E. H. Carr, *The Bolshevik Revolution 1917-1923*, Vol. 2, London and New
York, The Macmillan Company, 1952, pp. 160-161.

per cent to the city dwellers and the military. Subsequently he dropped the 30-70 per cent formula after having borrowed the stronger idea from Stalin in 1945 that the bourgeois-democratic revolution in China was, in essence, a peasant revolution.[94]

Mao Tse-tung did not discuss the land question in his *Hunan Report*. His views on this question found expression in a draft resolution on the land question which he worked out for the KMT-CCP joint land commission under the Wuhan regime in April. Like many others, he stood for what was called political confiscation, i.e., confiscation of the land of counterrevolutionaries but not of landlords as such. Only in Hunan, according to him, was there economic confiscation, i.e., confiscation of the land which was leased to a tenant. Interestingly, Mao alone defined land confiscation to be a mere refusal to pay the land rent. Both KMT and CCP members were dissatisfied with the draft resolution. A leading Communist complained that the draft resolution would amount to "evading a solution of the whole land problem". Finally the resolution was shelved.[95]

The purge of the Communists in the Nanking-Shanghai area on April 12 represented a turning-point in the Chinese Communist movement. As Stalin pointed out, it marked the desertion of the national bourgeoisie from the revolution and signified that a swing had begun away from the national united front toward a revolution of the vast masses of the workers and peasants, toward an agrarian revolution.[96]

3. The Showdown

The Eighth Plenum of the ECCI, held during May 8-30, 1927, set the long-awaited Chinese agrarian revolution afoot. Its impact on Chinese events was immediate and overwhelming. It led to the

---

[94] "Resolution on Some Historical Problems", adopted by the CCP Central Committee, April 20, 1945, section 3; Hsiao Tso-liang, *Power Relations Within the Chinese Communist Movement 1930-1934*, Vol. II, *The Chinese Documents*, Seattle and London, University of Washington Press, 1967, p. 793.

[95] Chiang Yung-ching, *Borodin and the Wuhan Regime*, Taipei, Commercial Press, 1963, pp. 278-306.

[96] Stalin, "Questions of the Chinese Revolution: Theses for Propagandists", Approved by the CC, CPSU (B), *Stalin's Works*, Vol. 9, p. 229.

KMT-CCP split in Wuhan, the change of the CCP leadership, and the ensuing Communist insurrections despite deviations.

Because of China's semi-colonial status, the character of the Chinese revolution was still a bourgeois-democratic revolution. Stalin declared that the bourgeois-democratic revolution in China was a combination of the struggle against feudal survivals and the struggle against imperialism. He emphasized that this was the starting point of the whole Comintern line on the Chinese revolution.[97]

As described previously, the national bourgeoisie which had played a leading role in the national united front period was now declared to have broken away from the revolution as a whole. Instead, the proletariat was assuming an increasing role of leadership in the revolution.[98] For the first time a revolutionary democratic dictatorship of the proletariat and the peasantry was proclaimed for China.[99]

The Eighth ECCI Plenum ordered the Chinese Communists to remain in the Kuomintang and secure the role of leadership within it. The Kuomintang on its part was to be converted into a mass and revolutionary democratic organization.[100] It followed that the workers' and peasants' soviets would not be formed at once, but deferred until a later period when the democratic revolution had begun to grow into a socialist revolution.[101] It is well known that Trotsky held the opposite view. He urged the Communist withdrawal from the Kuomintang and the immediate creation of soviets.[102].

It is interesting to note that the Comintern's urban policy in China was as mild as before. On the one hand, the workers were assured of what they could legitimately expect from a trade union movement marked by the eight-hour working day. On the other,

---

97 Stalin, "The Revolution in China and the Tasks of the Comintern", a speech delivered at the Tenth Sitting of the Eighth Plenum of the ECCI, May 24, 1927, *Stalin's Works*, Vol. 9, p. 292.

98 "Resolution on the Chinese Question", adopted by the Eighth Plenum of the ECCI, May 1927, section 2.

99 Ibid., section 4.

100 Ibid., section 5.

101 Ibid., section 6.

102 Leon Trotsky, *Problems of the Chinese Revolution*, second edition, New York, Pioneer Publishers, 1962, pp. 23-72, 83-111.

only the bourgeoisie which was found guilty of sabotage and destruction of property, thereby creating unemployment leading to an economic disorder and bankruptcy, was subject to expropriation.[103]

In contrast, the agrarian policy in China, as formulated by the Eighth ECCI Plenum, was considerably more radical than ever before. It will be recalled that the Fifth Congress of the CCP, opening on April 27 for a session of two weeks, decided to confiscate the part of a landlord's land which was rented to a tenant, while the small landlord was left untouched.[104]   Though this was the first land policy ever adopted by the CCP and was considered radical enough in Chinese Communist circles at that time, it failed to meet the demands of the Eighth ECCI Plenum which called for the direct action of the peasant masses to seize land without authorization of the government which on its part was required to help realize the agrarian revolution from above. "The most important thing at present", the Eighth Plenum declared, "is to make the hundreds of thousands of peasants carry out the agrarian revolution by means of the 'plebeian type' of direct struggle from below—and the Communist Party should stand at the forefront to direct the movement".[105]

Moreover, the Eighth ECCI Plenum decided upon a number of military measures to facilitate the work of agrarian revolution in China.   These were to reorganize the army, build up military units faithful to the revolutionary cause, establish contact between the troops and mass organizations, organize the workers and peasants of Wuhan into a reliable army, establish Communist influence in the troops and rid them of counterrevolutionaries, etc.[106]   In

---

103   "Resolution on the Chinese Question", adopted by the Eighth Plenum of the ECCI, May 1927, section 4.

104   [Ch'ü] Ch'iu-pai, "The Peasant Regime and the Land Revolution", May 14, 1927, *Guide Weekly*, No. 195, p. 2124; "Resolution on the Agrarian Question", adopted by the Fifth Congress of the CCP, May 9, 1927, printed in *M. N. Roy's Mission to China*, p. 262; but the land policy of the Fifth Congress of the CCP was never carried out, as can be seen from "Letter of the CCP 'August 7' Conference to All Members of the Party", section 4.

105   "Resolution on the Chinese Question", adopted by the Eighth Plenum of the ECCI, May 1927, section 4.

106   Ibid., section 6; but the last three points cited here appear in the Chinese version of this resolution as printed in *Red Documents*, but not in the English version as printed in *Inprecor.*, Vol. 7, No. 35, June 11, 1927, p. 740.

accordance with this military decision, the Comintern telegraphed to China in May 1927, urging the immediate organization of eight to ten divisions of peasants and workers as guards of Wuhan for the disarming of unreliable troops.[107]   Needless to say, all these military measures flowed from Stalin's maxim: "In China, armed revolution is fighting against armed counterrevolution".[108]

It must, however, be remembered that in adopting the above military measures, the Comintern did not mean to launch immediate armed insurrections in the large cities in China. Stalin was very cautious about this matter. It will be recalled that when the Communist-organized labor pickets were disarmed by the Nationalists in Shanghai on April 12, 1927, the Trotsky-Zinoviev Opposition suggested a Communist insurrection as a means of retaliation in that city but that the Stalin-Bukharin leadership rejected the suggestion.[109] Stalin was of the opinion that Shanghai was a world center where the cardinal interests of the imperialist powers intersected and that the imperialists would not lightly give up the city. He therefore took the position that it would be more expedient to build up sufficient military strength, develop the agrarian revolution to the full, and carry on intense work to demoralise Chiang Kai-shek's rear and front, and then, after that, to tackle the problem of Shanghai in all its magnitude.[110]

Stalin was a cool, circumspect strategist. At the time some Communist leaders were of the opinion that an offensive on all fronts would be the principal sign of revolutionary spirit. But Stalin did not think so. He declared that an offensive on all fronts at that moment would be stupidity, not a sign of revolutionary

---

[107] Stalin, "The International Situation", a speech delivered at the plenum of the Soviet Communist Party, August 1, 1927, op. cit.; Eudin and North, p. 379.

[108] Stalin, "The Prospects of the Revolution in China", a speech delivered at the Chinese Commission of the Seventh Plenum of the ECCI, November 30, 1926, as printed in his *Works*, Vol. 8, Moscow, Foreign Languages Publishing House, 1954, p. 379; Eudin and North, p. 352.

[109] N. Bukharin, "The Results of the Plenary Session of the ECCI", report given at the Plenum of the Moscow Committee of the CPSU on June 4, 1927, *Inprecor.*, Vol. 7, No. 39, July 7, 1927, p. 882; Ch'en Po-ta, *Stalin and the Chinese Revolution*, Peking, People's Publishing House, 1952, p. 13.

[110] Stalin, "Talk with Students of the Sun Yat-sen University", May 13, 1927, *Stalin's Works*, Vol. 9, p. 260.

spirit, and that stupidity should not be confused with revolutionary spirit.[111] He charged that the Opposition did not realize that a decisive battle must be avoided in unfavorable conditions, otherwise it would make things easier for the enemy.[112]

On the basis of Stalin's position, the Eighth Plenum of the ECCI went on record with a denunciation of the stand of the Trotsky-Zinoviev Opposition in favor of a Communist insurrection in Shanghai. It was pointed out that the Opposition was absolutely wrong when it suggested the tactics of staging an insurrection at the time of the Shanghai coup. For such tactics were bound to engage the imperialists and their agents with armed force on a wide front. If the Shanghai workers had risked an extensive armed insurrection despite their inferior strength, they would have been crushed by the enemy, and the blood of the Chinese proletariat would have been shed in vain in a fight which stood no chance of success at all. Accordingly, the Eighth Plenum of the ECCI laid down the principles of armed insurrection as follows: "The tactics of insurrection are: once an insurrection gets started, an offensive must follow. An insurrection can be launched only when it stands a fair chance of success. One cannot afford to 'play' with insurrection. The tactic of 'insurrection under all circumstances' is not a Leninist tactic".[113]

Needless to say, the above principles of armed insurrection were nothing new; they came from Engels and Marx. But they were now for the first time introduced into China and were to serve as guides to armed insurrections for the Chinese Communists from that time on. More important, Stalin's strategy to avoid an armed clash with the immeasurably stronger enemy in Shanghai, choosing instead to retreat to the countryside to build up adequate agrarian and military strength for an eventual capture of the city, provided a guide for the subsequent revolutionary strategy of the Chinese Communists. This strategy was of immediate practical importance at the time since the CCP was just beginning to shift its main opera-

---

111 Ibid.
112 Stalin, "Questions of the Chinese Revolution: Theses for Propagandists", Approved by the CC, CPSU (B), *Stalin's Works*, Vol. 9, p. 232.
113 "Resolution on the Chinese Question", adopted by the Eighth Plenum of the ECCI, May 1927, section 7.

tional base from the few large cities to the vast expanse of the countryside.[114]

As a result of the Eighth Plenum, the ECCI lost no time in sending a telegram to China containing the following points: (1) the actual seizure of land from below—that is, the seizure of land by the direct action of the peasant masses without governmental authorization; (2) drawing new leaders from the agrarian revolution into the KMT leadership and taking millions of workers and peasants into the KMT membership; (3) mobilizing about 20,000 Communists and 50,000 workers and peasants of Hunan and Hupeh, and forming a reliable Communist army; and (4) organizing a military tribunal, headed by prominent KMT members, to punish anti-Communist officers.[115]

The above Comintern telegram reached China toward the end of May.[116]   Not until June 1 did Roy show it to Wang Ching-wei, leader of the Wuhan regime. Understandably Wang Ching-wei rejected it.[117]

Thereupon, Moscow changed its attitude toward the Wuhan regime immediately. The Comintern, which had wanted to utilize the Wuhan regime to carry out the agrarian revolution since May, decided now that that regime had become a counterrevolutionary force and that any continued support for it would be disastrous to the CCP. Therefore, the Comintern, which had ordered the Chinese Communists to head the labor and peasant departments of the Wuhan government in March, now instructed them to withdraw from it but remain in the KMT party with a view to winning over the rank and file members of the party and removing

---

114 M. N. Roy, "Revolution and Counterrevolution in China", *M. N. Roy's Mission to China*, p. 312; *Inprecor.*, Vol. 7, No. 42, July 21, 1927, p. 926; *Guide Weekly*, No. 197, June 8, 1927, p. 2156.

115 The text of the telegram is cited in Stalin's speech on "The International Situation" at the Plenum of the Soviet Communist Party, August 1, 1927, printed in *Communist International*, October 15, 1927, pp. 204-310 and, in extract form, in Stalin's book *Marxism and the National and Colonial Question*, New York, International Publishers, n. d., probably 1935, pp. 232-252. The text of the telegram in the two different sources is not exactly the same.

116 Ch'en Tu-hsiu, "Letter to All Comrades of the Party", December 10, 1929.

117 Wang Ching-wei, "The Story of the Expulsion of the Communists at Wuhan", November 5, 1927, printed in *Wang's Selected Works*, Vol. 3, pp. 215-237, edited by Hsun Ju, Shanghai, Kuang Ming Bookstore, 1929.

their incumbent leaders.[118] In consequence, the Communists announced their withdrawal from the Wuhan government but not the KMT on July 13, and two days later, July 15, they were all expelled from the KMT party.[119] The Comintern had expected this Communist expulsion.[120] Stalin's policy to utilize the KMT to carry out the agrarian revolution in China ended in a complete failure.

Viewed from the angle of CCP-Comintern relationships, it is more important to remember that the Comintern telegram in question led to the downfall of the Ch'en Tu-hsiu leadership. Both Roy, the Comintern representative, and Borodin, who served as advisor to the Wuhan regime and led the Communist fraction in the KMT leadership and government in Wuhan,[121] were intimately involved in the Comintern-CCP conflict.

It need hardly be pointed out that Roy wanted to utilize the Wuhan regime to carry out the agrarian revolution, but not to overthrow that regime.[122] Proceeding from this premise, he endorsed the Comintern telegram. He asserted that the telegram was a response to his request for a reassurance, which he had cabled to Moscow a few days before.[123] But he disclosed that he met

---

118 N. Bukharin, "An Abrupt Turn in the Chinese Revolution", *Inprecor.*, Vol. 7, No. 41, July 14, 1927, p. 898; "Resolution of the ECCI on the Present Situation of the Chinese Revolution", *Inprecor.*, Vol 7, No. 44, July 28, 1927, p. 984; M. N. Roy, "The Significance of the Fifth Congress of the CCP", May 13, 1927, *Guide Weekly*, No. 195, May 8 [sic], 1927, p. 2119; *M. N. Roy's Mission to China*, p. 279.

119 "Manifesto of the Central Committee of the CCP on the Political Situation", July 13, 1927, *Guide Weekly*, No. 201, July 18, 1927, pp. 2214-17; "Letter of Resignation from T'an P'ing-shan and Su Chao-cheng", July 1927, *Guide Weekly*, No. 201, July 18, 1927, pp. 2219-21; Wang Ching-wei, op. cit.; Ch'ü Ch'iu-pai, *The Chinese Revolution and the Communist Party*, 1928, p. 120.

120 *Inprecor.*, Vol. 7, No. 41, July 14, 1927, p. 898 and No. 44, July 28, 1927, p. 984.

121 Ch'u Ch'iu-pai, *The Chinese Revolution and the Communist Party*, 1928, p. 102.

122 M. N. Roy, "Revolution and Counterrevolution in China", *Inprecor.*, Vol. 7, No. 42, July 21. 1927, p. 926; *M. N. Roy's Mission to China*, p. 310; *Guide Weekly*, No. 197, June 8, 1927, p. 2157; Ch'ü Ch'iu-pai, *The Chinese Revolution and the Communist Party*, 1928, pp. 107-108.

123 M. N. Roy, *Revolution and Counterrevolution in China*, Renaissance Publishers, Calcutta, 1946, p. 520n. There is no evidence to support Chang Kuo-t'ao's claim that Roy dismissed the Comintern telegram as being difficult for execution (Chang Kuo-t'ao, "My Memoirs", *Ming Pao Monthly*, No. 23, November 1967, p. 89).

with strong resistance from Borodin and the Ch'en Tu-hsiu leadership in regard to the agrarian revolution. He complained that though Moscow backed him up politically, Borodin was left in the controlling position in the Chinese Communist Party and that the top Chinese Communist leaders followed Borodin, disregarding repeatedly the instructions of the Comintern in defiance of its representative on the spot.[124]

Roy's complaint was confirmed by Ch'ü Ch'iu-pai who reported the situation in Wuhan around mid-1927 as follows: There were, according to him, three different views on the Chinese revolution after the CCP Fifth Congress. On the one hand, Borodin favored making concessions to landlords and gentry. On the other, Roy was more radical, wanting to make some concessions only to small landlords and revolutionary officers. The most conservative was the Ch'en Tu-hsiu leadership which took the position that the agrarian revolution could not be carried out at once but should be preceded by a suitable period of propaganda. In fact, Ch'ü Ch'iu-pai stated, Roy's policy was never put into practice. A mixture of the ideas of Borodin and the Ch'en Tu-hsiu leadership prevailed.[125]

It was reported that Borodin told one of the CCP Politburo meetings, presumably in the spring of 1927, that agrarian revolution did not necessarily mean the confiscation of land. He was quoted as saying that agrarian revolution meant: (1) reduction of rent and interest, (2) self-government of the village, (3) protection of the tenant, (4) armed self-defense, and (5) training of the peasant movement personnel who would not commit excesses.[126] Not unnaturally, he dismissed the Comintern telegram in question as unpractical at that moment.[127]

Close to Borodin's thinking was the position of the Ch'en Tu-hsiu leadership which was on record as being against the immediate execution of agrarian revolution through the instrumentality of the

---

[124] M. N. Roy, *Revolution and Counterrevolution in China*, 1946, pp. 552-553n.
[125] Ch'ü Ch'iu-pai, *The Chinese Revolution and the Communist Party*, 1928, pp. 105-108.
[126] Ts'ai Ho-sen, "A History of Opportunism", dated September 1927, printed in Li Min-hun, *Red Archives*, July 1928, section B.
[127] Chang Kuo-t'ao, "My Memoirs", *Ming Pao Monthly*, No. 23, November 1967, p. 89.

Wuhan regime. The party chief Ch'en Tu-hsiu who had started out as a prominent university professor advocating science and democracy for China and who had successfully led the Chinese Communists in a trade union movement within the framework of a national united front was still in favor of liberal democracy. He rejected the idea of the seizure of political power by the Communists during the period of national revolution. Even at the time of reconstruction after the success of the national revolution, he stated, the political form would be a revolutionary, democratic and mass regime, but not a workers' and peasants' government, much less a proletarian dictatorship.[128] He was cited by Pavel Mif as not favoring an agrarian revolution.[129] He complained that "while Zinoviev used to tell us to support the bourgeoisie, Stalin now wants us to carry out the agrarian revolution in twenty-four hours!"[130] In commenting on the Comintern telegram of June 1 ordering the Chinese Communists to implement ultraleftist policies within the KMT, he said that it sounded as if Moscow wanted them to bathe in a cesspool.[131]

In contrast, Ch'ü Ch'iu-pai stood for a radical program of agrarian revolution. He declared that the proletariat had seized the revolutionary leadership from the bourgeoisie which could not perform the democratic tasks in the Chinese revolution. He hated the village despots and gentry who exploited and oppressed the peasants ruthlessly and who impeded the progress of the free economic development through the feudal exploitation. He favored the reduction of rent and interest in general and the confiscation of the land of large landlords and counterrevolutionaries in particular. He maintained that there must be a thorough change of the existing land tenure and a complete elimination of the political power of the feudal despots and gentry in the villages. The peasants must have the right to own and use the land and they must establish their own political power. In other words, the national revolution should be based on the agrarian revolution.[132]

---

128 [Ch'en] Tu-hsiu, "For What Are We Struggling at Present?" *Guide Weekly*, No. 172, September 25, 1926, pp. 1752-54.

129 Pavel Mif, *The Chinese Revolution*, Chinese version, Moscow and Leningrad, Foreign Workers' Publishing House, 1933, pp. 141-142.

130 Ts'ai Ho-sen, "A History of Opportunism", section B.

131 Ch'en Tu-hsiu, "Letter to All Comrades of the Party", December 10, 1929.

132 [Ch'ü] Ch'iu-pai, "The Peasant Regime and Land Revolution", May 14, 1927, *Guide Weekly*, No. 195, May 8 [sic], 1927, pp. 2120-24.

In addition, he excused if not defended the "excesses" of the labor and peasant movement.[133]   He called upon the peasants to rise against the oppressors in order to liberate themselves.[134]

Apart from Ch'ü Ch'iu-pai, there was another group of young Chinese Communists who upheld Comintern policy as against the Ch'en Tu-hsiu leadership.   This was the Communist Youth League or CY for short.[135]   But this group had no power at the time. Its views on the agrarian revolution, according to Ch'ü Ch'iu-pai, were suppressed.[136]

Mao Tse-tung, who was then not a top-ranking upstart, had not yet developed a consistent ideology regarding the Chinese revolution.   On the one hand, he told Edgar Snow in 1936 that he recommended a widespread redistribution of land and a rapid intensification of the agrarian struggle to the CCP Fifth Congress but that his recommendations were rejected by the Ch'en Tu-hsiu leadership.[137]   On the other, there are the following pieces of information in documents.   The National Peasant Union, of which Mao became director in May 1927, was actually restraining the peasant movement.[138]   He was quoted as admitting that the peasant unions in Hunan did molest the families of the military men.[139] When the Communists planned a counter-attack following the Changsha coup of May 21, he notified the Hunan Provincial Committee to cancel the plan.[140]   Roy testified that "the chairman of the Federation of Peasant Unions, Mao Tse-tung, in the critical

---

[133] [Ch'ü] Ch'iu-pai, "The Crisis of the Revolutionary National Government", June 13, 1927, *Guide Weekly*, No. 198, June 15, 1927, pp. 2169-71.

[134] [Ch'ü] Ch'iu-pai, "The Question of Responsibility for the Failure of the Revolution", *Guide Weekly*, No. 200, July 8, 1927, pp. 2201-2203.   Ts'ai Ho-sen's claim that Ch'ü Ch'iu-pai agreed with Borodin's moderate approach to the agrarian revolution (See Ts'ai Ho-sen, "A History of Opportunism", section B) cannot be corroborated.

[135] N. Bukharin, "An Abrupt Turn in the Chinese Revolution", *Inprecor.*, Vol. 7, No. 41, July 14, 1927, p. 899; "Resolution of the ECCI on the Present Situation of the Chinese Revolution", *Inprecor.*, Vol. 7, No. 44, July 28, 1927, p. 984.

[136] Ch'ü Ch'iu-pai, *The Chinese Revolution and the Communist Party*, p. 117.

[137] Edgar Snow, *Red Star Over China*, pp. 161-162.

[138] "Letter of the CCP 'August 7' Conference to All Members of the Party", section 4.

[139] Chiang Yung-ching, *Borodin and the Wuhan Regime*, p. 347.

[140] Chang Kuo-t'ao, "My Memoirs", *Ming Pao Monthly*, No. 27, March 1968, p. 96.

days of 1927, represented the extreme right-wing view in the leadership of the Communist Party".[141]

Despite the different shades of opinion within the party, the Ch'en Tu-hsiu leadership had, of course, the power to make decisions. Obviously the Chinese party leadership represented a different line from Moscow. The differences were major and basic. Both Ch'ü Ch'iu-pai and Pavel Mif recognized this.[142] On June 15, Ch'en Tu-hsiu in the name of the Chinese Politburo telegraphed back to Moscow, saying that the CCP accepted the Comintern instructions but could not execute them all immediately.[143] Since the "excesses" of the peasant movement in Hunan had caused a general hostility to the Communists, especially from the landowning revolutionary officers whose families had been hard hit, the Chinese Politburo considered it necessary to make a policy of concessions to save the revolutionary cause. Specifically, the Chinese telegram contained these major points: (1) It was necessary to correct the "excesses" immediately, and then to moderate the practices of land confiscation. (2) A split with the KMT and an immediate conflict with the revolutionary army should be prevented, otherwise it would be difficult and even impossible to create Communist military forces. (3) It was impossible to achieve a democratic dictatorship in a short time. (4) It would be particularly difficult to eliminate Wang Ching-wei by means of reorganization. (5) The poor peasants should replace the landless peasants as the motive force in the peasant movement.[144]

After receiving the Chinese Politburo telegram, Comintern President Bukharin declared that the CCP had literally rejected the Comintern instructions as "unpractical". [145] Naturally the Comintern reacted strongly against the Chinese intransigence. It was charged that the Chinese party leadership, instead of leading the agrarian revolution, had stood out as a hindrance to it in many

---

141 M. N. Roy, *Revolution and Counterrevolution in China*, 1946, p. 615.
142 Ch'ü Ch'iu-pai, *The Chinese Revolution and the Communist Party*, p. 110; Pavel Mif, *The Chinese Revolution*, Chinese version, 1933, p. 181.
143 Ch'en Tu-hsiu, "Letter to All Comrades of the Party", December 10, 1929.
144 Telegram to the Comintern [sent by] Ch'en Tu-hsiu at the Instructions of the Politburo, June 15, 1927, printed in *M. N. Roy's Mission to China*, pp. 338-340.
145 N. Bukharin, "An Abrupt Turn in the Chinese Revolution", *Inprecor.*, Vol. 7, No. 14, July 14, 1927, p. 899

cases. It was disclosed that the ECCI had frequently sent instructions in criticism of the CCP with the warning that the criticism would be made public unless the errors were made good. Now that the CCP leadership had rejected the Comintern instructions, the ECCI considered it their duty to call upon the members of the Chinese Communist Party to fight openly against the opportunism of their leadership.[146]

Ch'en Tu-hsiu confirmed that the Comintern instructions which the ECCI referred to as having been rejected by the CCP leadership were none other than the instructions embodied in the Comintern telegram of June 1.[147]

To make matters worse, the Communist-organized labor pickets in Wuhan which were posing a mounting threat to the public safety were forced to surrender their arms to the KMT garrison on June 28. Borodin was in favor of the surrender because he thought that there was no alternative. Chou En-lai agreed with him in the belief that the thousand-odd worn-out firearms of the pickets were not very important. The surrender was made with the approval of the CCP Politburo.[148] But this surrender of the pickets provoked serious criticisms from Moscow because it ran counter to the forward policy of the Comintern at the time.[149]

It was not surprising that Moscow could no longer tolerate the Ch'en Tu-hsiu leadership under the circumstances. The members of the CCP were called upon to close their ranks on the basis of Comintern decisions and fight against the deviations of their leadership. It was pointed out that the Chinese party had adequate forces within itself to change the character of its leadership and to disavow those leaders who had violated the Comintern discipline.[150]

---

146 "Resolution of the ECCI on the Present Situation of the Chinese Revolution", *Inprecor.*, Vol. 7, No. 44, July 28, 1927, p. 984.

147 Ch'en Tu-hsiu, "Letter to All Comrades of the Party", December 10, 1929.

148 Chang Kuo-t'ao, "My Memoirs", *Ming Pao Monthly*, No. 23, November 1967, p. 93.

149 "Resolution of the ECCI on the Present Situation of the Chinese Revolution", *Inprecor.*, Vol. 7, No. 44, July 28, 1927, p. 984; N. Bukharin, "An Abrupt Turn in the Chinese Revolution", *Inprecor.*, Vol. 7, No. 41, July 14, 1927, p. 899.

150 "Resolution of the ECCI on the Present Situation of the Chinese Revolution", *Inprecor.*, Vol. 7, No. 44, July 28, 1927, pp. 984-985.

In early July, Borodin told Ch'en Tu-hsiu to step down from the party leadership and asked him to go to Moscow to discuss questions of the Chinese revolution with the Comintern.[151] Ch'en Tu-hsiu tendered his resignation on July 15.[152] Meanwhile, Borodin designated Chang Kuo-t'ao, Chang T'ai-lei, Li Wei-han, Li Li-san and Chou En-lai to organize a five-man Politburo to take care of party affairs for the moment.[153]

Borodin and Ch'ü Ch'iu-pai left Hankow for Lushan, a summer resort in Kiangsi, on July 13.[154] Ch'ü Ch'iu-pai returned to Hankow on July 21 with the news that Borodin would soon go back to Moscow by way of northwestern China and that a new Comintern representative by the name of Lominadze would arrive in a day or two. According to Borodin, this new Comintern representative, associated as he had been with the Communist Youth International, was not familiar with Chinese affairs and was noted for his leftist disposition.[155]

Lominadze, aged 29, arrived in Hankow on July 23. He met Chang Kuo-t'ao and Ch'ü Ch'iu-pai that evening with the information that he was the Comintern representative with full powers to direct the work of the Chinese Communist Party and correct the mistakes made by both the former Comintern agents and the Chinese party leadership in the Chinese revolution. He said that the CCP leadership had made serious mistakes of right opportunism in contravention of Comintern instructions and that the Comintern had decided to reorganize the CCP leadership and remove Ch'en Tu-hsiu as party secretary and even possibly as a party member. Chang Kuo-t'ao inquired precisely what mistakes the Chinese party leadership had committed. Lominadze was quoted as answering to the following effect:

"The Chinese party leadership has, above all, failed to fight for the proletarian leadership in the Chinese revolution. For example, it rejected the Comintern instructions of June 1 decreeing

---

151 Ts'ai Ho-sen, "A History of Opportunism", section C.

152 Chang Kuo-t'ao, "My Memoirs", *Ming Pao Monthly*, No. 24, December 1967, p. 90.

153 Ts'ai Ho-sen, "A History of Opportunism", section C.

154 Chang Kuo-t'ao, "My Memoirs", *Ming Pao Monthly*, No. 24, December 1967, p. 89.

155 Ibid., p. 92.

the arming of workers and peasants. It also voluntarily disarmed the labor pickets in Wuhan. The root cause of these mistakes lies in the fact that the CCP leadership has been dominated by petty bourgeois intellectuals who lack class consciousness and revolutionary steadiness and who have long misinterpreted correct Comintern instructions from the angle of opportunism. The Comintern now can no longer trust those wavering intellectuals. It will resolutely support unwavering worker comrades to undertake work of leadership in the CCP and enable them to form a majority in the central leadership." [156]

Roy and Borodin left Hankow for Moscow late in July after the failure of their missions in China. [157]

Ch'en Tu-hsiu left Hankow for Shanghai in disguise about the same time. [158] He was disgraced on a charge of opportunism. [159] It is interesting to note that the word "opportunism", used in the Ch'en Tu-hsiu case here, referred to Menshevist deviation in authoritative documents of the time. [160] A Menshevik believed in gradualism and reformism and allied himself with the liberal bourgeoisie to achieve socialism. This was certainly true of Ch'en Tu-hsiu. The ideas of reformism, gradualism, and cooperation with the liberal bourgeoisie, which symbolized the Ch'en Tu-hsiu leadership, finally gave way to the militant policy of the Bolshevik rulers in Moscow who imposed the agrarian revolution on the Chinese Communist Party and, when the latter found it impossible to carry out this militant struggle within the KMT, removed Ch'en Tu-hsiu from the party leadership.

Pavel Mif attributed the Menshevist tendency in China to the fact that the Chinese Communist leaders at the time were all petty bourgeois intellectuals who joined the party during the period of the national liberation movement and regarded that movement as

---

156 Ibid., p. 94.
157 M. N. Roy's Mission to China, p. 126; M. N. Roy, Revolution and Counterrevolution in China, 1946, p. vi; Chang Kuo-t'ao, "My Memoirs", Ming Pao Monthly, No. 24, December 1967, p. 96.
158 Chang Kuo-t'ao, "My Memoirs", Ming Pao Monthly, No. 28, April 1968, p. 73.
159 "Letter of the CCP 'August 7' Conference to All Members of the Party"; Ch'en Tu-hsiu, "Letter to All Comrades of the Party", December 10, 1929.
160 For Stalin's view, see Communist International, October 15, 1927, p. 295; for Ch'ü Ch'iu-pai's view, see his booklet entitled The Chinese Revolution and the Communist Party, 1928, pp. 101, 110.

incompatible with the class struggle. He revealed that since the CCP leadership refused to obey Comintern instructions, the Comintern had to bypass it and call upon the Chinese Party members to hold an emergency conference to change that leadership.[161] This emergency conference was the August 7 Conference.

161 Pavel Mif, *The Chinese Revolution*, Chinese version, 1933, pp. 180-181.

CHAPTER II

THE LAND REVOLUTION

1. The August 7 Conference

The August 7 Conference stands out in Chinese Communist annals as marking the beginning of the agrarian revolution—or "land revolution" as the Chinese Communists call it. It adopted the armed insurrection as the main method of struggle.

The conference was called by order of the Comintern.[1] It was under the personal charge of the Comintern representative Lominadze who, as described previously, had been sent to China to fight opportunism and reorganize the Chinese party leadership.[2] The Comintern president Bukharin had summarized Comintern policy in China in advance: extraordinary conference of the Party, new elections to the Central Committee, ruthless criticism of the leadership, execution of directions of the Comintern, etc.[3] This must have served as a guide to Lominadze in the August 7 Conference.

At first, the Chinese Communist leaders hesitated to call the conference for lack of a quorum.[4] But they yielded to the pressure of Lominadze who threatened to call the conference himself if the Chinese refused to cooperate.[5] Finally they decided to hold an emergency, as distinct from a formal, conference of the central party leadership, which was to go down in history as the August 7 Emergency Conference.[6]

---

[1] Ch'ü Ch'iu-pai, *The Chinese Revolution and the Communist Party*, p. 121; Pavel Mif, *The Chinese Revolution*, Chinese version, 1933, p. 183.

[2] Ch'ü Ch'iu-pai, *The Chinese Revolution and the Communist Party*, p. 121; Chang Kuo-t'ao, "My Memoirs", *Ming Pao Monthly*, No. 24, December 1967, p. 94.

[3] *Inprecor.*, Vol. 7, No. 41, July 14, 1927, p. 899.

[4] Ch'ü Ch'iu-pai, *The Chinese Revolution and the Communist Party*, p. 121.

[5] Ts'ai Ho-sen, "A History of Opportunism", section C.

[6] Ch'ü Ch'iu-pai, *The Chinese Revolution and the Communist Party*, p. 122.

The conference was held at Kiukiang according to Chinese Communist sources.[7] It was attended by twelve full members and three alternate members of the Central Committee, plus five representatives of the Communist Youth League and two representatives from local party units.[8] Among those present were Ch'ü Ch'iu-pai, Chang T'ai-lei, Su Chao-cheng, Li Wei-han, Jen Pi-shih, Teng Chung-hsia, Hsiang Chung-fa, Ts'ai Ho-sen, Mao Tse-tung, P'eng Kung-ta and Lo I-nung.[9]

The August 7 Conference created the Provisional Central Political Bureau to act for the Central Committee pending the convocation of the Sixth National Congress of the CCP.[10] This new Politburo was composed of seven members, namely, Ch'ü Ch'iu-pai, Su Chao-cheng, Li Wei-han, Chang T'ai-lei, Hsiang Ying, Hsiang Chung-fa and Lu Fu-yuan.   Four of them had worker backgrounds and were set up in the top posts to strengthen the proletarian leadership. They were Hsiang Ying, Hsiang Chung-fa, Su Chao-cheng and Lu Fu-yuan.[11]

The influence of the Communist Youth League made itself felt in the Politburo as well as the August 7 Conference. Jen Pi-shih played an active part in the August 7 Conference by reason of the fact that the Communist Youth League under his leadership had been fighting against the opportunism of Ch'en Tu-hsiu for some time.   As secretary of the League, Jen Pi-shih was to attend the meetings of the Politburo regularly.[12]   Besides, Chang T'ai-lei was one of the founders of the League in 1920 and served as its

---

7 Ho Kan-chih, *A History of the Modern Chinese Revolution*, Hong Kong, San-lien Bookstore, 1958, p. 124; Wang Shih, Wang Ch'iao, Ma Ch'i-ping and Chang Ling, *A Brief History of the Chinese Communist Party*, Shanghai, People's Publishing House, 1958, p. 102.   It seemed likely that Kiukiang was the place of the August 7 Conference, since practically all the Communist leaders and troops had gathered in the Kiukiang-Nanchang area shortly after the KMT-CCP split in mid-July.

8 Ch'ü Ch'iu-pai, *The Chinese Revolution and the Communist Party*, p. 121.

9 Ibid.; Ts'ai Ho-sen, "A History of Opportunism", section C; Chang Kuo-t'ao, "My Memoirs", *Ming Pao Monthly*, No. 27, March 1968, p. 96; Edgar Snow, *Red Star Over China*, New York, Modern Library, 1944, p. 166; cf. Jerome Ch'en, *Mao and the Chinese Revolution*, London, Oxford University Press, 1965, p. 130.

10 "Resolution on the Question of the Organization of the Party", adopted by the August 7 Conference, *Central Correspondence*, No. 2, August 23, 1927.

11 Chang Kuo-t'ao, "My Memoirs", *Ming Pao Monthly*, No. 27, March 1968, p. 96.

12 Ibid.

secretary in 1925. It was he who introduced Ch'ü Ch'iu-pai into the Chinese Communist Party in Moscow, probably in 1922.[13]

Ch'ü Ch'iu-pai was made the new party leader because of his radical approach to land revolution, as described previously. He published a number of statements against P'eng Shuh-chih, a close friend and theoretician of Ch'en Tu-hsiu, since late 1926, and also against them both prior to and during the CCP Fifth Congress in 1927.[14] His thesis has already been outlined in the preceding chapter and need not be recapitulated here.

On the eve of his execution in 1935 Ch'ü Ch'iu-pai confessed that he had no intention to replace Ch'en Tu-hsiu as the party chief but he could not help it. Unlike Ch'en Tu-hsiu with patriarchal authority, he said, he was only responsible for the issuance of general public statements, leaving party organization and military work in the hands of those in charge of such affairs.[15] Chang Kuo-t'ao confirmed that Ch'ü Ch'iu-pai was forced to take blind action.[16]

In contrast to the upstarts, a number of Communist leaders fell into disgrace as a result of the August 7 Conference. Ch'en Tu-hsiu and T'an P'ing-shan were mentioned by name as opportunists in the documents of the conference and were to be punished accordingly. The former was removed from the party leadership though his party membership was still retained for the moment. The latter was dismissed as a party member three months later. Chang Kuo-t'ao was charged with having allegedly opposed the Comintern and having given support to opportunism. Li Li-san was held responsible for his wrong leadership in the General

---

13 Ch'ü Ch'iu-pai, "In Memory of Comrade Chang T'ai-lei", *Bolshevik*, No. 12, pp. 385-86; Ch'ü Ch'iu-pai, *Superfluous Words*, May 22, 1935.

14 Ch'ü Ch'iu-pai, *Superfluous Words*, May 22, 1935; Pavel Mif, *Heroic China—Fifteen Years of the Communist Party of China*, Chinese version, 1936, p. 65.

15 Ch'ü Ch'iu-pai, *Superfluous Words*, May 22, 1935; cf. T. A. Hsia, "Ch'ü Ch'iu-pai's Autobiographical Writings: The Making and Destruction of a 'Tender-hearted' Communist", *China Quarterly*, No. 25, January-March 1966; for Li Wei-han as minister of organization under the Ch'ü Ch'iu-pai leadership and Chou En-lai in charge of military affairs from November on, see Chang Kuo-t'ao, "My Memoirs", *Ming Pao Monthly*, No. 27, March 1968, pp. 95, 97.

16 Chang Kuo-t'ao, "My Memoirs", *Ming Pao Monthly*, No. 24, December 1967, p. 94.

Labor Union of Hupeh. Chou En-lai was held responsible for the disbanding of the labor pickets in Wuhan. Ts'ai Ho-sen was in charge of propaganda literature filled with opportunist errors. Mao Tse-tung was held responsible for the many incorrect instructions issued by the National Peasant Union under his leadership. As described previously, he also notified the Hunan Provincial Committee to cancel the plan for a counter-attack on Changsha following the May 21 coup there. Accordingly, it was thought that he should share the responsibility for opportunism. [17]

In the sphere of ideology the August 7 Conference represented the CCP's acceptance of the basic China policy of the Eighth ECCI Plenum of May 1927. The conference addressed a long letter to all party members which, according to Chang Kuo-t'ao, was prepared by Lominadze and translated by Ch'ü Ch'iu-pai into Chinese. [18] This letter gives an exhaustive listing of the errors of opportunism attributed to the Ch'en Tu-hsiu leadership. By contrast, one can also get a general idea of what was described as the correct policies— policies predominantly based on the China resolution of the Eighth ECCI Plenum. Besides, the ECCI Resolution on the Present Situation of the Chinese Revolution of July 1927 was also mentioned as a guide to CCP action. The letter advocated the confiscation of the land of landlords despite the fact that it is not clear whether the Eighth ECCI Plenum stood for confiscation of the land of landlords or large landlords in China. [19] In addition, the conference adopted three resolutions on the peasant struggle, the labor movement and the party organization. It also approved a political platform which was soon to be used by the Politburo as the basis for the drafting and adoption of a resolution on political tasks and tactics of the CCP, embodying significant additions to the theory and tactics of the revolution. [20]

---

[17] Ibid., No. 27, March 1968, p. 96.

[18] Ibid., pp. 95, 96.

[19] While the English version of the "Resolution on the Chinese Question" adopted by the Eighth Plenum of the ECCI, as printed in Eudin and North, *Soviet Russia and the East 1920-1927*, provides for the confiscation of the land of "landlords", the Chinese version as printed in *Red Documents*, uses the term "large landlords". The *Inprecor.* version happens to skip over this key expression.

[20] For the text of all the four resolutions, see *Central Correspondence*, No. 2, August 23, 1927; cf. Ch'ü Ch'iu-pai, *The Chinese Revolution and the Communist Party*, p. 124.

Regarding the nature of the Chinese revolution, the August 7 Conference made clear that the Chinese revolution was still in the stage of bourgeois-democratic revolution. But it was pointed out that the bourgeois-democratic revolution could and should grow into a socialist revolution immediately and without interruption.[21] The CCP, it was stated, saw no sharp line that could divide the bourgeois-democratic revolution from the socialist revolution. The prospects of the transition from the democratic to socialist revolution, it was believed, would depend upon the organizational strength of the proletariat.[22]

The coalition of revolutionary classes consisted of workers, peasants, and the petty bourgeoisie (except the counterrevolutionary petty bourgeoisie). The political system adopted was a revolutionary democratic dictatorship of workers and peasants.[23]

It is interesting to note that the urban program of the August 7 Conference did not go beyond the scope of the trade union movement as prescribed by the Comintern. The national bourgeoisie which was regarded as having broken away from the revolution was not subject to expropriation unless it opposed the revolution by means of, say, sabotage or the closure of factories.[24] Foreign industry was not to be seized if the resistance of the imperialists was strong enough to topple the local Communist regime.[25] The workers on their part were to wage the economic rather than political struggle. Specifically, they were to struggle for the eight-hour working day, unemployment relief, wage raise, etc.[26]

In contrast, the agrarian program of the August 7 Conference was far more radical. It was based upon the call of the Eighth

---

[21] "Resolution on the Political Tasks and Tactics of the CCP", n. d., probably around mid-August 1927, *Central Correspondence*, No. 2, August 23, 1927, section 2.

[22] Ibid., section 6.

[23] "Letter of the CCP 'August 7' Conference to All Members of the Party", section 2; "Resolution on the Political Tasks and Tactics of the CCP", n. d., probably around mid-August 1927, op. cit.

[24] "Resolution on the Political Tasks and Tactics of the CCP", section 2; "Resolution on the Present-day Labor Movement", adopted by the August 7 Conference, *Central Correspondence*, No. 2, August 23, 1927.

[25] "Resolution on the Political Tasks and Tactics of the CCP", section 9, op. cit.

[26] "Resolution on the Present-day Labor Movement", adopted by the August 7 Conference, op. cit.

Plenum of the ECCI that "the most important thing at present is to make the hundreds of thousands of peasants carry out the agrarian revolution by means of the 'plebeian type' of direct struggle from below".[27]   This was literally a call for a peasant revolt.

The peasant revolt called for took the form of the autumn harvest insurrection which was decided by the CCP leadership before the August 7 Conference.[28] The background of this proposed insurrection was the peasant hostility to the landlords and rural despots following the outlawry of the peasant movement in provinces like Hunan, Hupeh, Kiangsi and Kwangtung in late spring or so in 1927. These counterrevolutionary people tried what they could to revenge themselves on the peasants who had earlier done them harm. The most pressing thing at the moment was that these people were extorting payment of the rents and loans which the peasants had refused to pay in the hectic days of the peasant movement. The autumn crops were becoming the immediate bone of contention. On the one hand, the landlords wanted to get them in payment for debts due to them, anyway. On the other, the peasants wanted to resist in hopes that their crops might not be taken away altogether by the landlords. Driven underground, the local Communists sought to take advantage of this situation to serve their political purpose. The Communist organizations in Hunan and Hupeh made suggestions for a peasant struggle at the time of autumn harvest. The party leadership considered the suggestions favorably and decided to expand them into an autumn harvest insurrection for the purpose of carrying out the agrarian revolution. Lominadze was the prime mover of the insurrectionary wave.[29]

It is thus clear that the autumn harvest insurrection was not intended as a mere struggle for Communist survival; it was a positive program of armed insurrection against the old regime. It was the first experiment of the Comintern-inspired agrarian revolution in China.

---

27 "Letter of the CCP 'August 7' Conference to All Members of the Party", section 4.
28 Ch'ü Ch'iu-pai, *The Chinese Revolution and the Communist Party*, p. 122.
29 Chang Kuo-t'ao, "My Memoirs", *Ming Pao Monthly*, No. 27, March 1968, p. 97.

In consequence, the August 7 Conference formally adopted the policy of a general peasant insurrection in as large a region as possible at autumn harvest time. Strong and active comrades were to be despatched to the key provinces to organize the peasant insurrection. The main slogans were: Vest political power in peasant unions. Arm the peasants. Suppress and expropriate village bosses, rural gentry and counterrevolutionaries. Confiscate the land of large and middle landlords. Reduce land rents due to small landlords. It was explained that the purpose of exempting small landlords from confiscation was to neutralize the large number of small proprietors in city and countryside. The Communists should have no objection if the peasants would oppose those small landlords who had land for rent.[30]

Some additional ideas were supplied immediately after the August 7 Conference. First of all, it was made clear that the CCP could not possibly plan a nationwide insurrection at the moment because of the widely diverse conditions in the various provinces and the lack of a central government. It followed that the success or failure of insurrection could not be judged by the criterion of whether or not the central government was overthrown. Accordingly, Communist policy for the moment was only to prepare and organize the armed insurrection in those provinces which had become the centers of the peasant movement.[31] The provinces which were originally selected for the proposed insurrection were Hunan, Hupeh, Kiangsi, and Kwangtung.[32] But after the Nanchang uprising of August 1 there were no immediate party organization and mass movement in Kiangsi. Therefore, there

---

[30] "Resolution on the Present-day Peasant Struggle", adopted by the August 7 Conference, No. 2, August 23, 1927; for Mao's claim that the program of the autumn harvest uprisings had not been sanctioned by the Central Committee, see Edgar Snow, Red Star Over China, New York, Modern Library, 1944, p. 169.

[31] "Resolution on the Political Tasks and Tactics of the CCP", section 4.

[32] Ch'ü Ch'iu-pai, The Chinese Revolution and the Communist Party, p. 122; "Report on the Autumn Harvest Uprising in Hupeh", leaf 4A, prepared by the Hupeh Provincial Committee toward the end of October 1927 and printed with many errors in mimeograph in Central Correspondence, No. 11, n. d., probably late November 1927, made legible in Chinese and translated into Japanese in 1961 by Taicho Mikami, Tadao Ishikawa and Minoru Shibata of the Institute of Oriental and Occidental Studies, Kansai University, Osaka, Japan.

was no autumn harvest uprising in the province.[33]   In Kwangtung there were, indeed, some preparations for the autumn harvest uprising.   But since the Kwangtung Provincial Committee pinned its hope on the help of the troops which were retreating from Nanchang and which were finally defeated at Swatow, the proposed autumn harvest uprising in Kwangtung never came off.[34]   In consequence, only Hunan and Hupeh turned out to be the actual scene of the autumn harvest uprisings.

For the sake of the autumn harvest uprisings, the CCP leadership laid down the general principles of insurrectionary tactics as prescribed by the Eighth Plenum of the ECCI.   It was made clear that one must not play with insurrection and that technical, organizational and political preparations must be made in advance. Once an insurrection was decided upon, it must not be abandoned halfway; rather it must be carried on unflinchingly to the end. Insurrection must always be on the initiative and offensive.   To take a defensive and wavering attitude at a crucial moment would be certain to result in the failure of the insurrection.[35]

The central office of the CCP remained in Wuhan for the time being for the supervision of the autumn harvest insurrection.   It was not until the end of September that it was transferred to Shanghai.[36]

2. Mao Versus the Party Leadership

The August 7 Conference laid down the general ideas of the autumn harvest insurrection as outlined above, but no detailed blueprint for action.   Armed with those general ideas, Mao was despatched by the party leadership to his home province of Hunan to reorganize the Hunan Provincial Committee for the purpose of carrying out the insurrection.   This new assignment made him

---

33 "Report of the Kiangsi Provincial Committee", December 12, 1927, *Central Political Correspondence*, No. 16, n.d.

34 "Letter to the Kwangtung Provincial Committee", October 12, [1927], *Central Correspondence*, No. 7, October 30, 1927.

35 "Resolution on the Political Tasks and Tactics of the CCP", op. cit., section 4.

36 Ch'ü Ch'iu-pai, *The Chinese Revolution and the Communist Party*, p. 125; "Report of Comrade I-nung to The Enlarged Conference of the Hupeh Provincial Committee", section 2, *Central Political Correspondence*, No. 20, April 12, 1928.

the central figure of the Hunan Provincial Committee, of which P'eng Kung-ta was the secretary.[37]

It will be recalled that in the critical days in late July the five-man Politburo wanted the prominent Communist leaders to leave Wuhan for reasons of security and that under this program it proposed to send Mao to Szechuan for his personal safety. But Mao did not comply. Regardless of danger, he volunteered to return to Hunan to arm the peasants among whom he had worked before.[38] There can be little doubt that Mao represented the radical trend of the peasant movement in Hunan since late 1926. [39] It was only natural that he should be entrusted with the important task of organizing the autumn harvest urpising in Hunan.

However, Mao like almost all other Chinese Communist leaders at the time had no experience of organizing a peasant uprising in a Communist way. Slogans like land revolution and peasant insurrection remained slogans of propaganda until then. It was easy to learn them from Communist literature but it was hard to translate them into practice. Thus, when the Chinese Communists were called upon to carry out the land revolution in the summer of 1927, few really knew how to do the job. Commenting on the Nanchang uprising of August 1, Chang Kuo-t'ao stated on October 9 that "although, politically, our comrades made active propaganda for land revolution, few realized how to make a land revolution". [40] Looking back at the beginnings of the autumn harvest uprising, the Hupeh Provincial Committee declared in late October that "though all our comrades admitted that the Chinese revolution had entered upon the stage of land revolution, even many leading comrades did not really understand what the land revolution was all about". [41] Summing up the insurrectionary experiences of the latter months of 1927, the party leadership declared on New Year's Day 1928 that it would be impossible to carry out a perfect party policy overnight when opportunism was being replaced by bolshevization and

---

[37] "Resolution on Political Discipline", November 14, [1927], sections (3)3, 5(6), *Central Correspondence*, No. 13, November 30, 1927.

[38] Chang Kuo-t'ao, "My Memoirs", *Ming Pao Monthly*, No. 24, December 1967, p. 91; Ts'ai Ho-sen, "A History of Opportunism", section C.

[39] Ts'ai Ho-sen, "A History of Opportunism", section C.

[40] "Chang Kuo-t'ao's Report", October 9, 1927, *Central Correspondence*, No. 7, October 30, 1927, par. 2.

[41] "Report on the Autumn Harvest Uprising in Hupeh", leaf 59A.

that adequate experience was needed to set the new policy on the right path. "Accordingly", it was stated, "many provincial committees were not able to employ the tactics of insurrection in the right way until they had gone through trial and error for a number of times".[42]   Commenting on the land law of December 1928, Mao admitted that he did not have any experience of land struggle before the winter of 1927-28.[43]

Against this background, Mao went to Hunan to organize his first peasant uprising. After arriving in Changsha, he called a meeting of the Hunan Provincial Committee to discuss the question of insurrection on August 18. He was cited as declaring in the meeting that the purpose of the autumn harvest uprising was to carry out a thorough land revolution and establish a democratic regime of workers and peasants and that, to that end, the party must do its best to lead the armed struggle and use firearms to seize political power and execute land revolution.[44]   In consequence, a plan for the insurrection in Hunan was drawn up with Changsha, the capital city of the province, as the starting point.[45]   The party leadership was asked to get two regiments of troops to attack Changsha on August 31.[46]

The above plan was in all probability embodied in a letter from the Hunan Provincial Committee to the central party leadership under date of August 20. Unfortunately the plan was omitted from the text of the letter when printed in the party organ *Central Correspondence*, No. 3, August 30, 1927. This letter which bears no signature in the incomplete reproduction available was most probably written by Mao on behalf of the Hunan Provincial Committee.[47]   It was delivered from Changsha to Hankow by an unidentified representative who made an oral report to the Central

---

[42] "Central's Letter to Hupeh Comrades", January 1, 1928, *Central Political Correspondence*, No. 20, April 12, 1928, section 6.

[43] Mao Tse-tung, *Investigations of the Rural Districts*, published at Yenan in 1941, reissued by Hsinhua Bookstore, Shantung, 1946, p. 88.

[44] Miao Ch'u-huang, *A Short History of the Chinese Communist Party* (First Draft), Peking, 1956, pp. 59-60.

[45] "A Reply to Hunan", August 23, 1927, *Central Correspondence*, No. 3, August 30, 1927.

[46] Ch'ü Ch'iu-pai, *The Chinese Revolution and the Communist Party*, p. 127.

[47] Stuart R. Schram, "On the Nature of Mao Tse-tung's 'Deviation' in 1927", *China Quarterly*, No. 18, April-June 1964, p. 59n.

Standing Committee which met in special session to discuss it almost immediately.[48]

Thus, the available incomplete text of the August 20 letter contains only two major points, namely, (1) the question of soviets, and (2) the land problem. Mao was pleased to hear that a newly arrived Comintern directive decreed immediate formation of workers', peasants' and soldiers' soviets in China. He thought that China had long reached her 1917 and that it was a great mistake to regard her as being still in her 1905. With the feeling that the CCP should have the determination to set up workers', peasants' and soldiers' regimes in Kwangtung, Hunan, Hupeh and Kiangsi at once, he expressed the hope that the party leadership would accept the Comintern directive without hesitation and carry it into execution in Hunan.[49]

Intimately associated with the proposed formation of soviets was the question of abandoning the KMT banner. Mao urged that the KMT banner be abandoned and that the Red flag be hung out immediately.[50]

Regarding the land problem, Mao advocated the confiscation of all land, including that of small landlords and owner-peasants.[51]

In reply, the party leadership declared on August 23 that it endorsed, in principle, the idea of using Changsha as a starting point of the insurrection, but pointed out the following two mistakes:

1. Preparatory work of insurrection among peasants in the counties surrounding Changsha was too weak, and therefore Changsha would have to be taken by military force. An undue

---

[48] "A Reply to Hunan", August 23, *Central Correspondence*, No. 3, August 30, 1927.

[49] "Letter from Hunan to the Central", August 20, *Central Correspondence*, No. 3, August 30, 1927; for Mao's claim that the Comintern opposed organization of soviets and not until later did it advance it as a slogan, see Edgar Snow, op. cit., p. 167.

[50] "Letter from Hunan to the Central", August 20, *Central Correspondence*, No. 3, August 30, 1927.

[51] Ibid.; Mao told Edgar Snow in 1936 that his program of the autumn harvest uprisings consisted of the following five points: (1) complete severance of the provincial Communist Party from the Kuomintang, (2) organization of a peasant-worker revolutionary army, (3) confiscation of the property of small and middle, as well as great, landlords, (4) setting up the power of the Communist Party in Hunan, independent of the Kuomintang, and (5) organization of soviets. (Edgar Snow, op. cit., p. 167).

emphasis on military force and an apparent distrust of the masses like this would only result in a military adventure.

2. With attention focused only on Changsha, the outlying districts were neglected. For example, southern Hunan was practically abandoned as a rising area. Also there were no active preparations for insurrection in the counties of Changsha, Hsiangtan, Liuyang, Liling, Hsianghsiang, Ninghsiang, etc.[52]

Accordingly, the party leadership suggested that southern Hunan with Hengyang as the center be made another starting point of insurrection, Paoching (Shaoyang) in central Hunan might also be slated for a third starting point, if possible. Southern Hunan should be coordinated with central Hunan, and northern Hunan should be coordinated with southern Hupeh. In fact, it was pointed out, the two regiments of troops requested could no longer be used by Communists. The most important thing for the Hunan comrades to do was to mobilize the great masses of poor people for the struggle.[53]

With regard to the question of soviets, the party leadership told Mao that it was wrong to think of China as having reached her 1917. China was still in the second stage of the bourgeois-democratic revolution in which the KMT banner should be used. Only in the third stage of the bourgeois-democratic revolution could soviets be created. It was pointed out that all this was laid down in Comintern instructions.[54]

As for the land question, the Central Standing Committee declared that the slogans of confiscating the land of small landlords and owner-peasants should not be raised. However, it was stated, the Communists should not fear the expropriation of the land of small landlords when it actually happened. Nor should they consciously avoid peasant attacks on the land of owner-peasants.[55]

But Mao and his fellow Hunan Communists were stubborn. They flatly rejected the position of the party leadership on the

---

[52] "A Reply to Hunan", August 23, *Central Correspondence*, No. 3, August 30, 1927.
[53] Ibid.
[54] Ibid.
[55] Ibid.

insurrectionary strategy. On August 30 Mao rejoined on behalf of the Hunan Provincial Committee as follows:

1. Changsha was intended merely as the starting point of the whole insurrection. The principal fighters there would be workers and peasants, while the two regiments of troops in question would be an auxiliary force only. The party leadership was really not clear about the local conditions in Hunan when it ordered the cancellation of the proposed Changsha rising. It was, indeed, a contradictory policy to give no heed to military effort on the one hand and call for an armed insurrection of the masses on the other.

2. The charge that the outlying districts were neglected was not true. Hengyang in southern Hunan was not made a second starting point of the insurrection because Communist strength in Hunan could afford an insurrection only in central Hunan with Changsha as the center. It was feared that even the insurrection in central Hunan could not materialize if the Communist strength was divided. It was contended that the insurrection plan for southern Hunan had been sent to the various organized counties for implementation and that once Changsha made a start on the insurrection, the various counties would follow suit simultaneously.[56]

It is interesting to note that Mao did not answer the two other questions: the soviets and the land problem. Obviously, he made a mistake in thinking that China had reached her 1917 which stood for the proletarian-socialist revolution. A year later, he corrected this mistake by stating that he agreed with the Comintern that China was still in the stage of the bourgeois-democratic revolution and that she must go through the democratic revolution before laying a real foundation for the transition to socialism.[57]

As to the question of the soviets, Mao was somewhat misinformed about Comintern instructions. Moscow did not advocate an unqualified immediate formation of soviets in China as Mao understood. It decided on August 9 that if the KMT could not be converted into a mass organization of workers and peasants and if the revolution

---

[56] "Letter from the Hunan Provincial Committee", August 30, *Central Correspondence*, No. 5, September 20, 1927.

[57] Mao Tse-tung, "Struggle in the Chingkang Mountains", November 25, 1928, in his *Selected Works*, Chinese edition, Vol. I, pp. 79-80, Peking, 1953, English edition, Vol. I, p. 99, New York, 1954.

was on the upsurge, it would be necessary to change the propagandist slogan of soviets into a slogan of direct struggle and to proceed at once to the organization of workers', peasants' and artisans' soviets.[58] The CCP accepted the Moscow decision on September 19 when it declared that the soviets should first be established in central locations like Canton and Changsha if decisive and firm victories were achieved there.[59] The priority given to central locations was eliminated in November,[60] after *Pravda* declared on September 30 that as the Chinese revolution spread to industrial centers, it would be possible to create soviets of workers, soldiers' and artisans' deputies there, but that the peasant unions must be converted into soviets of peasant deputies in the countryside.[61]

In regard to the land problem, Mao was obviously more radical than the party leadership. As to why Mao changed from his conservative attitude of confiscating the land of only counterrevolutionaries but not of landlords as such in April, as noted previously, to his radical position of confiscating all land including that of small landlords and owner-peasants in August, it is anybody's guess. It will be recalled that Mao advocated confiscation of all land, too, at Chingkangshan in December 1928 but that he soon found it to be a mistake and changed it to confiscation of the land of organizations and landlords in April 1929. [62] Needless to say, if owner-peasants meant middle peasants, the idea of seizing their land was also a mistake because the middle peasants were not supposed to be injured in China as in Russia.[63]

---

58 "Resolution of the Joint Plenum of the C.C. and the C.C.C. after hearing Comrade Bukharin's report of August 9, 1927", *Inprecor.*, Vol. 7, No. 48, August 18, 1927, p. 1076; Eudin and North, p. 383.

59 "Resolution on the Questions of the 'Left-wing Kuomintang' and the Soviet Slogan", adopted by Provisional Central Politburo, September 19, 1927, *Central Correspondence*, No. 6, September 30, 1927.

60 "Resolution on the Current Situation in China and the Tasks of the Party", section 9, *Central Correspondence*, No. 13, November 30, 1927, *Bolshevik* (Pu-er-se-wei-ke), No. 56, November 28, 1927.

61 *Inprecor.*, Vol. 7, No. 56, October 6, 1927, p. 1239.

62 See Mao's comments on the Chingkangshan land law of 1928 and the Hsingkuo land law of 1929 as printed in his *Investigations of the Rural Districts*, published at Yenan in 1941, reissued by Hsinhua Bookstore, Shantung, 1946, pp. 86-90.

63 E. H. Carr, *The Bolshevik Revolution, 1917-1923*, Vol. 2, p. 161, New York, The Macmillan Company, 1952; Hsiao Tso-liang, *The Land Revolution in China 1930-1934, A Study of Documents*, Seattle and London, University of Washington Press, 1969, pp. 30, 68, 107, 256.

Mao's letter of August 30 was delivered from Changsha to Hankow by a comrade who was described as having charge of the Hunan Provincial Committee. This could be none other than P'eng Kung-ta, secretary of the Committee. He made an oral report to the Central Standing Committee which met in special session to discuss the letter. On September 5 the party leadership answered Mao, reaffirming its position of August 23 that insurrection must be based on the peasant masses rather than the troops. It repudiated Mao's claim that its policy was contradictory and that work among peasants in the outlying districts in Hunan was not neglected. It contended that it ordered the cancellation of the proposed Changsha rising at the end of August because the Hunan comrades were interested in the two regiments of troops rather than in the peasants. Without a large-scale uprising in southern Hunan, it was stated, an insurrection in the Changsha area, even if successful, could not hold out for long. The question of the division of strength would not arise at all if the peasants were used as the main force of insurrection since the peasants of southern Hunan would take care of the insurrection in their own area. In conclusion, the party leadership stressed that the Hunan Provincial Committee must carry out the party policy of using the peasantry as the principal force of insurrection without hesitation.[64]

3. Insurrection Plan for Hunan and Hupeh

After the first round of debate with the Mao group, that is, after August 23, the party leadership drew up an insurrection plan for Hunan and Hupeh and sent it to the two provincial committees as their guide to action.[65] This was the first insurrection plan formulated by the Ch'ü Ch'iu-pai leadership without previous experience, apparently under the ideological impact of Lominadze. It set forth the purpose, strategy and tactics of the autumn harvest insurrection.[66]

---

[64] "Letter to the Hunan Provincial Committee", September 5, *Central Correspondence*, No. 5, September 20, 1927.

[65] Ibid.; "Report on the Autumn Harvest Uprising in Hupeh", leaf 7AB; Ch'ü Ch'iu-pai, *The Chinese Revolution and the Communist Party*, p. 128.

[66] The text of the "Insurrection Plan for Hunan and Hupeh" is printed in *Central Correspondence*, Nos. 4 and 11. Serious omissions in issue No. 4, dated September 12, 1927, are supplied in No. 11, n.d., probably late November. The numbering of item 7 of the plan in issue No. 11 is wrong: item 7 should be No. 7 under item 6, and item 8 should be item 7, and so on.

As described previously, the autumn harvest insurrection program flowed from the suggestions of the Hunan and Hupeh party units for a peasant struggle at autumn harvest time. Not unnaturally, the party leadership proceeded on the assumption that there was already an insurrection situation in Hunan and Hupeh. The immediate tasks facing the Communists, it was stated, were to carry out the land revolution, lead the working and peasant masses to stage an insurrection, overthrow the Wuhan government and establish a revolutionary regime of the common people instead.[67] For the sake of a thoroughgoing land revolution, it would be necessary to confiscate the land of large and middle landlords (actually all land in the end). Also, it would be essential to kill and expropriate village bosses, bad gentry and all reactionaries, vest political power in the peasant unions in villages, set up popularly elected regimes in cities and towns, eliminate reactionary armed forces and organize a revolutionary army.[68]

The autumn harvest insurrection in Hunan and Hupeh was scheduled for September 10,[69] the time-honored mid-autumn festival according to the lunar calendar.[70] Each of the two provinces was divided into a number of key areas for insurrection,[71] and a special committee in charge of the insurrection was to be set up in each area.[72]

The insurrection was to be staged in the name of the Revolutionary Committee of China. Prior to the insurrection, the peasants' self-defense army should be reorganized into the peasants' revolutionary army and the workers' pickets into the workers' revolutionary army. Both of these would combine to bear the title of the Workers' and Peasants' Revolutionary Army.[73]

Hunan was divided into three areas for insurrection, namely, southern Hunan, eastern Hunan and western Hunan. There were two routes in southern Hunan leading to the capture of

---

67 "Insurrection Plan for Hunan and Hupeh", item 1.

68 Ibid., items 9, 11.

69 Ibid. item 4.

70 "Political Report of the Hupeh Provincial Committte", September 10, section 9, *Central Correspondence*, No. 5, September 26, 1927.

71 "Insurrection Plan for Hunan and Hupeh", item 4.

72 Ibid., item 16.

73 Ibid., item 7.

Hengyang. One route comprised the counties in the extreme south such as Chenchou, I-chang, Jucheng and Yunghsing, and the other consisted of the three nearby counties of Hengyang, Luiyang and Hengshan. These two routes were to start insurrection on September 6 with the town of Hengyang as the objective. After achieving successes in this area, the insurrectionists should proceed to take Changsha.[74]

The counties in eastern Hunan were divided into three routes: (1) Anyuan (in Western Kiangsi), Liling, Hsiangtan, and Hsianghsiang; (2) Liuyang, Pingchiang, Ninghsiang, I-yang, and Anhua; and (3) Hsiangying, Yuehyang, and Changsha. All these three routes were to start insurrection on September 10 with Changsha as the focal point. After achieving successes, the three routes should each keep a part of their strength to maintain local insurrection and send their major strength to attack Changsha where an insurrection was expected to erupt on September 12 or 13 with a view to taking over the provincial government.[75]

In western Hunan two routes of insurrection were to converge on the key town of Changte. One route consisted of the counties of Nanhsien and Huayung and the other comprised the counties of Changte, Taoyuan and Hanshou. The insurrection here was scheduled for September 10 to provide a shield to Changsha.[76]

In addition, Paoching (Shaoyang) in central Hunan and Yuanling in western Hunan were also to rise up around September 10 to protect the main theaters of insurrection.[77]

Thus, the whole province would be engulfed in insurrection in the name of the Chinese Revolutionary Committee. An interim provincial government of Hunan would be set up upon a successful insurrection.[78]

Hupeh was divided into seven areas for insurrection, namely, southern Hupeh, central Hupeh, western Hupeh, northern Hupeh, Peking-Hankow railway zone, eastern Hupeh, and Wuhan. The

---

[74] Ibid., item 5.
[75] Ibid.
[76] Ibid.
[77] Ibid.
[78] Ibid.

insurrection was to start in southern Hupeh on September 10. At the same time it should be launched in central and western Hupeh which was to join with southern Hupeh in creating an independent situation (tu-li chü-mien) to threaten Wuhan or eventually Changsha.[79] It would appear that the idea of this "independent situation" was the embryonic concept of what was later to be called the revolutionary base area in the countryside.

It will be recalled that there was a Communist division commander by the name of Chang Chao-feng,[80] who was operating in southwestern Honan at the time and was sending two regiments of his troops to Hsiangyang, the focal point of insurrection in northern Hupeh.[81] The Communist authorities placed great hopes in his role in the projected insurrection. It was pointed out that if local conditions permitted and if his troops arrived in time, northern Hupeh should rise up on September 10 or thereabout. If the uprising in western Hupeh was also successful, then his troops should be transferred to attack Wuhan where, by this time, there should be emerging a large insurrection or at least a large disturbance if an insurrection was impossible. In the case of a successful insurrection in both central and western Hupeh, his troops should move to Hunan or return to northern Hupeh.[82]

After northern, western and central Hupeh had all risen up, eastern Hupeh and the railway zone should respond accordingly.[83]

From the above it has become apparent that the autumn harvest insurrection in Hunan and Hupeh was based on the strategy of fighting from the countryside to the city. Before the start of the insurrection, there must be slaughters of village bosses, bad gentry and reactionary large landlords as well as mass agitation in distant villages. Once the insurrection got started, all efforts must be made to attack the urban centers of a township or district, which actually meant the county seats or smaller towns. Changsha and Wuhan were subject to insurrection, but the insurrection in these cities was not covered by the Insurrection Plan for Hunan

---

79 Ibid., item 6; "Report on the Autumn Harvest Uprising in Hupeh", leaf 5B.
80 Ch'ü Ch'iu-pai, *The Chinese Revolution and the Communist Party*, p. 128.
81 "Report on the Autumn Harvest Uprising in Hupeh", leaf 56B.
82 "Insurrection Plan for Hunan and Hupeh", item 6.
83 Ibid.

PROJECTED INSURRECTION
AREAS IN HUNAN AND HUPEH

NORTHERN

HUPEH

PEKING
HANKOW
RAILROAD

WESTERN HUPEH

CENTRAL HUPEH

WUHAN

EASTERN

HUPEH

SOUTHERN

HUPEH

WESTERN

HUNAN

EASTERN   HUNAN

CENTRAL

HUNAN

SOUTHERN   HUNAN

centers of insurrection areas
routes of insurrection
boundaries of insurrection areas
insurrection area stimulated
supplied by outside

PROJECTED INSURRECTION AREAS IN HUNAN AND HUPEH

SHENSI

HONAN

ANHWEI

SZECHUAN

Yunhsi
Yunhsien
Chunhsien
Chuchi
Kucheng Kuanghua
Chushan Tsaoyang
Fanghsien Hsiangyang
Paokang Suihsien
Nanchang Yingshan
Tzuchung
Hsingshan Chunghsiang Aulu Huangan
Yuanan Yunmeng Macheng
Tzukuei Chingshan Yingcheng Hsiaokan Lotien
Patung Tangyang Tienmen Hanchuan Huangpei
Chienshih Changyang I-chang Wuhan Huangkang Hsishui
Enshih I-tu Chiangling Tutitang Aocheng
Wufeng Chihchiang Chienchiang Shanpo Tayeh Kuangchi
chuan Sungtzu Mienyang Chiayu HSC Chichun Huangmei
Hsuanen Kungan Chienli Luchikou Hsienning
Haofeng Shihshou Hsinti TSC Chunghopu Yanghsen
Hsienfeng Huayung Yanglouszu Puchi Tungshan
Laifeng Nanhsien Yuehyang Chungyang
Changte Tungcheng Hsiushui
Taoyuan Pingchiang
Hanshou Hsiangying
Yuanling I-yang Tungku Nanchang
Ninghsiang Liuyang
Anhua Changsha
Hsiangtan Chuchou Pinghsiang
Hsianghsiang Liling Anyuan Kian
Hengshan
Paoching
Hengyang KIANGSI
Hsinning
KWANGSI Luiyang
Hsintien Yunghsing
Chenchou Kanchow
I-chang Jucheng

KWEICHOW

KWANGTUNG

Chuchiang

50 100 150 Km

TSC = Tingszuchiao   HSC = Hoshengchiao

and Hupeh.   It was clearly indicated that the Hunan and Hupeh
Provincial Committees should formulate special plans for the
insurrection in Changsha and Wuhan.[84]   There is no evidence
that such special plans were ever formulated.   On September 10,
the first day of the autumn harvest insurrection, the secretary of
the Hupeh Provincial Committee, Lo I-nung, declared at a meeting
of the Central Standing Committee that the most important work
in Wuhan at the moment was to win over the masses and guide
them to wage the practical struggle—particularly to guide the
workers to wage the economic struggle and, as a second step, the
political struggle. "Would there be an insurrection in Wuhan"?
he asked. "We still need technical preparation", he answered
himself. "But when would the insurrection be launched"? "This
must be at a time when the peasant insurrection has erupted in all
places".   Accordingly, all the CCP could do in Wuhan at the time
was to develop the economic struggle—to instigate a strike, for
example. Even this, according to him, was extremely difficult
under the circumstances.[85]

In this connection, it should be remembered that the Chinese
term "ch'eng shih" literally means city and town but that it is
commonly translated as "city" in the English language. The
county seat is a "city" in Chinese but not in English. Not in-
frequently, cities like Changsha and Wuhan are referred to in
Chinese Communist literature as *ta ch'eng shih* (large cities), as
distinguished from county seats.[86] This semantic distinction is
important because large cities are not only militarily better protected
than county seats but are also inhabited by the industrial proletariat
which is generally not present in county seats in China.

It has become apparent that the above-mentioned strategy of
fighting from the countryside to the city was contrary to the thinking
of Mao who, as noted previously, asked for two regiments of troops
to attack Changsha and who, despite the instructions of the party
leadership to the contrary, declared on August 30 that once Changsha

---

[84] Ibid., item 15.

[85] "Political Report of the Hupeh Provincial Committee", September 10,
sections 9 ff.

[86] [Ch'ü] Ch'iu-pai, "The Question of Armed Insurrection", December 10,
1927, section 2, *Bolshevik*, No. 10, December 19, 1927; Ch'ü Ch'iu-pai,
The Chinese Revolution and the Communist Party, p. 139; Chang Kuo-t'ao,
"My Memoirs", *Ming Pao Monthly*, No. 26, February 1968, p. 92.

made a start on the insurrection, the various counties would follow suit simultaneously. Needless to say, his belief that China had reached her 1917 was also based on the idea of the urban proletarian revolution. No wonder the former party chief Ch'en Tu-hsiu stated that Mao was one of those who were primarily interested in the seizure of political power in the city.[87] It was from the autumn harvest uprising that Mao learned the strategy of encircling the city with the countryside.[88] As described previously, the idea of fighting from the countryside to the city came from Stalin.

Another basic idea underlying the Insurrection Plan for Hunan and Hupeh was the classical Communist conception of the masses as the principal force of insurrection. Troops which have been the most important fighting force in a non-Communist revolution are supposed to be merely a supplement to the masses in a Communist revolution. It is not that the troops are not important, but that they are auxiliary to the masses. Accordingly, it was made clear in the Insurrection Plan for Hunan and Hupeh that the land revolution must be based on the strength of the peasant masses and that the troops and bandits were to be only an auxiliary force of the peasant revolution. It would be sheer opportunism, it was stated, to wait idly for the action of the troops and bandits or to rely on the action of the troops without regard to the strength and action of the peasant organizations. If this was the way to lead insurrection, it would be bound to lose the insurrection. In fact, it was stressed, this was no insurrection; it was only a military adventure or military opportunism.[89]

The Communist idea at the time was that if the masses were really roused to a fiery and violent wave of insurrection, their strength would be irresistible. For the masses constituted the greatest part

---

[87] "Letter from Comrade Tu-hsiu", (No. 1), November 12, 1927, *Central Political Correspondence*, No. 14, n.d.

[88] Lo Jung-huan, "Early Days of the Chinese Red Army", *Peking Review*, Vol. 5, No. 31, August 3, 1962, p. 12; "Resolution on Some Historical Problems", adopted by the Central Committee of the CCP, April 20, 1945, section 4-(1)b. It remains to be seen whether Mao learned the strategy of encircling the city with the countryside immediately from the autunm harvest uprisings. As late as 1930, Mao supported Li Li-san's strategy of capturing Changsha and Wuhan, as can be seen from his poem "From Tingchow Toward Changsha", dated July 1930 (available in various editions of Mao's *Selected Poems*).

[89] "Insurrection Plan for Hunan and Hupeh", item 3.

of the population in any area which might be the scene of an insurrection. To the Communists, therefore, the question was whether the masses in a given area of insurrection had been roused fanatically enough to action. This question was uppermost in the Communist mind regardless of practical difficulties. For this reason, the pre-insurrectionary work was important. In order to arouse the revolutionary zeal of the peasants, according to the Insurrection Plan for Hunan and Hupeh, it was necessary to kill village bosses, bad gentry and reactionary large landlords in villages distant from the county seat. At the same time, peasant meetings should be held in all places to overwhelm the masses with political propaganda. Once the insurrection got started, all strength must be mustered to attack the local urban center, kill government officials and proclaim a revolutionary regime. Not until then could an overall insurrection be launched.[90]

It is interesting to note that Mao was quick to accept the theory of the priority of the peasants over the troops. As outlined above, he admitted on August 30 that the main fighters in his projected assualt on Changsha were to be the workers and peasants and that the two regiments of troops requested were supposed to supplement the inadequate strength of the workers and peasants, but were not the principal force. In other words, the two regiments were designed to cover the development of the insurrection, but were not the sole important factor in the insurrection.[91]

Despite his ready acceptance of theory, however, Mao in practice did lay undue emphasis on the troops and neglect the peasant masses. Even P'eng Kung-ta who personally explained the Hunan case to the party leadership had no evidence to indicate that the peasants were not neglected.[92] It is hard to understand how Mao, who in his *Hunan Report*, described the poor peasants as the revolutionary vanguard or main force, forgot them almost completely when he began to organize the autumn harvest insurrection.

With regard to the non-communist troops and bandits, the Communist policy was to emphasize propaganda in an effort to

---

90 Ibid., item 12.

91 "Letter from the Hunan Provincial Committee", August 30, [1927], *Central Correspondence*, No. 5, September 20, 1927.

92 "Letter to the Hunan Provincial Committee", September 5, [1927], *Central Correspondence*, No. 5, September 20, 1927.

win them over to the side of the revolution. The troops should be instigated to kill their counterrevolutionary officers. If possible, soldiers' councils should be created on a broad mass basis so that the rank and file might be made to join them during the insurrection and organize new revolutionary armies in the future.[93] As for the bandits, the Communists should persuade and organize them in order that they might become an important auxiliary force in the insurrection, only to be reorganized into the army afterwards.[94]

It was made clear in the Insurrection Plan for Hunan and Hupeh that as soon as the insurrection got started, it would be necessary to destroy the railways, pedestrian roads, waterways, post offices and telegraphic wires so as to create a terrific panic among the enemies and facilitate the development of the insurrection. But such disruption of communications should not be allowed to retard the work of insurrection itself. Even if their contacts with the outside world were cut off, the insurrectionists must continue their assaults on all targets as originally planned. Hesitation would make a successful insurrection impossible.[95]

Where the insurrection was successful, it was stated, it would be necessary to suppress the counterrevolutionaries ruthlessly. If they sabotaged or closed factories, the labor unions should occupy those factories and turn them over to the management of the revolutionary government. The property of counterrevolutionary village bosses and bad gentry was subject to seizure. But no lootings were allowed.[96]

In brief, the outstanding characteristics of the Insurrection Plan for Hunan and Hupeh were as follows: (1) The basic idea was to fight from the countryside to the city. This was opposite to Mao's idea that once the city of Changsha made a start on the insurrection, the counties would follow suit simultaneously. (2) The plan placed emphasis on the peasant masses as the main force of insurrection with the troops as the auxiliary force. But the trouble was that the potential of the peasant masses was overestimated since they were then not yet well organized. The framers of the plan

---

[93] "Insurrection Plan for Hunan and Hupeh", item 10.
[94] Ibid., item 8.
[95] Ibid., item 13.
[96] Ibid., item 14.

seemed to make the mistake of thinking that once a single spark was struck among the masses, the whole area of insurrection would burst into flames. (3) The county seats were made the starting points of insurrection. This seemed to be an adventurous decision. The fact was that the county seats were the best protected towns in the countryside and that they could not possibly be taken without the use of the troops as the main fighting force. (4) The plan proceeded on the assumption that once the uprisings erupted in the counties, they would lead directly and rapidly to insurrection in the cities of Changsha and Wuhan though the special insurrection plans for these cities were never drawn up. The concept of "independent situations" did not provide a prolonged intermediate stage like the later idea of revolutionary base areas to assure the strategical progress toward the eventual seizure of the cities.

Despite its merits in the sphere of Communist ideology, the Insurrection Plan for Hunan and Hupeh was, after all, not realistic. Its validity was to be tested by the practical experience of insurrection in the two provinces.

4. Uprising in Hupeh

The Communists started preliminary work of insurrection in Hupeh over a month earlier than in Hunan because they were directly subjected to the pressure of the Wuhan government. The Hupeh Communists decided on insurrection toward the end of July. They immediately began to organize peasant guerrilla brigades, only to be followed by an overall insurrection across the countryside. [97]

As outlined previously, Hupeh was originally divided into seven insurrection areas. It finally turned out that only southern Hupeh played a real role in the insurrection. At the outset, northern Hupeh looked hopeful for a while. The other areas accomplished practically nothing.

---

[97] "Report on the Autumn Harvest Uprising in Hupeh", leaves 4AB, 58A; "Political Report of the Hupeh Provincial Committee", September 10, [1927], section 1; Ch'ü Ch'iu-pai, *The Chinese Revolution and the Communist Party*, p. 124; "Report of the Standing Committee of the Hupeh Provincial Committee to the Enlarged Conference of the Hupeh Provincial Committee", conclusion, December 12, 1927, *Central Political Correspondence*, No. 20, April 12, 1928.

In western Hupeh, weak Communist organizations were penetrated by members of the local gentry. The embryonic form of the labor and peasant movements was devastated by the troops of Yang Shen who were coming down from Szechuan at the time. Consequently, the projected uprising in this area was postponed repeatedly and never came off.[98]

In eastern Hupeh, well-known Communists and pro-Communist workers and peasants could no longer operate after the KMT-CCP split. Accordingly, they received orders to leave Hupeh to join the troops of the Nanchang revolt of August 1 in an attempt to retreat to Kwangtung. But the local Communist decision was said to be more discouraging. It ordered all the leading Communists and active workers and peasants to escape to Nanchang with the result that nobody was left behind to take care of the proposed uprising.[99] It was not suprising that the Communist authorities attributed the wholesale escape to opportunism.[100]

It had been expected that an insurrection area would be created in central Hupeh. But this dream never came true. It was charged that the local cadres were only interested in the troops and bandits.[101]

The party units in Wuhan had little contact with the party branches in the rural districts. Some leading party officials in Wuhan did not even know that there were party organizations in the countryside. One day a district party official was surprised at meeting the head of the peasant department of the CCP Hankow branch since he had never heard of any peasant movement in the Hankow area, much less the head of the peasant department.[102]

It was charged that the Communist leaders in the Peking-Hankow railway zone understood neither the meaning of the land revolution nor the purpose of their work at first. It was not surprising that they accomplished nothing in the sphere of insurrection.[103]

Northern Hupeh emerged as a hopeful insurrection area at

---

[98] "Report on the Autumn Harvest Uprising in Hupeh", leaves 18B-24B.
[99] Ibid., leaf 25A.
[100] Ibid., leaves 25A-36A.
[101] Ibid., leaves 37A-45A.
[102] Ibid., leaves 46A-49B.
[103] Ibid., leaves 49B-56A.

first.   This was due to a number of reasons: First, the peasantry hated the local troops; therefore it could be counted on to support the insurrection.   Second, the secret society Red Spears had begun to clash with the local troops, killing some of their officers.   Third, the Communist division commander Chang Chao-feng, as described previously, could be depended upon to play an important role in the insurrection.   But unfortunately the Northern Hupeh Special Committee under the leadership of Lu Ch'en did not follow a correct policy in organizing the insurrection.   It neglected the peasants and relied on the troops.   It insisted on using Chang Chao-feng to get rid of the local warlord Fang Cheng-wu stationed in the town of Hsiangyang, focal point of insurrection in northern Hupeh.   All of a sudden, Chang Chao-feng was removed as division commander, and this dealt a great blow to the local Communist scheme.   He was then told to seek an appointment from another warlord Fan Chung-hsiu stationed in the neighboring town Tsaoyang.   It was hoped that if Chang Chao-feng obtained the desired appointment, he would be able to get back the troops which he had lost as a result of his disgrace.   But he failed to get an appointment.   On August 29 the Special Committee reported that it was simply impossible to carry out the insurrection as planned.[104]

But the party leadership did not rest there.   On September 13 when uprisings had already started in Hunan and Hupeh, the Ch'ü Ch'iu-pai leadership ordered the Northern Hupeh Special Committee to act promptly despite the loss of Chang Chao-feng's troops.   It expressed its great disappointment at the tactical mistake of the Special Committee in playing off one warlord against another without regard for work among peasants.   It was emphasized that the disbandment of Chang Chao-feng's troops should not be allowed to stop the insurrection and that the remnants of those troops, however small in number, should be made to participate in the insurrection.[105]

But no insurrection came off in northern Hupeh.

Thereupon, the Hupeh Provincial Committee shifted its attention to southern Hupeh which controlled the strategical railway and

---

[104] Ibid., leaves 7AB, 56A-57B; Ch'ü Ch'iu-pai, *The Chinese Revolution and the Communist Party*, pp. 128-129.

[105] "Letter to the Northern Hupeh Special Committee", September 13, *Central Correspondence*, No. 5, September 20, 1927.

waterway transportation between Changsha and Wuhan. An insurrection in southern Hupeh could not fail to have considerable effect on Wuhan and Hunan province. It was not surprising that southern Hupeh finally turned out to be the real theater of insurrection in Hupeh.[106]

After the Communists started work for insurrection in southern Hupeh, they made their main efforts to win over the bandits and local people's self-defence units. On August 16 they asked the Provincial Committee to send the troops under the command of the Communist officers in the Second Guard Regiment to help them. But they were told that the peasants should be the principal force in a peasant revolution while the troops and bandits were only an auxiliary which was not altogether reliable, and that the absence of confidence in the masses was opportunism or a military adventure.[107]

On September 8 the Southern Hupeh Special Committee reported that the projected insurrection could hope to succeed only if the troops at Hsiushui and Puchi could be won over. It was emphasized that it would be impossible to overpower the enemy troops at Puchi in particular for the Communists had only ten revolvers with 600 bullets at their disposal.[108]

In reply, the Hupeh Provincial Committee declared on September 12 that the comrades in southern Hupeh had made the opportunistic mistake of neglecting the strength of the masses and relying on the troops. It once again reaffirmed the party line, as lain down in the Insurrection Plan for Hunan and Hupeh, that the insurrection should be based on the peasant masses, but not the troops and bandits which were only an auxiliary force. The Southern Hupeh Special Committee was accused of having placed undue emphasis on the number of revolvers at its disposal and of having overestimated the strength of the enemy troops at Puchi. Such being the case, it was stated, the insurrection seemed certain to fail. Furthermore, it was stressed that the local Communists should by no means retreat to Hunan in case they failed. Instead, they must go underground in their own area to create disturbances and help the peasants in refusing to pay land rents.[109]

---

[106] "Report on the Autumn Harvest Uprising in Hupeh", leaf 7AB.
[107] Ibid., leaf 12A.
[108] Ibid., leaf 13AB.
[109] Ibid., leaves 13B-14A.

According to the insurrection plan for southern Hupeh, the county seats of Puchi and Hsienning were made the two starting points. A variety of pre-insurrectionary work was to be done in villages distant from the county seats. There should be widespread disturbances in which village bosses and bad gentry would be executed. Mass meetings were to be held in various districts to create a fiery, violent wave of revolution among the peasants. Once the insurrection got started, the two county seats should be taken on the first day so as to win over the peasants in southern Hupeh quickly and create an overall insurrectionary situation there. All railway, telegraphic and postal communications between Hunan and Hupeh should be cut. Government officials, particularly the county magistrates, and bad gentry should be executed. Land committees were to be organized under peasant unions to redistribute land. [110]

After the capture of Puchi and Hsienning, according to the plan, the insurrectionists should advance along the railway northward toward Hoshengchiao, Shanpo and Tutitang and then deploy southward in an effort to seize the county seats of Chiayu, Chungyang, Tungcheng and Tungshan. If possible, they should threaten Wuhan directly or capture Yuehchou (Yuehyang) to threaten Changsha. Otherwise, they should defend Shanpo, Hoshengchiao, Yanglouszu, etc. along the railway and cross the Yangtse River at Luchikou in Chiayu county in order to establish contacts with the bandits and peasant troops in the counties of Hsinti, Mienyang, Chiangling, Kungan, and Shihshou in midwest Hupeh with a view to the establishment of an independent situation. If this could not be achieved, the insurrectionists would, in the last resort, have to retreat to the mountains near Tungcheng and Tungshan. [111] It should be noted that this Communist idea of retreating to the mountains as the last resort in a desperate situation foreshadowed the subsequent retreat of Mao Tse-tung to Chingkangshan.

The insurrection in southern Hupeh started on the night of September 8, two days ahead of schedule. That night a large amount of Chinese dollars was being shipped by train from Wuhan to Changsha to meet military expenditures. As the Communists could not afford to miss the chance, they raided the train when it

---

110 Ibid., leaf 14B.
111 Ibid., leaves 14B-15A.

stopped over at Chunghopu near Puchi. They succeeded in getting the money. But they did not retain the train nor cut the telegraphic communications with the result that the information about the raid was leaked to the enemy in Changsha almost immediately.[112]

Moreover, the insurrectionists failed to capture the two county seats of Puchi and Hsienning on the first day of their insurrection, as originally planned, on the ground that the enemy was militarily too strong there. Instead, they chose to work outside the county seats and set up a revolutionary government on September 12 at Hsikeng, a small mountain town ten miles east of Tungshan.[113]

At the same time the Southern Hupeh Special Committee moved to Hsintien, a small town near Puchi, in order to get the support of the local people's self-defence army in an attempt to capture Chiayu. After that was done, the insurrectionists were to move southward to take the railway station Tingszuchiao from where they were to sweep back to Puchi. In case this could not be achieved, they would proceed to attack Yuehchou with a view to helping the insurrection in Hunan.[114]

But the people's self-defense army of Puchi was a group of former bandits armed with thirty-eight rifles. The commander of the army, Liu Pu-i, was an unscrupulous man of bad faith. He had the full confidence of the Southern Hupeh Special Committee as a result of fairly long contacts and negotiations. The Committee moved everything to Hsintien after it had decided to give up the strategy of capturing the county seats of Puchi and Hsienning first. The Communists had hardly expected that they were falling into a trap. They were all disarmed the moment they arrived in Hsintien. Consequently, the Special Committee disintegrated and the whole cause of insurrection in southern Hupeh collapsed.[115]

5. Uprising in Hunan

The unfolding of insurrection in Hunan was as haphazard as that in Hupeh. The Hunan Provincial Committee, of which Mao

---

[112] Ibid., leaf 15AB.
[113] Ibid., leaf 15B.
[114] Ibid.
[115] Ibid., leaves 16AB, 18AB.

was the central figure, did not follow the insurrectionary policy of the Ch'ü Ch'iu-pai leadership, either. Although P'eng Kung-ta, secretary of the Hunan Provincial Committee, yielded superficially to the position of the party leadership after the policy debate described previously, Hunan remained recalcitrant.[116]

As pointed out above, the party leadership attached primary importance to the southern Hunanese region around Hengyang where the insurrection was scheduled to start on September 6. However, no uprising ever erupted there. Accordingly, as late as September 17, the Hunan Provincial Committee was urged to act in Hengyang and other main counties without delay, otherwise uprisings which had already been under way in eastern Hunan would be crushed by the enemy one by one.[117]

Similarly, little work of insurrection was done by the Hunan Provincial Committee in western Hunan.[118]

It finally turned out that only eastern Hunan became the scene of actual insurrection. But what happened there was not along the lines set forth in the Insurrection Plan for Hunan and Hupeh.

Any investigation of the insurrection in eastern Hunan must begin with a brief account of the Lu Te-ming regiment which was the core of the insurrectionary force there. This regiment, manned largely by Communists, was originally known as the garrison regiment attached to the Second Front Army of Chang Fa-k'uei with a total of more than a thousand troops. Both the commander and deputy commander, Lu Te-ming and Yü Shai-tu, were Communists. Toward the end of July, they received orders from the Communist Party to move their troops from Wuchang to Nanchang. They took a boat down the Yangtse River. In view of the fact that the Kiukiang area was heavily protected by KMT forces, they decided to give up the boat halfway and march to Kiangsi on foot instead. There were a few mutinies in the ranks on the way but were all suppressed. On arriving in Fenghsin, a neighboring county west of Nanchang, they found out that it was too late to catch the Nanchang insurrectionists who had already abandoned

---

116 "Resolution on Political Discipline", November 14, [1927], section (3)3, *Central Correspondence*, No. 13, November 30, 1927.

117 "Comrade Ma's Letter to the Hunan Provincial Committee", September 17, 1927, item 7.

the provincial capital and marched southward to Kwangtung. They, then, decided to move their troops westward to Hsiushui in north-western Kiangsi. Lu Te-ming was to proceed to the central party headquarters for consultations. During his absence Yü Shai-tu was to act for him on the understanding that they would meet again in Hsiushui a few weeks later.

Shortly after arriving in Hsiushui, Yü Shai-tu received orders from the Hunan Provincial Committee giving his band the title of the First Division of the First Army of the Chinese Workers' and Peasants' Revolutionary Army. A Communist flag took the place of the Nationalist flag which had hitherto been in use. Yü Shai-tu himself became the division commander with Yü Fen-min as his assistant. The division consisted of four armed units called regiments. The first regiment was under the command of Chung Wen-chao. A second was headed by Ch'iu Kuo-hsien who had started out as a bandit. A third was composed of the Pingchiang-Liuyang self-defense corps led by Su Hsien-Chün, a graduate of the Wuchang branch of the Whampoa Military Academy. The commander of the fourth regiment was Wang Hsin-ya in charge of the Pinghsiang-Liling self-defense corps.[119] There can be little doubt that a great many troops of the third regiment were not peasants while the fourth regiment was composed largely of the unemployed miners of the Anyuan-Pinghsiang area.[120] In addition, the division had a general staff, a supplies department, a health station, a transportation service and an "administrative service" battalion composed of both the self-defense corps of Chungyang county in southern Hupeh and the local garrison brigade of Hsiushui county.[121]

As soon as the army was organized, the military and political training was started. There was a party committee in the division and a party cell in each company responsible for political work.

---

[118] "From Wuhan to Chingkangshan", n. p., n. d., an official documentation on the origins of the Chinese Red Army, prepared probably in the 1950's; Yang Li-san, "The Garrison Regiment at the Time of the 'August 1' Revolt", printed in *Reminiscences About the Struggle in the Chingkangshan Area*, Peking, Workers' Publishing House, 1956, pp. 1-3.

[119] "From Wuhan to Chingkangshan", op. cit.

[120] Roy Hofheinz, Jr., "The Autumn Harvest Insurrection", *China Quarterly*, No. 32, October-December 1967, pp. 69-70.

[121] "From Wuhan to Chingkangshan", op. cit.

But political work was poor in the initial stage. So, too, was party work.[122] This was confirmed by Mao when he told Edgar Snow in 1936 that in his army, discipline was poor, political training was at a low level, and many wavering elements were among the men and officers. There were many desertions.[123]

After its hurried organization in Hsiushui, the division set out for the autumn harvest insurrection on September 8 or 10. The idea was that this division was the basic force to be supplemented by the local workers and peasants in eastern Hunan. When the advanced post of the first regiment reached Chaching near the Hunan border, Lu Te-ming returned. He immediately became the commander-in-chief of the army with Yü Shai-tu as his deputy.[124] According to one source, the real power was still in the hands of Yü Shai-tu as the division commander.[125]

The division marched from Kiangsi to Hunan along three routes: (1) the first and second regiments from Hsiushui to Pingchiang, (2) the third regiment from Tungku to Liuyang, and (3) the fourth regiment from Anyuan to Liling. Their common destination was Changsha.[126]

After the first regiment left the county seat of Hsiushui, it was joined by the bandit-infested second regiment at a point west of Chaching near the Hunan border. Unexpectedly, the second regiment deserted. This incident also caused heavy losses in the first regiment. As a result, the first regiment had to be reorganized and replenished in eastern Pingchiang before it could carry on the fighting.[127] It soon became clear that this incident turned out eventually to be a deadly blow to the military operations of the autumn harvest uprisings.

The third regiment which had come down from Tungku was engaged by the enemy at Paisha in Liuyang. It could not go any further. The fourth regiment had, indeed, occupied the county seat

---

122 Ibid.

123 Edgar Snow, pp. 168-69.

124 "From Wuhan to Chingkangshan", op. cit.

125 T'ieh Hsin, "Mao Tse-tung Became a Bandit in Chingkangshan", *Modern Historical Materials*, Vol. 3, pp. 232-253.

126 "From Wuhan to Chingkangshan", op. cit.

127 Ibid.; T'ieh Hsin, op. cit.

of Liling and penetrated as far as the enemy's rear in Liuyang. But owing to poor security and intelligence work, the whole regiment was destroyed by the enemy who had been closing in upon it from all sides. The regiment commander was missing.[128] The poor security and intelligence work of the Communists at the time is confirmed by the fact that their secret plan for insurrection had long been leaked out and made known to the public in newspapers.[129]

Apparently owing to the truculence of the Hunan Communists as manifested in the policy debate following Mao's arrival in Changsha in August, the party leadership despatched one Comrade Ma to Changsha to supervise insurrection on the spot. This man, called Ma Ke-fu in Chinese transliteration, was probably a Russian. He did not speak Chinese. According to him, the Communists scored one victory after another in eastern Hunan from September 8 to 12. The number of their rifles increased considerably: from 700 to 1,300 at Pinghsiang and from 500 to 2,100 at Anyuan. Thousands of peasants, armed with hand weapons, joined them. They occupied the major counties in eastern Hunan like Pingchiang, Liuyang and Liling as well as Pinghsiang in western Kiangsi. Chuchou, a strategical town on the railway to Changsha, was captured by peasants armed with only sixty rifles. There was a panic in Changsha on September 13.[130]

Allowing for possible exaggerations and inaccuracies, what Comrade Ma said was probably true in the general survey that the tide of the insurrection was on the flow in the first five days. He did not necessarily mean the county seats when he spoke of the occupation of the major counties.

From September 13 to 16, however, the tide turned suddenly for the worse. According to Comrade Ma, the forces from Anyuan began to retreat without a fight in the vicinity of Liling when they

---

128 "From Wuhan to Chingkangshan", op. cit. For information that the county seat of Liuyang was occupied by insurgents from Anyüan, see Liu Hsien-sheng, "The Armed Workers of Anyüan", *A Single Spark Can Start a Prairie Fire*, Peking, People's Literature Publishing House, 1958, Vol. 1, pp. 179-187, sections 2-3.

129 Shen Pao, September 16, Changsha, as cited by Roy Hofheinz, Jr., "The Autumn Harvest Insurrection", *China Quarterly*, No. 32, October-December 1967, p. 71.

130 "Report from Comrade Ma in Hunan", September 16, 1927, printed in *Central Correspondence*, No. 6, September 30, 1927.

learned that enemy troops were assembling on the east and west sides. In a panic, they abandoned Liling and refused to advance on Chuchou. They did all this with the approval of the Hunan Provincial Committee. Ten firearms and sixty peasants were lost in Pingchiang. But acting on the false report that a whole battalion was destroyed there, the insurrectionists were quick to retreat toward Tungku and Tungcheng. The Provincial Committee connived at this. In the Changsha area the Communists had already occupied some territory on the east and west sides. Accidentally a peasant was wounded or killed by another fellow peasant who did not know how to use a firearm properly. But the Provincial Committee jumped to the conclusion that the peasants were not able to rise against the local militia. [131]

To make matters worse, according to Comrade Ma, the Hunan Provincial Committee on September 15 called off its plan for a Changsha rising scheduled for the night of September 16 on the pretext that the enemy was too strong in the city. But, he thought, the enemy strength was exaggerated while the Communist potential was underestimated. It was his belief that a Communist uprising was not impossible in Changsha despite the large number of the government garrison troops. He believed that if Changsha could be taken and occupied for a week or more, a general peasant uprising in the whole province could erupt before the Communist forces retreated to Kiangsi. He held that the Communists must go to the countryside if they were unable to hold Changsha. [132]

Comrade Ma was very angry at the cowardice of the Hunan Communists. On the afternoon of September 16 he wrote to the Hunan Provincial Committee, saying that the indefinite postponement of the Changsha rising was at once wrong and harmful and that the rising must be staged on that night or the next morning. He explained that there were only partial defeats in eastern Hunan, that the situation in Changsha was not so bad as was imagined, and that an attack on Changsha was the only way to stop further retreats, restore the morale of the troops and prevent a possible debacle in southern Hupeh and eastern Hunan. [133]

---

[131] "Report from Comrade Ma in Hunan", September 16, 1927.
[132] Ibid.
[133] "Letter from Comrade Ma to the Hunan Provincial Committee", September 16, 1927.

As the expected rising of Changsha did not come off on the night of September 16, Comrade Ma wrote again to the Hunan Provincial Committee on the morning of the 17th. A whole list of instructions was given as follows: stop the retreat to Tungku or southern Hupeh immediately; retake Liuyang, Pingchiang and, if possible, also Liling; attack Yuehchou, a strategic town on the railway to Hupeh; send two members of the Provincial Committee to direct work between Yuehchou and Pingchiang; disrupt railway transportation to prevent government troops from putting down revolts in southern Hupeh; launch immediate uprising in key counties like Hsiangtan and Hengyang; reconsider the decision to postpone the Changsha rising or, if it did not come off right away, make it impossible for the enemy to send troops immediately from Changsha to suppress peasant revolts in the outlying counties.[134]

On September 16 Comrade Ma made a report to the CCP leadership on the situation in Hunan. He deplored the retreat in eastern Hunan and the cancellation of the uprising in Changsha. He put the blame on P'eng Kung-ta, secretary of the Hunan Provincial Committee, who was branded as being a radical in words but a coward in deeds. Scolded and pressed by Comrade Ma, P'eng promised to persuade the Hunan Provincial Committee to act. In the same breath, however, he was quoted by Comrade Ma as whispering to a Chinese interpreter: "He does not understand anything. A bookish person and intellectual. He does not realize that the objective conditions are no good and we can not help it". In fact, P'eng never tried to persuade his committee to act at this crucial moment. Comrade Ma became impatient with P'eng's false promise, complaining that all this was a typical Chinese trick.[135]

In order to turn the tide of insurrection in Hunan, therefore, Comrade Ma made three recommendations to the CCP leadership: (1) to despatch a responsible member of the Central Committee to watch over work in Hunan; (2) to proclaim the Hunan Provincial Committee guilty of both disobedience of order and escape from battle; (3) to reorganize the Hunan Provincial Committee.[136]

---

134 "Letter from Comrade Ma to the Hunan Provincial Committee", September 17, 1927.

135 "Report from Comrade Ma in Hunan", September 16, 1927.

136 Ibid.

Acting on the recommendations of Comrade Ma, the Party leadership sent a certain Comrade Jen (probably Jen Pi-shih) to Hunan on September 19 with full powers to execute the original insurrection plan. The Hunan Provincial Committee was charged with calling off the Changsha rising and conniving at the retreat in eastern Hunan. This was believed to have affected the insurrection in Hunan and southern Hupeh unfavorably. Once again, the Hunan Provincial Committee was instructed to order the insurrectionists in the Pinghsiang-Liuyang-Pingchiang area to advance on Changsha and to launch a rising in Changsha itself without delay. Comrade Jen was authorized to make an investigation of the responsibility for the cancellation of the Changsha rising in order to mete out necessary punishment to those responsible.[137]

After his arrival in Hunan, Comrade Jen called an emergency meeting of the Hunan Provincial Committee. As a result, the Hunan Provincial Committee was apparently reorganized.[138] But that was all. Comrade Jen, like Comrade Ma, could do nothing more. The proposed rising of Changsha never came off. This led the Communist historian Hua Kang to conclude that there was literally no labor movement in Changsha at the time of the autumn harvest insurrection in Hunan.[139]

In this connection, it should be noted that Comrade Ma's advocacy of the proposed Changsha rising in September was different from Mao's in August. While Mao's was a strategy of fighting from the city to the countryside, Ma's was one of fighting from the countryside to the city. Comrade Ma stood for the proposed Changsha rising since he knew that uprisings had already broken out in the countryside in eastern Hunan. This was apparently in agreement with the strategy laid down in the Insurrection Plan for Hunan and Hupeh. Of course, Ma's strategy, though an improvement over Mao's, also turned out to be unpractical because it was not easy to take county seats, much less the provincial capital. That was why, as we shall see later, this strategy was revised in the enlarged session of the Central Politburo less than two months later.

---

[137] "Letter to the Hunan Provincial Committee", September 19, [1927], *Central Correspondence*, No. 6, September 30, 1927.

[138] Ch'ü Ch'iu-pai, *The Chinese Revolution and the Communist Party*, p. 128.

[139] Hua Kang, *A History of the Liberation Movement of the Chinese Nation*, Vol. 2, 1940, Cock-crow Bookstore, n.p., third edition, 1946, p. 498.

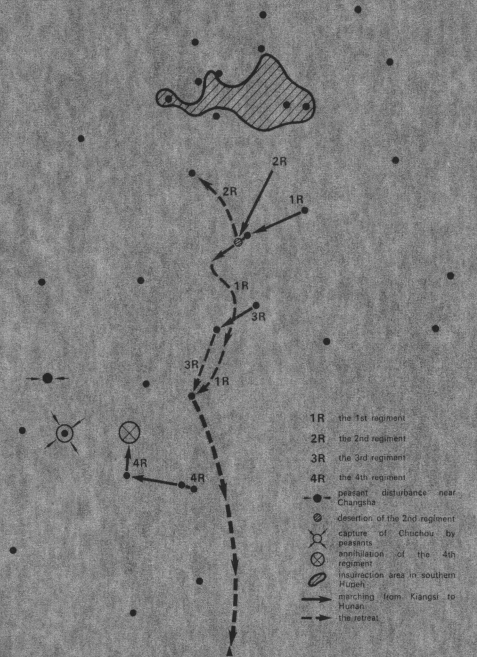

CENES OF AUTUMN
ARVEST UPRISINGS

2R

2R

1R

1R

3R

3R

1R

4R

4R

1R the 1st regiment

2R the 2nd regiment

3R the 3rd regiment

4R the 4th regiment

peasant disturbance near Changsha

desertion of the 2nd regiment

capture of Chuchou by peasants

annihilation of the 4th regiment

insurrection area in southern Hupeh

marching from Kiangsi to Hunan

the retreat

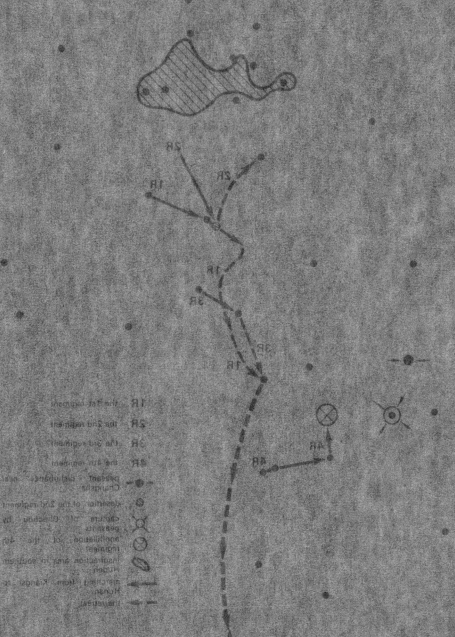

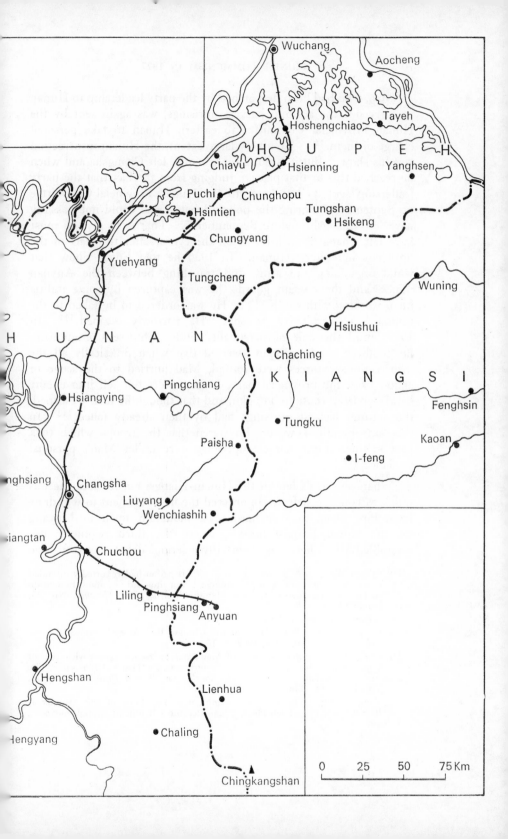

Mao, who had been despatched by the party leadership to Hunan to carry out the autumn harvest uprisings, was again sent by the Hunan Provincial Committee to eastern Hunan to take personal charge of them.[140]   To a very large extent, the Hunan insurrection was his show.   But it is not clear when he left Changsha and when he reached this or that place.   Judging from the fact that the party leadership sent its last letter to the Hunan Provincial Committee on September 5 during the policy debate, Mao could not possibly have left Changsha before September 7.   That is to say, he must have left Changsha in a hurry on the eve or after the start of the uprisings in eastern Hunan.   In 1936 he told Edgar Snow that while organizing the army and travelling between the Anyuan miners and the peasant guards, he was captured by some militia men, working with the KMT.   He was ordered to be taken to the militia headquarters to be shot.   He narrowly escaped.[141]   In 1957, amid the cult of personality under Chinese Communism, his follower Lo Jung-huan asserted that when practically all the insurrectionary forces were routed, Mao hurried to the scene of action from the provincial party headquarters but fell into enemy hands while en route to Tungku, and that though he finally escaped, the autumn harvest uprisings had by then already failed.[142]   In the same breath, however, Lo stated that the troops which took part in the autumn harvest uprisings were under Mao's personal guidance.[143]

Whatever Mao's fate in the Hunan-Kiangsi border area, he was quick to concede defeat. He ordered the first regiment to withdraw from Pingchiang to Wenchiashih, a mountain town in Liuyang on the Hunan-Kiangsi border, where the third regiment also assembled.[144]   There was reportedly a serious debate between Mao

---

140 "From Wuhan to Chingkangshan", op. cit.; Mao had reportedly intended to join the Nanchang revolt of August 1, but time did not allow him to do so (see Chang Kuo-t'ao, "My Memoirs", *Ming Pao Monthly*, No. 25, January 1968, p. 94).

141 Edgar Snow, pp. 167-68.

142 Lo Jung-huan, "Early Days of the Chinese Red Army", *Peking Review*, Vol. 5, No. 31, August 3, 1962, p. 10.

143 Ibid., P. 12. Another account of Mao's narrow escape agrees with that of Edgar Snow, but not with Lo Jung-huan, see Hsieh Chio-tsai, "The Accident in Liuyang", *A Single Spark Can Start a Prairie Fire*, 1958, Vol. 1, pp. 145-146.

144 Yang Li-san, "The Garrison Regiment at the Time of the 'August 1' Revolt", op. cit.; T'ieh Hsin, "Mao Became a Bandit in Chingkangshan", op. cit.

and Yü Shai-tu in Wenchiashih. Yü insisted on a counter-attack on Liuyang with the view of taking Changsha. He did not think that the setback resulting from the desertion of the second regiment in the Pingchiang sector would mean a defeat. A defeat, he stated, could only come from a Communist decision to fall back. But Mao emerged victorious. At his suggestion it was decided that the battered insurrectionary forces retreat to Chingkangshan.[145]

Of course, as laid down in the insurrection plan for southern Hupeh, the Communists could retreat to the mountains in the last resort. The question is whether this applied to the Wenchiashih decision. Yü Shai-tu answered in the negative. His position happened to be in agreement with that of Comrade Ma who had warned against playing with insurrection.[146]

When Mao led his little band to retreat to Chingkangshan in October, there were only about one thousand. Yü Shai-tu had left.[147] Lu Te-ming had been killed in battle.[148]

Party chief Ch'ü Ch'iu-pai summed up Mao's insurrectionary tactics in Hunan in the term "keep time-ism" (ho-pe chu-i) meaning that Mao had tried to fix the times and places of the military operations in advance and then fit the worker and peasant insurrections in with them.[149]

6. Disciplinary Measures

After the failure of the antumn harvest uprisings, the CCP leadership discussed the matter in October and deplored the mistakes made by the Communists in Hunan and Hupeh. At first, it was charged, the Hunan comrades wanted only to use two regiments of troops to attack Changsha but not to launch a peasant rising across the province. By September 13 Changsha was seized with a panic, but no insurrection came off. In northern Hupeh, it was said, Chang Chao-feng was originally designated to help organize a peasant uprising, but the local Communist leaders told him to play off one warlord against another despite the peasant hostility

---

[145] T'ieh Hsin, op. cit.
[146] "Report from Comrade Ma in Hunan", op. cit.
[147] Edgar Snow, p. 169.
[148] "From Wuhan to Chingkangshan", op. cit.
[149] Ch'ü Ch'iu-pai, The Chinese Revolution and the Communist Party, p. 130.

to all warlords alike. In southern Hupeh, it was added, some twenty to thirty thousand peasants had assembled with intent to attack the county seat of Puchi but the local leading cadres ordered them to retreat on the ground that they were underarmed and did not know how to do the fighting. [150]

In November, the party leadership rendered its verdict. In the Politburo session of November 9-10, almost all the party organizations and personnel entrusted with responsibility to stage uprisings were punished. The Hunan Provincial Committee was accused of having completely violated the party policy of using the peasant masses as the main insurrectionary force as laid down in the Insurrection Plan for Hunan and Hupeh. Despite the fact that P'eng Kung-ta, secretary of the Hunan Provincial Committee, had been warned against military opportunism and that he had nominally accepted the viewpoint of the central leadership, the Hunan Provincial Committee was held responsible for a variety of blunders as follows:

1.   P'eng Kung-ta regarded insurrection as a simple military action in contravention of party instructions. He had dealings only with bandits and motley troops and failed to stir up the broad peasant masses to rise in insurrection. Consequently, once the insurrection got started, only the workers in Anyüan participated in the struggle courageously while the peasant masses took no action at all in the various places.

2.   No clear programs of land revolution and political power were proclaimed in areas of insurrection with the result that the peasants suspected the Communists of making trouble and that even the Hunan Provincial Committee doubted the peasant demand for land and objected to the enforcement of the eight-hour working day.

3.   The policy of slaughtering village bosses and bad gentry was not carried out in areas where the Workers' and Peasants' Army was passing. Consequently, the peasants looked upon the army as ordinary troops which were just passing through those areas on a routine mission. [151]

---

150 "A Report on the Recent Political Situation", *Central Correspondence*, No. 7, October 30, 1927.

151 "Resolution on Political Discipline", November 14, [1927], section (3)3, *Central Correspondence*, No. 13, November 30, 1927.

Thus, the autumn harvest uprising which was intended to be a peasant revolt had turned out to be a military adventure in Hunan. The party leadership was indignant at this. It enforced political discipline on an unprecedented scale. All the leading members of the Hunan Provincial Committee, including P'eng Kung-ta and Mao Tse-tung, were dismissed. P'eng and Mao were also removed as alternate members of the Provisional Central Politburo. In addition, P'eng was placed on probation as a party member for half a year. The part of the *Resolution on Political Discipline* which meted out this punishment read:

> P'eng Kung-ta, Mao Tse-tung, I Li-yung and Hsia Ming-han, members of the Hunan Provincial Comittee, shall be removed from their present membership of the Provincial Committee. Comarde P'eng Kung-ta shall be dismissed as an alternate member of the Central Political Bureau and placed on probation as a party member for half a year. Comrade Mao Tse-tung was despatched by the Central after the August 7 Emergency Conference to Hunan as special representative to reorganize the Hunan Provincial Committee and carry out the Central's autumn harvest insurrection policy. In fact, he was the center in the Hunan Provincial Committee. Comrade Mao should bear serious responsibility for the mistakes made by the Hunan Provincial Committee. He shall be dismissed as an alternate member of the Provisional Central Political Bureau.[152]

As to the autumn harvest uprising in Hupeh, the Communists did a better job than in Hunan. The Hupeh Provincial Committee committed no deviations from the party line. The peasant masses had noticeably though inadequately been roused to action in southern Hupeh which was the scene of actual insurrection.

The trouble was with northern Hupeh. The November session of the Politburo maintained that the Northern Hupeh Special Committee did not pay due attention to the peasant hostility to taxes and warlords. On the contrary, the Special Committee looked down upon the strength of the masses and waited idly for the coming of Chang Chao-feng's troops to their aid. After his troops were disbanded, they ordered Chang Chao-feng to play off the peasants [sic!] against the warlord Fan Chung-hsiu by dint of military op-

---

152 Ibid., section (5)6; English translation made with assistance from Karl Wittfogel's translation appearing in *China Quarterly*, No. 2, April-June 1960, p. 33.

portunism. All this was at variance with the policy of the central leadership.[153]

But the record of southern Hupeh was not perfect despite the agitation of the peasant masses. The party leadership charged the Southern Hupeh Special Committee with having abandoned the strategy of attaching the county seat of Puchi as originally planned. The Communist organisers in southern Hupeh feared that the peasants were underarmed and their fighting strength was not equal to that task. For this reason, they were accused of having no confidence in the masses and escaping in the heat of action.[154]

Yet no one in the Southern Hupeh Special Committee was subjected to censure. The northern Hupeh case was more serious. The November session of the Politburo adopted the following resolution:

> As the Northern Hupeh Special Committee disobeyed the Central's orders, all its members shall be given a warning. Lu Ch'en, secretary of the Special Committee, shall be removed as a member of the Central Committee for he stood largely for the mentality of military opportunism and did no work whatever for the peasant movement.[155]

153 "Resolution on Political Discipline", November 14, [1927], op. cit., section (3)4.
154 Ibid.
155 Ibid., section (5)7.

CHAPTER III

FROM NANCHANG TO SWATOW

1. The Military Coup

On August 1, a week before the August 7 Conference, the Nanchang revolt occurred.[1] This was a basically urban military coup unleashed against the wishes of Moscow.

It will be recalled that simultaneously with the removal of the Communists, the Wuhan regime was moving its troops down the Yangtse Valley to put up a fight against the Nanking government. To that end, the Fourth Army under the command of Chang Fa-k'uei was gathering around Nanchang, the capital city of Kiangsi province. In the Fourth Army lurked the strongest Communist military potential at the time, as represented by Yeh T'ing, commander of the 24th Division, and Chou Shih-ti, commander of the Independent Regiment. Also, a large number of Communists were proceeding to Nanchang with a view either to operating underground under the shelter of Chang Fa-k'uei or plotting rebellion with the military support of Yeh T'ing in case of need.[2]

Interestingly, Chang Fa-k'uei meant no harm to the Communists despite the KMT-CCP split. Communist military commanders like Yeh T'ing and Chou Shih-ti were old members of the Fourth Army and were treated as such by their fellow soldiers. The Communist-inspired peasants' excesses against military men's families in Hunan did not affect the Fourth Army which came from

---

[1] C. Martin Wilbur published English translations of eight *Central Correspondence* documents on the Nanchang revolt in *China Quarterly*, No. 18, April-June 1964, with the cautionary note that the reports by participants may have been edited before printing. Allowing for possible inaccuracies of all Communist literature, however, these documents are found to be generally authentic. New Comintern representatives after the KMT-CCP split in July 1927, like Besso Lominadze and Pavel Mif, were all not mentioned by name in Chinese Communist statements.

[2] Chang Kuo-t'ao, "My Memoirs", *Ming Pao Monthly*, No. 24, December 1967, p. 91.

Kwangtung. Not unnaturally, the Fourth Army was not enthusiastic about the anti-Communist cause.[3]

Moreover, the leftists were generally disappointed in the realities of the revolution at the time. They were thinking of returning to Kwangtung to start the revolution all over again. This was particularly true of the Fourth Army which was predominantly manned with people from Kwangtung. Above all, the commander of the Fourth Army Chang Fa-k'uei was a most popular military leader at the time, not only respected by his fellow KMT left-wingers, but also trusted by Communists and the Russian military adviser Galen (Vassili Blücher). Galen took the position that the Communists should maintain friendly relations with Chang Fa-k'uei and accompany him on a return trip to Kwangtung. Under cover of the Fourth Army, he said, the Communists would have a much better chance to return to Kwangtung than to go all alone by themselves. Chang Kuo-t'ao and Ch'ü Ch'iu-pai raised no objections to Galen's idea but doubted its practicability.[4]

However, some Chinese Communist leaders held a different view. Li Li-san, T'an P'ing-shan and others met in Kiukiang on July 19. They found that there was little likelihood of winning over Chang Fa-k'uei in view of the fact that he had already asked Yeh T'ing and other Communists to quit his army or else abandon their membership of the Communist Party. They also found that KMT troops were closing in upon Nanchang in order to encircle the Communist-controlled forces there. In such a critical situation, they decided that the Communists had no alternative but to launch an uprising in Nanchang as a way of survival.[5]

When the above decision of the Kiukiang conference was reported to the party leadership at Hankow, it met with the immediate approval of the military minister Chou En-lai, who was of the opinion that if the Communists relied on Chang Fa-k'uei to take them back to Kwangtung, they would run the risk of being destroyed in a lump should he betray them. Chou En-lai, therefore, suggested that the Communists raise the standard of revolt at Nanchang under

---

[3] Ibid., p. 92.
[4] Ibid.
[5] "Li Li-san's Report", section 1, *Central Correspondence*, No. 7, October 30, 1927.

the military direction of Yeh T'ing, *et al.*, and at the same time try to win over the workers and peasants in Hunan, Hupeh and Kiangsi in order to form a power center against both Nanking and Wuhan. Since Nanchang was militarily indefensible, he was in favor of a retreat to Kwangtung to establish a revolutionary base in the region of the East River. He reasoned that the enemy was weak in that region while the peasant movement was strong in Hai-lu-feng and that Swatow was a seaport from where contacts with the Soviet Union could be established. Accordingly, Chou En-lai asked the party leadership to make immediate decisions on a number of important questions such as the political program and strategy of the proposed revolt, the manner of cooperation with friendly forces and the KMT left-wingers, the method of arousing the masses of workers and peasants in Hunan, Hupeh, Kiangsi and Kwangtung, and the quickest way to secure military and other material aid from the Comintern. To the mind of Chou En-lai, Russian aid was the most important of all the items requested.[6]

As time was short, there was no detailed discussion at Hankow. In the name of the Central Standing Committee, Chang Kuo-t'ao and Chou En-lai decided to launch the proposed revolt and, to that end, create a Front Committee to be composed of T'an P'ing-shan, Li Li-san, Yeh T'ing, etc. with Chou En-lai as secretary. Thereupon, Chou En-lai was sent to Nanchang to organize the revolt along the lines he had suggested himself. He arrived in Nanchang on July 22. Chang Kuo-t'ao alone was left behind in Hankow to take care of the work of the party leadership. Chang Kuo-t'ao flattered himself that the Nanchang revolt was a major decision made by the Chinese party leadership without the approval of Moscow.[7]

Meanwhile, the Wuhan KMT leaders were calling a conference at Lushan, a summer resort in Kiangsi, to devise ways and means to deal with the Communists. When Ho Lung, commander of the Twentieth Army, arrived at Kiukiang on July 23 or so, he became the object of contention between the two opposing sides. On one hand, KMT men invited him to attend the Lushan conference. On the other, T'an P'ing-shan tried what he could to draw him into

---

[6] Chang Kuo-t'ao, "My Memoirs", *Ming Pao Monthly*, No. 24, December 1967, pp. 91-92.

[7] Ibid., p. 92.

the Communist ranks. T'an frankly confided to him the Communist plan of revolt at Nanchang and urged him to join it. Ho Lung decided to work on the Communist side. Having started out as a bandit in western Hunan, he was politically ambitious. He aspired to the sole leadership of the Communist forces and did not like Chang Fa-k'uei to work with the Communists.[8]

Soon afterward, Chang Kuo-t'ao received word from Kiukiang that the projected Nanchang revolt could be launched with the support of Ho Lung. Chou En-lai and company sought instructions regarding basic political and military policies. They asked the party leadership to mobilize workers and peasants in various places to help the revolt. They were anxious to know if the Soviet Union would give them practical support. They badly needed the help of Russian military advisers and a large amount of financial aid. They hoped that they would get arms and other material support from the Soviet Union after they reached the region of the East River in Kwangtung.[9]

Of course, Chang Kuo-t'ao could not answer the above questions himself. He put them to Lominadze who had just arrived in Hankow. Lominadze said that he had to seek instructions from Moscow. Pointing out that this was a matter of extreme urgency brooking no delay, Chang Kuo-t'ao inquired if it would be possible to work out some practical measures for Chou En-lai and company to act upon while instructions were being sought from Moscow. Lominadze stated that the CCP leadership might tell Chou En-lai, et al, to make active preparations and that it might also mobilize the workers and peasants according to local circumstances. As for the other questions, Lominadze said, he had to ask for instructions from Moscow.[10]

The Central Standing Committee met in Hankow on July 26 at 4 p.m. at the request of Lominadze. It was attended by Chang Kuo-t'ao, Ch'ü Ch'iu-pai (both members of the Central Standing

---

8 "Li Li-san's Report", section 1, op. cit.; "Chou I-ch'ün's Report", section 1, *Central Correspondence*, No. 7, October 30, 1927; "Comrade Kuo-t'ao's Letter to the Enlarged Session", November 8, [1927], section 7, *Central Correspondence*, No. 13, November 30, 1927.

9 Chang Kuo-t'ao, "My Memoirs", *Ming Pao Monthly*, No. 24, December 1967, p. 95.

10 Ibid.

Committee), Li Wei-han, Chang T'ai-lei (both members of the Central Committee), Lominadze, Galen, Fanck, an unidentified representative of the Communist Youth International, and two interpreters. The meeting began with a report by Galen who had met Chang Fa-k'uei earlier that day. Galen said that Chang Fa-k'uei had agreed to stop his troops at the Nanchang-Kiukiang railway line and move gradually in the direction of Kwangtung. He stressed that the Communists should go back to Kwangtung with Chang Fa-k'uei if he agreed to do so and not to force Yeh T'ing and others to withdraw from the Communist Party. Without the support of Chang Fa-k'uei, he pointed out, the Communists could collect only 5,000 to 8,000 troops to stage the Nanchang rising and would find it difficult to reach the East River of Kwangtung with the odds against them. Of course, Galen added, the Communists would have to act independently if Chang Fa-k'uei refused to cooperate.[11]

By this time Lominadze had already received an answer from Moscow. He disclosed that no funds were available for the projected Nanchang uprising and that Moscow did not allow Russian advisers to participate in the uprising under any circumstances. In addition, he quoted the Comintern telegram as saying: "If the uprising has no hope of success, it would be better not to launch it, and the Communists in Chang Fa-k'uei's army should all be pulled out and sent to work among the peasants".[12]

Lominadze asked Chang Kuo-t'ao to deliver the Comintern telegram to the Communist leaders in Kiangsi at once. Chang Kuo-t'ao accepted the errand of messenger with reluctance since he said he realized that the Comintern telegram was meant to stop the projected Nanchang uprising which the Chinese party leadership had approved. He quoted Lominadze as admitting that the Comintern telegram, which was decided by Stalin and issued under the name of Bukharin, was really a serious order to stop the Nanchang uprising under preparation, but that as a Comintern order, it had to be obeyed. According to Chang Kuo-t'ao, all those present at

---

[11] Ibid.; "Comrade Kuo-t'ao's Letter to the Enlarged Session", section 2, op. cit.

[12] Ibid.; English translation of the Comintern telegram was based on C. Martin Wilbur's translation in *China Quarterly*, No. 18, April-June 1964, p. 46, see also pp. 11 and 52 for slightly different versions of the telegram.

the meeting agreed with Lominadze who had made clear his intention of stopping the Nanchang uprising according to the Comintern order. Under such circumstances, all were inclined to accept Galen's suggestion to seek the cooperation of Chang Fa-k'uei in a return trip to Kwangtung. If this also proved impossible, they felt, the Communists would then have to be sent to work in the rural districts. Chang Kuo-t'ao asserted that it was with this understanding that he agreed to take the Comintern telegram to Kiangsi in person. [13]

Chang Kuo-t'ao left Hankow by boat on the evening of July 26 and arrived in Kiukiang the next morning. He immediately reported the content of the Comintern telegram to those Communist leaders who were left behind there. But he was told that the die was already cast and that it was no longer possible to change the insurrection plan, no matter how the Comintern and the party leadership felt about it. [14] He wired twice to Nanchang on the 29th, counseling caution and warning against a decision before his arrival. But the Front Committee at Nanchang ignored him and went ahead with the insurrection plan. [15]

Chang Kuo-t'ao arrived at Nanchang on the morning of the 30th. The Front Committee plunged immediately into a meeting with Chou En-lai, Li Li-san, T'an P'ing-shan, Chang Kuo-t'ao, P'eng P'ai, Yung Tai-ying, Yeh T'ing and Chou I-ch'ün present. Chang Kuo-t'ao made a report on the Comintern telegram and the cautious position of the party leadership. He personally was still inclined to win over Chang Fa-k'uei whose support was considered indispensable to a successful march to Kwangtung. Yeh T'ing agreed with him. But all others were insistent on an insurrection. Chou En-lai even threatened to resign if the insurrection was called off. The discussion lasted several hours without a decision being reached. Since Chang Kuo-t'ao spoke on behalf of the party leadership, his opinion could not be overridden by a majority vote.

---

13 Chang Kuo-t'ao, "My Memoirs", *Ming Pao Monthly*, No. 24, December 1967, p. 96.

14 Ibid., p. 91; "Comrade Kuo-t'ao's Letter to the Enlarged Session", section 2, op. cit.

15 "Li Li-san's Report", section 1, op. cit.

The date of the revolt, which had already been postponed from the 28th to the 30th, had to be changed once again.[16]

When the Front Committee met again on the morning of the 31st, the situation had undergone a dramatic change. Since Ho Lung and Yeh T'ing had rejected an invitation to the KMT conference at Lushan, their military leader Chang Fa-k'uei wanted to come to Nanchang to see them, and he was scheduled to arrive on August 1. This new development was so urgent that it left the Communists no option but to launch the revolt right away without deliberation. In such critical circumstances, Chang Kuo-t'ao also changed his mind and was willing to abide by a majority decision. Finally the time of the revolt was set for the early morning of August 1.[17] Owing to an information leak, the mutiny started at 12:30 a.m.[18] The insurrectionary army consisted of approximately 21,000 men with those under the command of Yeh T'ing and Chou Shih-ti as the core.[19] About one per cent of them were Communists and Communist Youths. Ho Lung and Yeh T'ing served as the commander and deputy commander of the rebel forces respectively. As the KMT garrison at Nanchang consisting of about 3,000 troops was caught unprepared, it was disarmed without much fighting. No more gunfire was heard by nine o'clock in the morning.[20]

Moscow still had misgivings concerning the Nanchang uprising after it had erupted. On August 13 *Pravda* carried a report from Wuhan, beginning with the following statement:

> The insurrection in Nanchang is the central point of general interest. Whether this insurrection is merely a heroic episode or whether it is really the beginning of a decisive phase in the

---

[16] Ibid.; "Comrade Kuo-t'ao's Letter to the Enlarged Session", section 7; Chang Kuo-t'ao, "My Memoirs", *Ming Pao Monthly*, No. 25, January 1968, pp. 91-92.

[17] "Li Li-san's Report", section 1; "Chou I-ch'ün's Report", section 1; "Comrade Kuo-t'ao's Letter to the Enlarged Session", section 7; Chang Kuo-t'ao, "My Memoirs", *Ming Pao Monthly*, No. 25, January 1968, p. 92.

[18] "Chou I-ch'ün's Report", section 1; Kung Ch'u, *The Red Army and I*, South Wind Publishing Co., Hong Kong, 1954, p. 53.

[19] "Chang Kuo-t'ao's Report", October 9, [1927], *Central Correspondence*, No. 7, October 30, 1927; Chang Kuo-t'ao, "My Memoirs", *Ming Pao Monthly*, No. 25, January 1968, p. 94.

[20] Kung Ch'u, pp. 52, 54, 57; Chang Kuo-t'ao, "My Memoirs", *Ming Pao Monthly*, No. 25, January 1968, pp. 93-94.

Chinese revolution, cannot yet be said. Much depends upon the courage and determination of the leaders, upon whether the Communist Party of China shows itself big enough to deal with the situation and upon the success of the insurrection in securing support from the broad masses of the peasantry.[21]

2. The Exodus

The Nanchang rebels were interested in the capture of large cities [22] rather than in land revolution, guerrilla warfare, etc.[23]

As soviets were not the aim of Chinese Communist policy at this time, the rebels set up an interim regime at Nanchang, known as the Revolutionary Committee of the Kuomintang. T'an P'ing-shan served as chairman of the Revolutionary Committee with Chou En-lai in charge of the staff corps, Li Li-san leading the political security bureau, and Chang Kuo-t'ao directing the worker and peasant movement. Some KMT left-wing leaders including Chang Fa-k'uei were listed as members of the Revolutionary Committee without their previous knowledge.[24]

Chu Teh who was originally a regiment commander stationed in Linchuan (Fuchou), about ninety miles south of Nanchang, was made the police chief in the city of Nanchang. He was also appointed the commander of the Ninth Army in order that he might use his influence to win over the KMT troops with whom he had worked.[25]

The political program of the new regime was generally the same as that of the KMT during the first phase of the Northern Expedition in 1926. What was new was the policy that a landlord who owned more than 200 *mow* of land was subject to confiscation.[26]

---

21 *Inprecor.*, Vol. 7, No. 8, August 18, 1927, p. 1069.

22 Chang Kuo-t'ao, "My Memoirs", *Ming Pao Monthly*, No. 26, February 1968, p. 92.

23 Ibid., No. 25, January 1968, p. 94.

24 Ibid.

25 Ibid., pp. 94, 96; Kung Ch'u, pp. 61, 62.

26 Chang Kuo-t'ao, "My Memoirs", *Ming Pao Monthly*, No. 25, January 1968, p. 95.

There was no real cooperation among the leaders of the rebellion. T'an P'ing-shan, though politically ambitious, was not a good political leader. His colleagues did not like him. Chou En-lai was then more interested in military affairs than in politics. He seemed to think that all political dreams would be empty without a military victory. Li Li-san seemed to think so, too.[27] Chang Kuo-t'ao, who had tried to stop the revolt, no longer enjoyed the confidence of his colleagues.[28]

Li Li-san reported that the Front Committee was weak and provided little political leadership. Its leading members worked independently of one another and seldom got together for a meeting. Practically all the major tasks of the revolt were carried out by them individually at will. Although the revolt was launched in the name of the Communist Party, it was actually run by individual Communists, particularly T'an P'ing-shan.[29]

According to Chang Kuo-t'ao, defeatism developed from the outset. Some thought that they would have to go to the mountains like bandits if there was no way out. Others were of the opinion that they should return to Kwangtung first, leaving all problems open for the moment. Still others simply sought to escape to save their lives.[30] On the whole, the morale was not so good as that of the initial stage of the Northern Expedition.[31]

Since the Nanchang revolt was a purely military mutiny, there was no support from the masses. No workers and peasants participated. After the Communists took over, the people at large did not know what it was all about.[32]

Nobody believed from the beginning that the revolt would be successful.[33] That meant that the Communists had no intention to stay at Nanchang for a relatively long time. In fact, as described

---

[27] Ibid., p. 93.

[28] Ibid., p. 91.

[29] "Li Li-san's Report", section 10, op. cit.

[30] "Chang Kuo-t'ao's Report", October 9, [1927], section 1, op. cit.

[31] Chang Kuo-t'ao, "My Memoirs", *Ming Pao Monthly*, No. 25, January 1968, p. 95.

[32] Kung Ch'u, p. 56.

[33] Chang Kuo-t'ao, "My Memoirs", *Ming Pao Monthly*, No. 24, December 1967, pp. 95, 96.

previously, they wanted to return to Kwangtung right away. Accordingly, they discussed the question of the route of retreat on the first evening of the rebellion. Some of them wanted to take the main road in western Kiangsi leading from Changshu through Kian to Kanchow and then follow the Canton-Hankow railway zone all the way down to Canton. The majority preferred the out-of-the-way route in eastern Kiangsi leading from Fuchou through Juichin and Hsunwu to eastern Kwangtung. Finally it was decided to take the latter route on the ground that this route had the advantage of avoiding enemy attacks and connecting quickly with the peasant revolts in eastern Kwangtung. Almost all the top-ranking Communist leaders including Chou En-lai, Yeh T'ing and the Russian adviser by the name of Chikung were in favor of this route.[34]

On August 3, the Communists began to withdraw from Nanchang. Yeh T'ing left the city the next day while Ho Lung and all the remaining troops pulled out August 5.[35] It was difficult to tell this Communist-led army from the KMT troops.[36] The exodus was financially supported with 700,000 Chinese dollars in banknotes and 100,000 Chinese dollars in silver, all grabbed in Nanchang. The banknotes were actually useless.[37]

It took the rebels three days to reach Linchuan in extremely difficult conditions. They marched quickly on foot in summer heat and were overloaded with arms and ammunition. Owing to the bad discipline of the vanguard of Ho Lung's troops who had largely started out as bandits, plus the lack of the support of a peasant movement in the Kiangsi countryside, all the peasants, except the aged, had fled before the rebel troops. In consequence, there was no food for sale. Many soldiers deserted or died. More than one-third of the rebel military strength was reportedly lost in the first three days of retreat.[38]

34 "Li Li-san's Report", section 2; "Chou I-ch'ün's Report", section 3; for Ho Lung's advocacy of moving to Hunan, see Chang Kuo-t'ao, "My Memoirs", *Ming Pao Monthly*, No. 25, January 1968, pp. 94, 96n.

35 "Chou I-ch'ün's Report", section 4.

36 Chang Kuo-t'ao, "My Memoirs", *Ming Pao Monthly*, No. 25, January 1968, p. 95.

37 "Chang Kuo-t'ao's Report", October 9, [1927], section 2.

38 "Li Li-san's Report", section 2B; "Chou I-ch'ün's Report", section 4; "Chang Kuo-t'ao's Report", October 9, [1927], section 1; Kung Ch'u, pp. 59-60.

In collaboration with Ho Lung and Yeh T'ing in the Nanchang mutiny was a former KMT division commander by the name of Ts'ai T'ing-k'ai. He was entrusted with the task of guarding the left wing during the southern march. When he reached Chinhsien north of Linchuan, he deserted back to the KMT with his 5,000 troops, killing a Communist regiment commander under his command. This dealt a great blow to the Communists.[39]

After a stopover of three days at Linchuan, the rebels continued to march southward. They were now better off than before with fewer desertions reported. But the peasants were still hostile to them. The peasants avoided them and did not hesitate to kill them if caught alive.[40]

The Nanchang insurgents reached Juichin on August 19 after some fighting with KMT troops in the northeastern suburbs who had come to intercept their escape. They stayed in Juichin for about a week under the protection of a fighting going on in Huichang, a neighboring county about 30 miles to the southwest.[41] Ho Lung joined the Chinese Communist Party in Juichin.[42]

Shortly after their retreat from Nanchang many staff officers fled with the result that there was the danger of a leakage of the military plan. In addition, it was feared that there would be no adequate food supply in southern Kiangsi. Consequently, the Communist leaders decided to give up their original plan of traversing southern Kiangsi as the short cut to Kwangtung but to take the roundabout way from western Fukien to eastern Kwangtung.[43]

There was a discussion of the question of the strategy to take Kwangtung when the rebels reached Tingchow in western Fukien. Some wanted to take the main route from Sanhopa southwestward

---

[39] "Li Li-san's Report", section 2B; "Chang Kuo-t'ao's Report", October 9, [1927], section 1; Kung Ch'u, p. 58; Chang Kuo-t'ao, "My Memoirs", *Ming Pao Monthly*, No. 25, January 1968, p. 95.

[40] "Li Li-san's Report", section 2B; "Chang Kuo-t'ao's Report", October 9, [1927], section 2.

[41] "Chou I-ch'ün's Report", sections 5, 6; "Li Li-san's Report", section 2B.

[42] Chang Kuo-t'ao, "My Memoirs", *Ming Pao Monthly*, No. 26, February 1968, pp. 89-90; cf. Kung Ch'u, pp. 62-63; "Chou I-ch'ün's Report", section 9.

[43] "Li Li-san's Report", section 2B.

to Meihsien, Hsingning and Huichow, sending only a small detachment to Swatow where the KMT garrison was believed to be weak. Others preferred to use the principal force to take Swatow first, leaving only a small column at Sanhopa to guard against the enemy at Meihsien, and then proceed from Chiehyang through Hsingning and Wuhua to Huichow. As the latter course was thought to have the advantage of getting possible Russian aid, it was accepted by the majority of the rebel leaders. In fact, there was no fighting all the way from western Fukien to Swatow. When the rebels reached Swatow on September 24, the government troops had evacuated the city two days before.[44]

There were interesting policy discussions and decisions during the march of the Communist rebels to Kwangtung. As described previously, a landlord who owned more than 200 *mow* of land was subject to confiscation. But, in fact, there were few landlords who owned that much land in China. Therefore, as soon as the Communists reached Juichin, this unrealistic policy was abandoned and changed to a simple "confiscation of land" program without fixing a definite amount of land as the criterion for confiscation. [45] This simple "confiscation of land" program was retained during a discussion at Shanghang in western Fukien. It was reinforced by a "land to the tiller" slogan adopted there. Chang Kuo-t'ao suggested 50 *mow* as the criterion for confiscation with a view to winning the support of the small landlords, but he did not get immediate support from his colleagues. His suggestion was not accepted until it was learned that 30 to 50 *mow* of land was the criterion for confiscation being actually carried out by Communists in Kwangtung.[46]

It is interesting to note that the Nanchang rebels did not give any attention to the labor question at first. Not until after their arrival in Juichin did the Front Committee begin to discuss this question. Consequently a labor protection program was adopted, providing for the eight-hour working day, etc.[47]

---

44 "Li Li-san's Report", section 2C; "Central's Circular", (No. 13), October 24, [1927], section 2, *Central Correspondence*, No. 7, October 30, 1927; Kung Ch'u, pp. 74-75.

45 "Li Li-san's Report", section 4.

46 Ibid.; "Chang Kuo-t'ao's Letter to the Enlarged Session", section 8.

47 "Li Li-san's Report", section 5.

It was natural that the question of raising funds confronted the Nanchang rebels from the beginning. There were two different currents of opinion regarding this question. Some wanted to use the traditional method of entrusting the local gentry with the task of collecting the contributions. This method had the advantage of a simple and easy procedure of getting the necessary financial support, but it had the danger that the gentry class would try what they could to diminish their own share of the contributions and collect an unduly considerable share from the poor people. Therefore, another segment of the Communist leaders wanted to approach the question in a different way by imposing the financial burden on all persons other than the poor people. But this approach had the practical difficulty of having nobody make the contributions at all because there was no peasant movement in eastern Kiangsi to make it possible to identify the landlords and gentry who should bear the financial burden. Consequently, there was considerable confusion regarding this financial question. Ideals squared seldom with realities. In fact, the traditional method proved much more effective than the revolutionary approach during those hectic days of retreat. In the city of Swatow the Communists refrained from requisition and confiscation for fear of economic disorder and possible intervention of the imperialists.[48]

Intimately associated with the confused financial policy was the Communist treatment of the reactionaries at the time. Legally there was a political security department entrusted with the task of suppressing the reactionaries ruthlessly. In practice, however, it was impossible to carry out the stern policy of suppressing the reactionaries because there was no peasant movement in support of it. Besides, the Communist cadres were not yet quite clear about the true nature of this sort of work. Though having broken away from the old regime, they were still living under the influence of old traditions. They were as mindful of their good discipline as ever and tried their best to spare human life on grounds of humanity. In consequence, only a few dozens of the so-called reactionaries were executed all the way from Nanchang to Swatow. Interestingly, it was charged that three poor people had been shot

---

[48] Ibid., section 6.

on charges of looting in Swatow before steps were taken to punish the reactionaries.[49]

It is understandable that the organization of the Communist Party should have been weak at the time. There was no party organization in eastern Kiangsi. The party apparatus in eastern Kwangtung was no more than a loose conglomeration of party members; it was by no means an organization for mass struggle. In preparing for insurrections in some places, the Communists simply did not bother to infiltrate into the masses.[50] Workers and peasants were extremely weak in eastern Kwangtung on the whole.[51]

Moreover, the Communist military potential was also weak. Though the Eleventh Army in which Yeh T'ing served as a division commander was heavily infiltrated by Communists, it could not be said to be a Communist army. Ho Lung's Twentieth Army was in fact an old-fashioned bandit army which was at best sympathetic to the Communist cause. Only more than a hundred troops were left in Chu Teh's Ninth Army on reaching Juichin, and soon afterward the title of the Ninth Army was canceled. As pointed out previously, the rebels boasted some 21,000 troops at Nanchang, but lost 5,000 or so when the division commander Ts'ai T'ing-k'ai deserted about a week after Nanchang. Approximately 7,000 men were missing owing to sickness, flight, etc., while about 1,000 were killed in the battles at Juichin and Huichang. Only 8,000 combat troops or so were left at Juichin.[52] This figure was probably also true of the Communist strength while in Swatow in view of the fact that there was no fighting from western Fukien to Swatow.

3. Disillusion at Swatow

The Nanchang rebels captured Swatow on September 24 and stayed there during the last week of September. There was no communication between them and the party leadership in the

---

49 Ibid., section 7; "Chang T'ai-lei's Report", October 15, [1927], section 2, *Central Correspondence*, No. 7, October 30, 1927.

50 "Li Li-san's Report", section 10.

51 "Chang Kuo-t'ao's Report", October 9, [1927], section 3.

52 Ibid., sections 2, 5; Chang Kuo-t'ao, "My Memoirs", *Ming Pao Monthly*, No. 25, January 1968, p. 96.

seven-week interval between Nanchang and Swatow.[53] The
Nanchang events were not seriously discussed at the August 7
Conference [54] which, in turn, remained unknown to the Nanchang
rebels until Swatow. [55] Swatow was designed for the provisional
capital city of the projected Communist regime. The rebels were
prepared to start a grandiose political upheaval from there.[56] As
it was, Swatow was relatively quiet under the Communist occupation.
It suffered only a small-scale assault from the KMT marines on
September 29.[57]

About two days after the fall of Swatow into the Communist
hands, Chang T'ai-lei arrived from Hong Kong, armed with important
instructions from the party leadership. He told the Communist
rebels to change the Revolutionary Committee to a soviet and give
up the KMT banner. He also wanted them to abandon Swatow
and move their troops to Hai-lu-feng in order to join with the
peasants in organizing a Worker-Peasant Red Army. In addition,
Chang Kuo-t'ao and Li Li-san were told to proceed to Shanghai
immediately to discuss party policy with the central leadership.
Chou En-lai was to be left behind. With the dissolution of the
Revolutionary Committee, T'an P'ing-shan was also to leave
Swatow.[58]

The Communist leaders at Swatow were stunned by the above
party instructions. They were given to understand that their
whole group from Nanchang was to disintegrate, that they were
not to remain in Swatow, and that their troops must be sent to
Hai-lu-feng to join the peasants. This was, indeed, a new orientation diametrically opposed to their own way of thinking. They
felt that something must be wrong, but they could not tell why.[59]

A few days later, September 30, *Pravda* published a leading
article on the victorious southern march of the Nanchang rebels,

---

53 Kung Ch'u, p. 75; Pavel Mif, *Heroic China: Fifteen Years of the Communist Party of China*, Chinese version, p. 74, English version, p. 54; Ch'ü Ch'iu-pai, *The Chinese Revolution and the Communist Party*, p. 127.

54 Ts'ai Ho-sen, "A History of Opportunism", section C.

55 "Li Li-san's Report", section 10.

56 Chang Kuo-t'ao, "My Memoirs", *Ming Pao Monthly*, No. 26, February, 1968, p. 93.

57 Kung Ch'u, p. 75.

58 Chang Kuo-t'ao, "My Memoirs", *Ming Pao Monthly*, February 1968, p. 93.

59 Ibid.

which threw considerable light on the above-mentioned instructions of the Chinese party leadership. *Pravda* began by declaring:

> After the southern revolutionary army had achieved important successes, it became perfectly clear that there would be a new revolutionary *èlan* in China. Contrary to the preceding revolutionary *èlan*, this one did not originate in towns, in centers of the industrial proletariat where counter revolution has for the time being gained the upper hand, but in the peasant guerrilla movement and those revolutionary divisions of the former Canton army which are winning victories with the help of the peasant risings over the oppressors of the Chinese people.[60]

Thus, *Pravda* made clear that by the later months of 1927 the Chinese Communists had begun to shift their primary revolutionary base from the city to the countryside and that the revolution in the countryside was being carried out by means of peasant guerrilla tactics, peasant risings and military operations. This was a policy switch of basic importance. It not only accounted for the proposed transfer of the Communist-led troops from the city of Swatow to the rural districts of Hai-lu-feng but also foreshadowed the subsequent development of Chinese Communism for many years to come.

It need hardly be emphasized that the countryside should now come first as the revolutionary base. This was evident from the *Pravda* thesis that the new revolutionary *èlan* which originated in peasant areas was to spread to industrial centers:

> As revolution spreads to industrial centers it will be possible to create there soviets of workers', soldiers' and artisans' deputies on which the new revolutionary government or governments will rest in the beginning, if they will spring up at first in various parts of South Chinese [sic] at a distance from each other. The soviet slogan, from being a propaganda slogan, must develop into an action slogan. As to the Chinese countryside the so-called peasant unions have shown their worth as revolutionary organizations, and all power should go to them in these districts, of course, under the control of revolutionary committees. These peasant unions and committees must be converted into soviets of peasant deputies and their business must be to rouse as large sections as possible of the Chinese peasantry for revolution.[61]

---

[60] *Inprecor.*, Vol. 7, No. 56, October 6, 1927, p. 1238.
[61] Ibid., p. 1239.

Thus, as noted above, Moscow took the position that while the conversion of the peasant unions and committees into peasant soviets in China was a "must", the creation of the soviets of workers, soldiers and artisans would be "possible" as revolution spread to industrial centers.

It may be recalled that it was made clear in the Eighth Plenum of the ECCI in May 1927 that soviets should be created in China when the democratic revolution began to develop into the socialist revolution. Now that the creation of soviets was demanded, the question naturally arose as to whether the socialist revolution had begun. This question was negatively answered by *Pravda* in its leading article of September 30:

> The tasks of the new power are tasks of *Anti-Imperialist Revolutionary-Dictatorship*. Socialist tasks do not yet directly confront this power.

Pravda pointed out that the Chinese Communist regime "must first of all awaken the masses, leaving it to the creative initiative of all toilers to carry out energetically *agrarian revolutions*, confiscate land, abolish all feudal privileges, gaining thereby the allegiance of large sections of peasants, crush relentlessly all counter revolutionaries, confiscate in towns the property of people supporting counter revolutions, impose taxes on the big bourgeoisie to satisfy the immediate needs of the army. . . . . . ."[62]

It must be remembered that Swatow was still in the hands of the Communists when Chang T'ai-lei arrived there and when the *Pravda* article was published. It was then debatable whether Swatow should be held or given up. However, the situation underwent a dramatic change after a decisive Communist defeat at Tangkeng, a strategic town about 35 miles northwest of Swatow, around the beginning of October. The Communists were forced to leave Swatow on the morning of October 1 and retreat in the direction of Hai-lu-feng where P'eng P'ai had set up a sort of rural power center.[63]

---

[62] Ibid.

[63] "Li Li-san's Report", section 2D; "Ch'en Kung's Report", October 18, [1927], *Central Correspondence*, No. 7, October 30, 1927; Kung Ch'u, pp. 76, 86-87; the Tangkeng defeat is dated October 3 in Chang Kuo-t'ao's "My Memoirs", *Ming Pao Monthly*, No. 26, February 1968, p. 93.

When most of the Communist leaders reached Liusha on October 4, Chou En-lai, as secretary of the Front Committee, announced that the soviet flag must replace the KMT flag in accordance with party instructions. Chang Kuo-t'ao and Li Li-san were the first to flee to Hong Kong by way of Chatzukong. Chou En-lai, T'an P'ing-shan, Ho Lung, Yeh T'ing, etc. followed suit. Except for a small number of survivors, all the rebel troops were smashed.[64]

Interestingly, the peasants in Hai-lu-feng also availed themselves of the opportunity to harass the rebel survivors. They disarmed and looted them in order to make fortunes, and the local Communists could not help it.[65]

The party leadership in Shanghai made two major decisions on October 12. First, as it was no longer possible to seize Kwangtung, the original plan of the rebels to capture Canton must be stopped at once. If necessary, the remaining Communist forces should retreat to southern Hunan and eventually to the mountains. Second, all important Communist leaders were to go to Shanghai except those whose duties required them to stay behind.[66]

Chu Teh who was caught up in Sanhopa on the northern flank of Swatow took several hundred troops including Lin Piao and Ch'en Yi to escape in the direction from the Fukien-Kiangsi border through southern Kiangsi and northern Kwangtung to southern Hunan. Chu Teh joined Mao in Chingkangshan in April 1928.[67]

Needless to say, the Swatow debacle killed all hope of the Kwangtung Communists to stage an insurrection in the province. Like their comrades in other provinces, the Communists in Kwangtung based their projected insurrection on the troops. They waited for the arrival of the rebel troops retreating from Nanchang,

---

[64] "Chang Kuo-t'ao's Report", October 9, [1927], sections 1, 4; Chang Kuo-t'ao, "My Memoirs", *Ming Pao Monthly*, No. 26, February 1968, pp. 94-95; Kung Ch'u, pp. 76-78, 80, 85, 87.

[65] Kung Ch'u, pp. 78-80, 87.

[66] "Letter to the Kwangtung Provincial Committee", October 12, [1927], *Central Correspondence*, No. 7, October 30, 1927.

[67] "Chou I-ch'ün's Report", section 7; Chang Kuo-t'ao, "My Memoirs", *Ming Pao Monthly*, No. 26, February 1968; Huang Ho, *A Short History of Thirty-five Years of the Chinese Communist Party*, Peking, Popular Readings Publishing House, 1957, pp. 31-33; Li Wei, *Chingkangshan*, Shanghai, New Knowledge Publishing House, 1956, pp. 16-18.

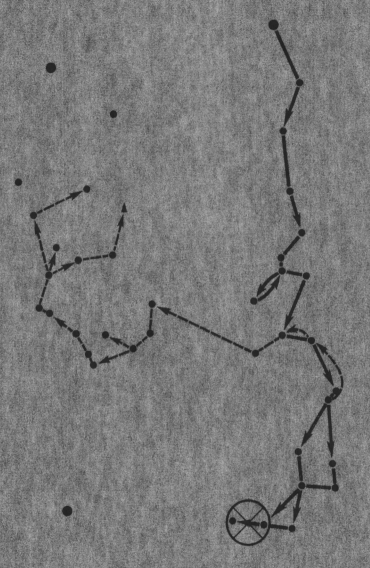

THE EXODUS FROM
NANCHANG

⊗ utter dissolution of insurrectionists

→ direction of retreat

-·-·→ escape of Chu Teh's column

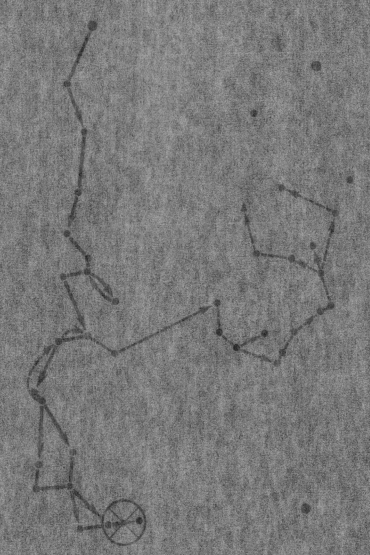

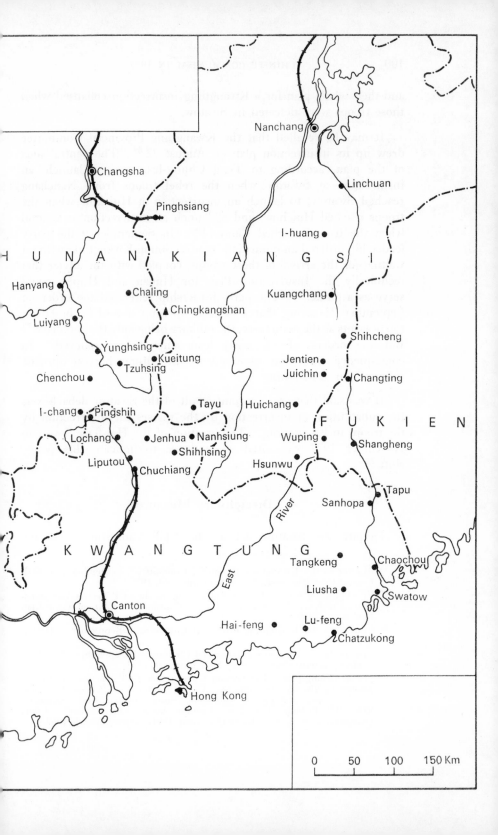

and their whole plan for a Kwangtung insurrection collapsed when those troops were defeated in Swatow.

It may be recalled that the Kwangtung Provincial Committee drew up its insurrection plan on August 22.[68]   The central idea of the plan, according to Teng Chung-hsia, was to launch an insurrection at Swatow when the rebel troops from Nanchang reached Swatow, to launch an insurrection at Huichow when the troops reached Huichow, and to launch an insurrection at Canton when the troops reached Canton.[69]   On September 9 the party leadership ordered an immediate insurrection in Kwangtung without waiting for the arrival of those troops, coupled with the advice that technically the Insurrection Plan for Hunan and Hupeh could serve as a guide.[70]   The party leadership reiterated the order on September 23 saying that a peasant uprising should be based on the peasants as the main force, the military being only the auxiliary.[71] But the orders of the party leadership were disobeyed.   In consequence, no rising came off in the autumn harvest uprising program in Kwangtung.

It was said that an important result of the Swatow debacle was the substitution of insurrection by the masses for insurrection by the troops in Kwangtung.   The creation of the Hai-feng Soviet in November 1927 was cited as evidence to indicate this policy shift.[72]

4. Disciplinary Measures

Despite the Swatow defeat, the CCP leadership found the

---

[68] "Letter to the Kwangtung Provincial Committee", September 9, [1927], *Central Correspondence*, No. 5, September 20, 1927.

[69] [Teng] Chung-hsia, "The Canton Uprising and the CCP Tactics", section 2, printed in Lozovsky, *et al*, *The Canton Commune*, in Chinese, Proletarian Bookstore, 1930.

[70] "Letter to the Kwangtung Provincial Committee", September 9, [1927], op. cit.

[71] "Letter to the Kwangtung Provincial Committee", September 23, [1927], *Central Correspondence*, No. 6, September 30, 1927.

[72] [Teng] Chung-hsia, "The Canton Uprising and CCP Tactics", section 2, printed in *The Canton Commune;* Chung I-mou, *The Peasant Movement in Hai-lu-feng*, Kwangtung Publishing Store, October 1957; Shinkichi Eto, "Hai-lu-feng—The First Chinese Soviet Government", *China Quarterly*, Nos. 8, 9, October-December 1961, January-March 1962.

revolutionary tide rising rather than falling. It was their belief that the failure of the whole revolt from Nanchang to Swatow was due to the mistake of relying on the military force rather than the peasant masses. They thought that the Yeh-Ho troops were just an auxiliary force and that their defeat was a military defeat which would not affect the revolution of the masses. In addition, it was stated, the rebel leaders made a number of mistakes such as expropriating the land of only the landlords owning more than 200 *mow* and avoiding military clashes with the enemy by marching through eastern rather than western Kiangsi.[73]

Lominadze took the position that the defeat of the Yeh-Ho forces was due mainly to the opportunistic errors of the military leaders.[74]

Against this background, most of the leaders of the Nanchang revolt were summoned to Shanghai where the whole course of events from Nanchang to Swatow was reviewed.[75] Chang Kuo-t'ao and Li Li-san submitted each a report on the events but were not asked to take part in discussions.[76] On October 24 the party leadership issued a statement on the subject, enlarging on the old argument that the defeat was a military defeat which would not change the course of the revolution and that the rebel leaders had committed a host of political and military blunders. More important, the statement contained a program of workers' and peasants' revolution through armed insurrection. Two new planks were added to the party platform: (1) nationalization of land, coupled with a ban on the purchase and sale of land, and (2) confiscation of all large enterprises of Chinese and foreign capitalists.[77]

---

73 "A Report on the Recent Political Situation", dated around mid-October 1927, "Chang T'ai-lei's Report", October 15, [1927], both in *Central Correspondence*, No. 7, October 30, 1927.

74 *Communist International*, London edition, January 5, 1928, p. 33.

75 Kung Ch'u, p. 85; Chang Kuo-t'ao, "My Memoirs", *Ming Pao Monthly*, No. 27, March 1968.

76 Chang Kuo-t'ao, "My Memoirs", *Ming Pao Monthly*, No. 27, March 1968, p. 95; for English translations of these two and other related documents, see C. Martin Wilbur, "The Ashes of Defeat", *China Quarterly*, April-June 1964.

77 "Central's Circular", (No. 13), October 24, 1927, section 5, *Central Corespondence*, No. 7, October 30, 1927.

Learning of the above party statement, Ch'en Tu-hsiu, former party chief, worried about the dangerous possibilities of such new trends in the party line. He wrote to the party leadership on November 13 saying that the new party line, based as it was on the proletarian revolutionary program of the October revolution, was a program of "workers' and peasants' revolution through armed insurrection", but that Comintern resolutions had made clear that it would be incorrect to consider the national revolution in China ended and the workers' and peasants' revolution already commenced. He, therefore, suggested that the party soon determine the nature of the present state of the revolution and send it to the Comintern for approval. [78] The party leadership turned down Ch'en Tu-hsiu's suggestion on the ground that the nature of the Chinese revolution was already prescribed in the resolutions of the Politburo enlarged session held November 9-10. [79]

As described previously, on the eve of the Nanchang uprising, July 26, the Comintern sent a telegram to Lominadze to counsel caution. Chang Kuo-t'ao and Chang T'ai-lei, neither of whom had seen the original text of the telegram, interpreted it differently. While the former believed it to be a warning against rashness, which seemed to agree with the position of the Comintern, [80] the latter regarded it as an encouragement to insurrection, [81] which seemed to agree with the thinking of the Politburo Enlarged Session of November. No wonder that the party leadership took sides against Chang Kuo-t'ao immediately following the Politburo enlarged session. [82]

On November 14 the Provisional Central Politburo adopted a resolution on political discipline in which the Nanchang-Swatow events were reviewed. It was pointed out that the Front Committee had made serious political and military mistakes of an opportunistic

78 "Letter from Comrade Tu-hsiu" (No. 2), November 12, 1927, Central Political Correspondence, No. 14, n.d.; "Resolution on the Chinese Question", adopted by the Eighth Plenum of the ECCI, May 1927, section 5.

79 "Reply to Comrade Tu-hsiu's Letter" (No. 1), from the Central Standing Committee, December 9, [1927], Central Political Correspondence, No. 14, n.d.

80 "Comrade Kuo-t'ao's Letter to the Enlarged Session", November 8, [1927], section 9; "Resolution on the Chinese Question", adopted by the Eighth Plenum of the ECCI, May 1927, section 7.

81 "Chang T'ai-lei's Report", October 15, [1927], op. cit.

82 "Central's Reply", Central Correspondence, No. 13, November 30, 1927.

nature. Politically, it had failed to work out a clear-cut program relating to land revolution and to a worker-peasant regime. Also, it had not issued a firm "land-to-the-tiller" slogan, but wavered between 50 and 200 *mow* of land as the criterion for confiscation. In the sphere of political strategy, village bosses, gentry and capitalists were not slaughtered in areas traversed by the insurrectionary army, nor were their socio-political organizations and armaments destroyed. On the contrary, some poor people who were found looting were shot. In addition, the insurrectionists had not confiscated the property of village bosses and gentry to solve their financial problem but had used the old warlord method of raising funds to exploit the poor and toiling people. In the military sphere, they did not march into Kwangtung by way of western Kiangsi where the peasant movement had a better background, but by way of the backward eastern Kiangsi to avoid enemy attacks. Likewise, they did not march directly to Meihsien in eastern Kwangtung following their victories at Juichin and Huichang, but took the round-about way through western Fukien to Swatow. To make matters worse, they had illusions about Chang Fa-k'uei from the beginning and failed to take precautionary measures against Ts'ai T'ing-k'ai who deserted shortly after he joined the revolt. All this was the result of military opportunism without confidence in the masses.[83]

In consequence, the Provisional Central Politburo meted out the following punishments:

1. T'an P'ing-shan was dismissed from the party on a number of charges such as objecting to land revolution and advocating organization of a Third Party.

2. Chang Kuo-t'ao was removed as an alternate member of the Provisional Politburo and as a member of the Central Executive Committee on charges of doubting and even objecting to the Nanchang revolt, attempting to make a deal with Chang Fa-k'uei, and opposing confiscation of all land.

3. All the members of the Front Committee were given a warning.

---

[83] "Resolution on Political Discipline", November 14, [1927], section (3)1, *Central Correspondence*, No. 13, November 30, 1927.

4. Hsü Kuang-ying was placed on probation as a party member for he as Swatow's police chief ordered the execution of three poor people on a charge of looting.

5. The South Bureau and the Kwangtung Provincial Committee were given a warning for their errors in dealing with peasant uprisings and agrarian problems and relying on military actions rather than the masses.[84]

---

[84] Ibid., section (5)1-5.

CHAPTER IV

SOCIALIST DEVIATION
AND INSURRECTIONARY TACTICS

1. Political Line of the Politburo Enlarged Session

After the failures of the autumn harvest insurrection and the Nanchang-Swatow expedition, the policy of armed insurrection which was the party line since late July was brought into question. Did those failures mean the irretrievable loss of the revolution? Was the forward policy of the August 7 Conference basically correct and sound? All these and related questions should be examined and answered before the future course of the revolution was charted. For this purpose, the Provisional Central Politburo met in enlarged session in Shanghai on November 9-10, 1927.[1]

Among those present at the Politburo enlarged session were Ch'ü Ch'iu-pai, Li Wei-han, Su Chao-cheng, Chang T'ai-lei, Lo I-nung, Jen Hsu, Ch'en Ch'iao-nien and Liu Ch'ang-chun. Mao Tse-tung who was then in the Chingkangshan area was not present. Li Li-san and Chang Kuo-t'ao, though in Shanghai at the time, were excluded from the meeting. Despite his share of responsibility for the Nanchang-Swatow discomfiture, Chou En-lai was not only allowed to attend the meeting, but was also returned to the Politburo and put in charge of military and intelligence work. It would appear that Lominadze was present at the meeting.[2]

---

[1] Lü Mo, "The Significance of the CCP Central's Recent Enlarged Session", *Bolshevik* (Pu-er-se-wei-ke), No. 11, December 26, 1927, p. 333; for Shanghai as the site of the session, see "Report of Comrade I-nung to the Enlarged Conference of the Hupeh Provincial Committee", December 12, [1927], section 2, *Central Political Correspondence*, No. 20, April 12, 1928; for the date of November 9-10, see "Central's Circular" (No. 16), November 18, [1927], *Central Correspondence*, No. 13, November 30, 1927.

[2] Chang Kuo-t'ao, "My Memoirs", *Ming Pao Monthly*, No. 27, March 1968, pp. 95, 96-97; "Report of Comrade I-nung to the Enlarged Conference of the Hupeh Provincial Committee", December 12, 1927, op. cit.; Ch'ü Ch'iu-pai, *The Chinese Revolution and the Communist Party*, p. 144.

The enlarged session of the Politburo adopted a number of resolutions including the one on the current situation in China and the tasks of the party, in which the theory and strategy of the new party line were set forth.[3] The large-scale disciplinary punishments, with which we have dealt in the preceding two chapters,[4] reflected the policy of further bolshevization of the party as formulated by the Politburo enlarged session.[5] That some of the resolutions bear the date of November 14 suggests that the operation of the enlarged session continued after the close of the formal session officially dated November 9-10.

The new political line of the party was based on the assumption that the revolutionary tide was flowing rather than ebbing despite the failures of Communist uprisings in August and September.[6] It was said that a revolutionary ebb must be due to three factors: (1) stability of the bourgeois and warlord rule, (2) success of reformism, and (3) disintegration and demoralization of the revolutionary masses. None of these factors, it was stated, existed at the time. Mere enemy attacks and slaughters which had been going on since August did not mean revolutionary setbacks. On the contrary, they signified a flow of the revolutionary wave. As a matter of fact, the internecine fights among warlords, the increasing wave of peasant risings and worker struggles, the growing economic crisis, etc. bore witness to the revolutionary upsurge.[7]

Moreover, it was pointed out that there was a direct revolutionary situation in China. This did not mean that the revolution would succeed in a short time. The direct revolutionary situation could not be a matter of weeks or months, but a matter of years. The Chinese revolution, it was said, had a permanent and, indeed, uninterrupted character. This, it was stated, could be seen from the following two facts:

---

3 The text of this resolution is available in *Bolshevik*, No. 6, November 28, 1927, and *Central Correspondence*, No. 13, November 30, 1927.

4 "Resolution on Political Discipline", November 14, [1927], op. cit.

5 "Resolution on the Important Tasks in the Recent Organizational Question", November 14, [1927], *Central Correspondence*, No. 13, November 30, 1927.

6 "Central's Circular" (No. 16), November 18, [1927], section 3, op. cit.

7 "Resolution on the Current Situation in China and the Tasks of the Party", sections 6, 7, *Bolshevik*, No. 6, November 28, 1927, *Central Correspondence*, No. 13, November 30, 1927; "Central's Circular" (No. 16), November 18, [1927], sections 1-3; [Ch'ü] Ch'iu-pai, "What Kind of Revolution Is the Chinese Revolution?" November 16, 1927, section 1, *Bolshevik*, No. 5, November 21, 1927.

First, since the Chinese bourgeoisie did not have the ability to carry out the democratic revolution aimed at the overthrow of the feudal warlords, the democratic revolution would not constitute a separate period in the process of the Chinese revolution. The democratic revolution would grow immediately and directly into the socialist revolution.

Second, the Chinese revolution had been progressing without interruption despite repeated setbacks. The conflicts among reactionary rulers made their own position unstable. The revolutionary struggle of the masses, especially the peasant risings, had continued unabated. All these facts showed the uninterrupted character of the Chinese revolution.

In brief, it was stressed, the Chinese revolutionary struggle was bound to go beyond the democratic scope, though it had not yet started resolving its democratic tasks. The process of the revolution would make it necessary to resolve its democratic tasks thoroughly and take the socialist road immediately.[8]

However, Ch'ü Ch'iu-pai explained that the Chinese revolution was not yet a purely socialist revolution.[9] His position was basically confirmed by the correction of an editorial mistake in the party organ *Bolshevik*, No. 11, December 26, 1927, in which it was said that the political system of China would be either a bourgeois warlord regime or a proletarian dictatorship and that there was no third road ahead. The editorial of the journal, No. 14, January 16, 1928, was quick to point out that the former editorial was not approved by the chief editor and that it was wrong to refer to the Chinese revolutionary regime as a proletarian dictatorship. It was contended that a proletarian dictatorship could only emerge in a socialist revolution and that the Chinese revolution at the time was a worker-peasant revolution, but not a socialist revolution.[10]

Ch'ü Ch'iu-pai subsequently revealed that many people had made the mistake of socialist deviation. In the enlarged session

---

[8] "Resolution on the Current Situation in China and the Tasks of the Party", section 6, op. cit.; cf. "Central's Circular" (No. 16), November 18, [1927], sections 1, 3.

[9] [Ch'ü] Ch'iu-pai, "What Kind of Revolution Is the Chinese Revolution?" November 16, 1927, section 3, op. cit.

[10] "The Chinese Soviet Regime and Socialism", *Bolshevik*, No. 14, January 16, 1928.

of the Politburo, he said, some persons thought that it was quite unfair that the peasants were allotted land while the workers were given only the eight-hour working day. To those persons, he stated, the best way would be for the chauffeurs to confiscate the cars, for the workers to confiscate the factories, and for the sales personnel to confiscate the shops. In a meeting of the Kwangtung Provincial Committee, he disclosed, many people suggested that the property of all capitalists be expropriated.[11]

Intimately associated with the question of the socialist revolution was the soviet system which the Politburo enlarged session formally adopted as the main slogan of the party.[12] The soviet was defined as the organ of political power which took the form of a council of deputies of the masses. By masses in the Chinese revolution, it was indicated, were meant the workers in large cities and the peasants, handicraftsmen, sales personnel and the general poor people in villages and county seats. It was made clear that the soviet was to organize or help organize the insurrection in a revolutionary upsurge and that it was to become the organ of government after the success of the insurrection.[13] It was pointed out that the soviet could only be a proletarian dictatorship if it was organized in a capitalist country in Europe or America but that it could be nothing but a revolutionary democratic dictatorship of workers and peasants in a pre-capitalist country like China. This was because China was still in the bourgeois-democratic stage of the revolution with land revolution as the main task and the features of land revolution such as the confiscation of the land of landlords were democratic but not socialist in nature.[14]

Furthermore, it was made clear that the soviet in China could not be organized until "a firm victory of the insurrection" was assured. By "a firm victory of the insurrection" the Politburo

---

11 Ch'ü Ch'iu-pai, *The Chinese Revolution and the Communist Party*, p. 155.

12 "Resolution on the Current Situation in China and the Tasks of the Party", section 9.

13 "The Chinese Soviet Regime and Socialism", op. cit.; Leon Trotsky, *Problems of the Chinese Revolution*, New York, Pioneer Publishers, 1932, p. 152; "Resolution on the Chinese Question" adopted by the 9th Plenum of the ECCI, February 25, 1928, section 10, Chinese version in *Red Documents*, pp. 289-296, English version in *Inprecor.*, Vol. 8, No. 16, March 15, 1928, pp. 321-323.

14 "The Chinese Soviet Regime and Socialism", op. cit.

enlarged session meant that the insurrection could be maintained in a given area for a relatively long time. The peasant union, which was the sole instrument of the rural revolution following the August 7 Conference, would now serve only as a preliminary step to the soviet. Urban mass organizations like strike committees were to help engineer the insurrection and should be converted into soviets upon its success. [15]

As was natural in a bourgeois-democratic revolution, the traditional trade union policy of the CCP in urban centers remained unchanged. But the large factories and shops, banks, mines, railways, etc. of big capitalists were subject to seizure and nationalization. Factories were to be managed by workers. Small proprietors were to be deprived of their factories if they sabotaged or closed down their plants. The property of the bourgeoisie could be requisitioned to improve the living conditions of the poor people. [16]

It was not surprising that the Politburo enlarged session raised the slogan of expropriating the land of all landlords, [17] because this policy, as noted previously, had been inaugurated shortly after the August 7 Conference. The interesting thing was that a draft party program on the land question was submitted under the name of one Comrade Li Fu, but the enlarged session was so cautious that it merely released it and referred it to the forthcoming Sixth National Congress of the party for a decision. The draft program stood for seizure of the land of all landlords and for common ownership of all private land by the toiling people who were to form the soviet state. [18]

2. Principles of Insurrection

Of particular interest was the fairly elaborate system of armed insurrection worked out by the Politburo enlarged session on the basis of the strategy of fighting from the countryside to the city. The new system offered quite a few significant improvements over the tactics of the autumn harvest insurrection. The Ch'ü Ch'iu-pai

---

[15] "Resolution on the Current Situation in China and the Tasks of the Party", section 9.

[16] Ibid.

[17] Ibid.

[18] "Draft Party Program of the CCP on the Land Question", *Bolshevik*, No. 6, November 28, 1927; *Central Correspondence*, No. 13, November 30, 1927.

leadership proceeded on the assumption, held since the August 7 Conference, that as China was not a unified country, the revolution could not hope to succeed at a stroke by seizing the "capital". Accordingly, the revolution was bound to take the form of scattered peasant uprisings in one place after another.[19]

It will be recalled that the autumn harvest insurrection started with attacks on county seats and smaller towns following violence in distant villages. In contrast, the November Politburo program of armed insurrection started with guerrilla warfare around the villages with particular attention to the avoidance of attacks on county seats. Guerrilla warfare was not intended to occupy county seats and large areas, nor to make a prolonged effort to build up a big army. It meant the use of small but solid armed units to make surprise attacks on enemy troops from time to time.[20]

Moreover, guerrilla tactics, though adopted by the Hupeh Communists from the beginning, were not set forth in the Insurrection Plan for Hunan and Hupeh which governed the autumn harvest uprisings. But following the *Pravda* article of September 30, in the wake of the failure of the autumn harvest uprisings, guerrilla tactics became the main form of struggle in China,[21] and were prescribed as such in the resolutions of the November enlarged session of the Politburo.[22]

Party chief Ch'ü Ch'iu-pai explained that guerrilla warfare was a natural growth of the peasant struggle within the context of the Chinese life. It was an inevitable development in the initial stage of insurrection. To be successful, it must fulfil two conditions: First, it must be an armed struggle of the masses. Guerrilla troops which were alienated from the masses were bound to fail. Second, it must grow into a higher stage in which revolutionary base areas would be created and expanded. Failing this, it could not hope to succeed even if it had the support of the masses.[23]

---

[19] [Ch'ü] Ch'iu-pai, "The Question of Armed Insurrection", December 10, 1927, section 1, *Bolshevik*, No. 10, December 19, 1927.

[20] "Resolution on the Current Situation in China and the Tasks of the Party", section 8.

[21] "Yangtse Bureau's Recent Political Resolution", October 29, 1927, section (4)3, *Central Political Correspondence*, No. 14, n.d., No. 20, April 12, 1928.

[22] "Resolution on the Current Situation in China and the Tasks of the Party", sections 8, 9; "Central's Circular" (No. 16), November 18, [1927], section 7.

[23] "The Question of Armed Insurrection", December 10, 1927, section 1.

Of course, the idea of revolutionary base areas was nothing new. As described previously, it emerged in embryonic form in the Insurrection Plan for Hunan and Hupeh in late August. It was recognized toward the end of October that it would be necessary to seize county seats or occupy several counties in order to carry out the land revolution.[24]   Accordingly, Ch'ü Ch'iu-pai pointed out that guerrilla warfare must develop into the establishment of revolutionary base areas.   Once the struggle of the peasant masses got started, it must proceed forward and could not stay in the guerrilla phase.[25]

To the Politburo enlarged session, guerrilla warfare was only a preliminary type of peasant insurrection which, in turn, was a part of the whole insurrectionary program which included urban insurrection.[26]   The whole insurrectionary program consisted of the following: (1) unleash and organize the latent, spontaneous uprisings of the peasants as far as possible, (2) unleash an extensive economic struggle in cities and lead it to a revolutionary high tide so as to make armed insurrection possible, and (3) combine the insurrectionary forces of the workers and peasants in order to seize political power.[27]

In this connection, it must be remembered that the purpose of urban insurrection was to seize political power, but not to carry out socialism which, as described above, was banned by the Comintern in the stage of the bourgeois-democratic revolution.   As the peasant uprisings were scattered in the countryside, they needed a central force to lead them to the seizure of political power.   This central force could be none other than insurrection in urban centers.[28]

The Politburo enlarged session declared that the urban insurrection of workers was very important in itself and that it would be wrong to look upon it as a supporting force to the peasantry. The Communists, therefore, had the duty to lead the daily struggle

---

24 "Yangtse Bureau's Recent Political Resolution", October 29, 1927, section (4)3.

25 [Ch'ü] Ch'iu-pai, "The Question of Armed Insurrection", December 10, 1927, section 1.

26 "Resolution on the Current Situation in China and the Tasks of the Party", section 8.

27 "Central's Circular" (No. 16), November 18, [1927], section 4.

28 [Ch'ü] Ch'iu-pai, "The Question of Armed Insurrection", December 10, 1927, section 2.

of the workers into a vast revolutionary upsurge aimed at the armed insurrection. They should make the insurrectionary city the center and the guide of the peasant uprisings. The urban insurrection of workers was a pre-condition of the success of the revolution in the great insurrectionary wave.[29]

Ch'ü Ch'iu-pai explained that urban insurrection would become the key to the success of the revolution when uprisings erupted in quick succession in all parts of the countryside. The city would naturally become the center and the guide of insurrection when the revolutionary force engulfed a number of counties or half a province or when the uprisings of workers and peasants could hope to succeed in one or two provinces.[30] He declared that the armed struggle of the peasantry must proceed from guerrilla tactics to the establishment of revolutionary areas and finally to the capture of cities.[31]

Of course, it was the duty of the Communist Party to coordinate the uprisings of the peasants and workers to the best advantage.[32] In notifying all the party members about the major policy decisions of the Politburo enlarged session on November 18, the Ch'ü Ch'iu-pai leadership pointed out the following six possible mistakes which should be avoided in organizing an insurrection:

1. Neglecting the economic struggle and urban insurrection; waiting for the peasant army to come to liberate the workers; regarding the city as representing the military force in support of the peasant uprisings.

2. In peasant uprisings, relying on armed force, motley troops and bandit leaders, but not mobilizing the masses nor carrying out the basic tasks of land revolution such as killing village bosses and gentry, redistributing land, etc.

3. Dismissing spontaneous peasant uprisings as premature and refusing to lead them; stopping the revolutionary action of the masses; mobilizing the troops rather than the masses with the

---

29 "Resolution on the Current Situation in China and the Tasks of the Party", section 8.

30 [Ch'ü] Ch'iu-pai, "The Question of Armed Insurrection", December 10, 1927, section 2.

31 Ch'ü Ch'iu-pai, *The Chinese Revolution and the Communist Party*, p. 149.

32 "Resolution on the Current Situation in China and the Tasks of the Party", section 8.

result that a desperate sacrifice would have to be made before the revolutionary zeal of the masses became ripe for insurrection.

4. In peasant uprisings, paying attention only to attacking county seats with armed force and even capturing and occupying county seats regardless of the relative military strength on both sides; after the seizure of political power in a county, issuing only a proclamation decreeing the confiscation of land without doing any actual work in that regard, not even mobilizing and leading the masses to suppress the reactionaries and seize land by direct action.

5. Having scruples about the petty bourgeoisie, thereby serving the interests of the counterrevolutionaries and alienating the revolutionary masses and restraining their revolutionary action.

6. Being interested only in military technical preparation; waiting idly for opportunities of insurrection; failing to lead the daily struggle to an armed insurrection.[33]

As indicated above, there were no insurrection plans for the cities of Changsha and Wuhan during the autumn harvest uprisings. This gap was filled by the Politburo enlarged session which provided for various steps and conditions indispensable to the launching of an urban insurrection. First of all, the workers must be made to wage the daily economic struggle by asking for better wages, less working time, etc. Then, they should go forward to the political struggle culminating in political strike.[34] The importance of the political strike could not be overestimated. It was intended not only to rouse the masses to action but also to test the preparedness of the masses for insurrection. The normal urban insurrection would always be preceded by a strike.[35]

Accordingly, the Politburo enlarged session provided for the following four pre-conditions for an insurrection in the city: (1) the upsurge of the revolutionary fervor of the workers—the intensification and expansion of the daily economic struggle had developed into a general political struggle; (2) the likely collapse of the regime of the ruling class; (3) the city dwellers at large hating and opposing

---

[33] "Central's Circular" (No. 16), November 18, [1927], section 6.
[34] Ibid.
[35] *Armed Insurrection*, Introduction (1)2, Kung-Hsüeh-She, n. p. 1929.

the ruling class and favoring its downfall; and (4) the technical preparation and organization of the revolutionary force of the working class.[36]

In explaining the above pre-conditions for an insurrection in the city as worked out by the Politburo enlarged session, Ch'ü Ch'iu-pai was careful to use the term "large city" to replace the word "city".[37]

The enlarged session of the Politburo concluded that though the time for a general insurrection had not yet come, the party was striving to stir up a revolutionary high tide in city and countryside in order to create a situation for a general insurrection.[38]

It seems superfluous to add that the former party chief Ch'en Tu-hsiu objected to the policy of armed insurrection, as recorded in a letter to the party leadership dated November 12. He stood for the economic struggle, saying that the KMT was too powerful to be overthrown by insurrection.[39] Understandably, his view was rejected by the Ch'ü Ch'iu-pai leadership.[40]

3. The Dispute Over a Wuhan Rising

By a coincidence, the insurrectionary tactics worked out by the Politburo enlarged session were soon put to test in an intraparty dispute over a proposed uprising at Wuhan around the time of the session.

As a result of the KMT-CCP split at Wuhan in mid-July, the Nationalists managed to set up a unified regime of their own at Nanking. But T'ang Sheng-chih, the KMT military leader at Wuhan, rebelled against that unified regime. Nanking decided to send troops to fight him on October 24.[41]

---

36 "Resolution on the Current Situation in China and the Tasks of the Party", section 8.
37 Ch'ü Ch'iu-pai, *The Chinese Revolution and the Communist Party*, p. 139.
38 "Resolution on the Current Situation in China and the Tasks of the Party", section 8.
39 "Letter from Comrade Tu-hsiu (No. 1)", November 12, 1927, *Central Political Correspondence*, No. 14, n. d.
40 "A Reply to Comrade Tu-hsiu", December 9, 1927, *Central Political Correspondence*, No. 14, n. d.
41 Lei Hsiao-ch'en, *Thirty Years of Turmoil in China*, Vol. 1, Hong Kong, The Asia Press, Ltd., 1955, p. 101.

This KMT civil strife led immediately to an intraparty power struggle on the part of the Communists in the form of a dispute over the wisdom of a proposed insurrection at Wuhan in the event of T'ang Sheng-chih's defeat.

Having learned of the armed clash between Wuhan and Nanking, the military commission of the CCP Hupeh Provincial Committee met to discuss the situation, probably on the evening of October 25, 1927.   The meeting was apparently held under the influence of the CY (Communist Youth League).   It was the concensus of opinion there that T'ang Sheng-chih, the military leader at Wuhan, would fall.   Consequently, it was decided that at the time of his fall an uprising of workers should be staged to create a soviet at Wuhan and that rural guerrilla warfare should be intensified to establish local independent areas in the countryside.   Three persons including the CY leader Liu Ch'ang-chun were entrusted with the task of drafting a resolution to this effect for discussion at the Standing Committee of the Hupeh Provincial Committee the next day.[42]

On October 26, the Standing Committee of the Hupeh Provincial Committee met to discuss the draft resolution prepared by the three persons.   It was finally adopted with some revisions under the title of "Resolution on the Current Urgent Struggle".   This resolution, like its draft, stood for an uprising and a soviet at Wuhan and for guerrilla tactics and local independent areas in the countryside. In addition, this resolution set forth a political program consisting of the following items: kill and expropriate the property of all village bosses, bad gentry and government officials; confiscate the land of landlords; loot and burn reactionary agencies; raid prisons and set free prisoners; occupy factories; kill and expropriate the property of big capitalists and counterrevolutionaries.[43]

Meanwhile, the Standing Committee of the Hupeh Provincial Committee adopted more than a dozen slogans, some of which

---

42 "Report on the Hupeh Question by the Hupeh CY Representatives, Liu Ch'ang-chun and Han Kuang-han", December 13 [?], 1927, *Central Political Correspondence*, No. 20, April 12, 1928.

43 "Resolution on the Current Urgent Struggle", October 26, 1927, embodied in the "Report of the Standing Committee of the Hupeh Provincial Committee to the Enlarged Conference of the Hupeh Provincial Committee", December 12, 1927, section 1 (1), *Central Political Correspondence*, No. 20, April 12, 1928.   This resolution also bears the date of October 27 because it was sent out to the various local party units on that date.

began with the term "insurrection". The idea of insurrection was emphasized because it was believed that the fall of T'ang Sheng-chih was imminent and that it was possible to seize power through insurrection in Hupeh. Though a small number of Communists were inclined to think that the right thing to do in the circumstances was to prepare for insurrection but not to stage it at once, they nevertheless considered it necessary to raise the slogan of insurrection as a fillip to the morale of their comrades. They attached importance to the seizure of power through insurrection and to the proclamation of a soviet even for a very short time.[44]

Having adopted the above resolution and slogans, the Hupeh Provincial Committee lost no time in making preparations for the proposed insurrection. It looked as if a great catastrophe was forthcoming in Hupeh.[45]

All of a sudden, the tense atmosphere relaxed after Lo I-nung, the local CP (Communist Party) leader and secretary of the Yangtse Bureau, returned to Hankow on the morning of October 28 after a two-week trip to Changsha, the capital of Hunan province. He was surprised to find that the mood of his comrades had changed so fast that after the lapse of only two weeks many of them were feeling strong enough to stage an armed insurrection with a view to the seizure of power in Hupeh. Speaking before the Standing Committee of the Hupeh Provincial Committee that evening, he warned that his comrades should not overestimate their own strength and underestimate the strength of the enemy, otherwise they would run the risk of putschism by playing with insurrection. He stated that the new civil war had, indeed, inaugurated an objective situation for seizing power through insurrection, but that the subjective strength of the Communists in the sphere of organization and technical preparation was inadequate.[46]

Lo I-nung disclosed that following the above speech he met with an unidentified woman representative of the International of Labor Unions, who had just arrived from Shanghai, serving

---

concurrently as the personal representative of the Comintern delegate Lominadze. Since she sounded out Lo I-nung's opinion of the proposed insurrection, he told her about his ideas in the above-mentioned speech. She was quoted as saying:

> Your opinion is perfectly right. I am of the same opinion as yours. After I had talked to the comrades in the Provincial Committee, it seemed that my words were not quite convincing to them. I hope you will talk to them right away.

Lo I-nung said that the representative of the Communist Youth International was also there and expressed the same opinion. This man invited Lo to meet with his principal opponent, Liu Ch'ang-chun of the local CY leadership.[47]

On October 29 the CCP Yangtse Bureau, which had jurisdiction over eight provinces in the Yangtse valley, held a meeting to discuss the question of insurrection. Lo I-nung, who was the chief of the Bureau, introduced a resolution which was unanimously adopted. Liu Ch'ang-chun, who was a member of the Bureau, was not reported to have raised any objections on the spot.[48] The resolution was known as the "Yangtse Bureau's Recent Political Resolution". Its gist was as follows: The revolutionary tide was flowing. But the party and mass organizations were not strong enough to launch an immediate insurrection for the seizure of power. Under such circumstances, the party should create a new big tide of revolution in preparation for a general insurrection to seize political power. But the present time was by no means the time for continuing a general insurrection.[49]

Lo I-nung disclosed that following the adoption of the above resolution he called on the woman representative of Lominadze and told her about the content of the document. He remembered that the document was later translated into Russian. He stated that the woman supported the resolution and telegraphed it to Lominadze and through him to the CCP leadership at Shanghai. On November 2 he learned from her that Lominadze had wired

---

[47] Ibid.
[48] Ibid.
[49] "Yangtse Bureau's Recent Political Resolution", October 29, 1927, op. cit.

back his approval.   But it was later found out that Lominadze did not send a copy of the telegram to the CCP leadership.[50]

Incidentally, it may be helpful to us to understand Lominadze's position on urban insurrections at this time if we remember that he stopped a Chinese Communist plot of insurrection at Shanghai amidst the political confusion following the resignation of Chiang Kai-shek in August.[51]

On November 4 Lo I-nung left for Shanghai to attend the Politburo enlarged session scheduled for the 9th.   He stated that as he had not received any instructions from the party leadership after its transfer from Hankow to Shanghai in September, he had been very careful in drafting the Yangtse Bureau's Recent Political Resolution.   In fact, he heard of no criticisms of his work in the Politburo enlarged session.   On the contrary, he had received favorable comments from quite a few individual members of the party leadership.[52]

In a letter dated October 30, the Yangtse Bureau sent the gist of its Recent Political Resolution to the Hupeh Provincial Committee, saying that it was evidently impossible to launch an immediate insurrection, that T'ang Sheng-chih would definitely not collapse at once and that advocating insurrection at the moment was mere boasting.[53]   Later, it was found out that this letter was drafted by the chief of the secretarial staff and sent off on November 4 or 5 without the approval of Lo I-nung.[54]

The Communist program of action as laid down in the Yangtse Bureau's Recent Political Resolution consisted of these items: A propaganda week against new militarist wars, expanding guerrilla

---

50 "Report of Comrade I-nung to the Enlarged Conference of the Hupeh Provincial Committee", December 12, 1927, section 1, *Central Political Correspondence*, No. 20, April 12, 1928.

51 Ch'ü Ch'iu-pai, *The Chinese Revolution and the Communist Party*, p. 129.

52 "Report of Comrade I-nung to the Enlarged Conference of the Hupeh Provincial Committee", December 12, 1927, op. cit., section 2.

53 "Letter from the Yangtse Bureau to the Hupeh Provincial Committee", October 30 [?], [1927], *Central Political Correspondence*, No. 20, April 12, 1928.

54 "Report of Comrade I-nung to the Enlarged Conference of the Hupeh Provincial Committee", December 12, 1927, section 1; "Central Politburo's Resolution on the Hupeh Intraparty Question", January 3, 1928, section 1, *Central Political Correspondence*, No. 20, April 12, 1928.

tactics and occupying revolutionary bases, intensifying the economic struggle in cities, and capturing the enemy's arms.[55]   When the Hupeh Provincial Committee accepted the Recent Political Resolution on October 30, it automatically accepted these items of the program of action. Accordingly, the propaganda week was at once scheduled for November 7-14.[56]   It need hardly be pointed out that all these steps were taken to create a new big tide of revolution, but not to stage an insurrection at once.

In contrast, the CY maintained that T'ang Sheng-chih would fall anyway, that an insurrection should be launched at the time of his fall, and that the formation of a soviet for even a few days would be meaningful.   While the CP charged the CY with "immediate insurrection", the CY accused the CP of "abandoning insurrection".[57]

The situation underwent a dramatic change on November 9 when T'ang Sheng-chih's forces began to withdraw from Wuhan after sustaining crushing defeats down the Yangtse River.   The Communists wanted to make the most of the disorder during T'ang Sheng-chih's retreat.   They decided to raid prisons.   They scheduled a general strike for the morning of November 13 to be followed that afternoon by an attack on Hankow's Yu-I Street where a number of government agencies, including the labor union, were located.   It was decided that this Yu-I Street attack should not be made if the general strike in contemplation had not taken place beforehand.[58]

---

55 "Yangtse Bureau's Recent Political Resolution", October 29, 1927, op. cit.

56 "Report of the Standing Committee of the Hupeh Provincial Committee to the Enlarged Conference of the Hupeh Provincial Committee", December 12, 1927, section 3, *Central Political Correspondence*, No. 20, April 12, 1928.

57 "Report on the Hupeh Question by the Hupeh CY Representatives, Liu Ch'ang-chun and Han Kuang-han", December 13 [?], 1927, op. cit.; "Report of the CY Hupeh Provincial Committee to the Special Committee", n. d., received December 12, 1927, *Central Political Correspondence*, No. 20, April 12, 1928.   Dates given in these two documents should be consulted with caution.

58 "Report on the Hupeh Question by the Hupeh CY Representatives, Liu Ch'ang-chun and Han Kuang-han", December 13 [?], 1927, op. cit., section 4; "Report of the Standing Committee of the Hupeh Provincial Committee to the Enlarged Conference of the Hupeh Provincial Committee", December 12, 1927, op. cit., section 4; "Report of the CY Hupeh Provincial Committee to the Special Committee", n. d., op. cit., section 2.

T'ang Sheng-chih resigned on the 12th. But the Communist plot to fish in troubled waters did not materialize. Since the 13th was a Sunday, there was no possibility of a strike of industrial workers. Apart from a handful of railway workers already on a walkout for higher wages, none of the coolies and other poor people went on strike. In consequence, the plan for an attack on Yu-I Street was cancelled. But the cancellation was not made known to the Communist rank and file. As a result, some Communists went to Yu-I Street on time, only to be captured by the enemy. A leading rickshaw coolie was executed.[59]

It was admitted that there was little or no mass work carried out by the Communists during November 11-15. The workers had not been brought together for a meeting. The peasants in the vicinity of Wuhan had not been roused to action. Practically all work was military or intelligence in nature, and official information regarding this sort of work did not go beyond the confines of the Wuhan cities. Wuhan fell to the hands of the Nanking forces on November 16.[60]

4. Special Committee Investigation

On December 3 Liu Ch'ang-chun and Han Kuang-han, CY representatives from Hupeh, filed a complaint to the party leadership against what they called the opportunistic mistakes made by Lo I-nung and the Hupeh Provincial Committee during T'ang Sheng-chih's defeat. The two men charged that the defendants made two major miscalculations, namely, that T'ang Sheng-chih would definitely not quit and that the strength of the party and the masses at Wuhan was inadequate for an insurrection. But the fact was that T'ang Sheng-chih did quit quickly.[61]

---

59 Ibid.

60 "Report on the Hupeh Question by the Hupeh CY Representatives, Liu Ch'ang-chun and Han Kuang-han", December 13 [?], 1927, op. cit.; "Report of the Standing Committee of the Hupeh Provincial Committee to the Enlarged Conference of the Hupeh Provincial Committee", December 12, 1927, op. cit., section 4; "Report of the CY Hupeh Provincial Committee to the Special Committee", n.d., op. cit., section 2.

61 "Report on the Hupeh Question by the Hupeh CY Representatives, Liu Ch'ang-chun and Han Kuang-han", December 13 [?], 1927, op. cit.

The party leadership acted swiftly on the above CY accusation. By December 5 it had made a number of decisions. First, Lo I-nung was suspended from office as party inspector for Hunan and Hupeh, an office to which he had been appointed following the November enlarged session of the Politburo presumably in succession to his position in the Yangtse Bureau. Second, the Standing Committee of the Hupeh Provincial Committee was ordered to cease to function. Third, a Special Committee for Hupeh was appointed with responsibility to investigate the mistakes of the Yangtse Bureau and the Hupeh Provincial Committee and to call an enlarged conference of the Hupeh Provincial Committee for the purpose of electing a new provincial committee and examining the Hupeh case. Pending the election of the new provincial committee, the Special Committee was to take over the functions of the party in Hupeh. The Special Committee was composed of three persons, namely, Su Chao-cheng, Kuo Liang and Ho Ch'ang, with the first as secretary.[62]

Subsequently, the party leadership admitted that it was a mistake to include Ho Ch'ang in the Special Committee since he as a CP man had all along supported the CY accusation.[63] Acting on their own, Ho Ch'ang and Li Li-san also impeached Lo I-nung and the Hupeh Provincial Committee.[64]

The three members of the Special Committee left Shanghai on December 5 and arrived at Hankow on the 9th. They immediately delivered an identical note from the party leadership to the local CY and CP headquarters, informing them of its position on the Hupeh dispute and the mission of the Special Committee. It happened that the Standing Committee of the Hupeh Provincial Committee was holding a meeting that evening. They went to the meeting and announced the immediate cessation of the functioning of the Standing Committee on the spot. They then accompanied Lo I-nung back to his home for further conversations. Lo I-nung

---

62 "Central's Letter to Comrade I-nung, Inspector for Hunan and Hupeh, and the Hupeh Provincial Committee", December 5, [1927], *Central Political Correspondence*, No. 20, April 12, 1928.

63 "Central's Letter to the Hupeh Comrades", January 1, 1928, section 4, *Central Political Correspondence*, No. 20, April 12, 1928; cf. Note 70, section (4)5.

64 "Central's Letter to the Hupeh Comrades", January 1, 1928, section 4, op. cit.

frankly admitted that he had not expected the quick collapse of
T'ang Sheng-chih. But he added that the central leadership and
the Comintern representative had not expected it, either. He
pointed out that nobody had realized that T'ang Sheng-chih's
troops would be weary of fighting for lack of pay for eight months
and that Nanking would send a surprisingly strong army to fight
them.[65]

By the time of the arrival of the Special Committee at Hankow,
representatives from different localities had already arrived for a
provincial party conference which had been called by the Standing
Committee of the Hupeh Provincial Committee to study the resolutions of the November enlarged session of the Politburo. Now
that the Standing Committee had ceased to function and that the
Special Committee was to call another provincial party conference
to resolve the Hupeh crisis, it was natural that the same representatives would be used for the new conference.[66]

Interestingly, the Special Committee took some drastic
preliminary steps to manipulate the conference. First, it forced
Lo I-nung to leave for Shanghai on the eve of the conference for
fear of his influence in the party in Hupeh.[67] Second, the former
members of the Standing Committee who had been suspended
from office were allowed to attend the conference without vote.[68]
Third, all pertinent agencies and individual leaders were requested
to submit written statements which, except for those by Lo I-nung
and the Provincial Committee, plus a defense of the Hupeh autumn
harvest uprising by a participant, all turned out to be critical of the

---

65 "Letter from the Hupeh Special Committee to the Central (No. 2)", n. d.,
  probably December 15 or 16, 1927, section 1, *Central Political Correspondence*, No. 20, April 12, 1928; "Report on the Hupeh Question by
  the Hupeh CY Representatives, Liu Ch'ang-chun and Han Kuang-han",
  December 13 [?], 1927, op. cit.; "Report of Comrade I-nung to the
  Enlarged Conference of the Hupeh Provincial Committee", December 12,
  1927, op. cit., sections 2, 3.

66 "Letter from the Hupeh Special Committee to the Central (No. 2)", n.d.,
  op. cit., sections 1, 3.

67 Ibid., section 5; "Letter from the Hupeh Special Committee to the Central
  (No. 1)", December 13, [1927], *Central Political Correspondence*, No. 20,
  April 12, 1928.

68 "Central Politburo's Resolution on the Hupeh Intraparty Question",
  January 3, 1928, op. cit., section 4.

defendants.[69]   This tended to confirm the feeling of the defendants that the Special Committee had purposely come to find fault with them.[70]

The Hupeh provincial party conference was held at Hankow during December 14-15.[71] A total of 39 representatives was present, among them 15 listed as workers, 19 intellectuals, and 5 peasants. When newspaper reports on the Canton uprising of December 11-13 reached the conference hall, all those present rose in tribute to it.[72] Su Chao-cheng, the most powerful figure in the conference, did not seem to realize that he was made chairman of the Canton Soviet in his absence.[73]

It turned out that the conference was primarily concerned with the charges against Lo I-nung and the Hupeh Provincial Committee rather than with the discussion and formulation of party policies. As before, the defendants admitted in the conference that they had misjudged the timing of T'ang Sheng-chih's fall, but they pointed out that the party leadership had made the same mistake. They were insistent that conditions were inadequate for an uprising at Wuhan at the time of T'ang Sheng-chih's fall. They pointed out that none of the four pre-conditions of an urban insurrection

---

69 "Report of Comrade I-nung to the Enlarged Conference of the Hupeh Provincial Committee", December 12, 1927, op. cit., sections 8, 18; "Report of Comrade Huang Chih-kuang from Southern Hupeh", December 15; "Report of the CY Hupeh Provincial Committee to the Special Committee", n. d.; "Resolution of the CY Hupeh Provincial Committee", December 10; "Resolution of the Wuchang Municipal Committee", December 12; "Resolution of the Hanyang County Committee Criticizing the Work of the Provincial Committee", n.d.; "Resolution of the Joint Conference of Hankow's 1st, 2nd, and 3rd Districts", December 11; "Letter from the Hsu-chia-peng District Committee to the Special Committee for Hupeh", [December] 12; "Letter from Comrade Lin Chung-tan to the Special Committee for Hupeh", December 12——all these documents are available in *Central Political Correspondence*, No. 20, April 12, 1928.

70 "Report of the Three Comrades, Ch'en Ch'iao-nien, Jen Hsu and Huang Wu-i, to the Central Politburo", December 31, 1927, *Central Political Correspondence*, No. 20, April 12, 1928.

71 "Central's Letter to the Hupeh Comrades", January 1, 1928, op. cit. section 1.

72 "Letter from the Hupeh Special Committee to the Central (No. 2)", n. d., op. cit., section 3.

73 "The Red Flag Extra", December 11, 1927, in *Huston Report*.

as worked out by the Politburo enlarged session were present at Wuhan.[74]

In contrast, the CY charged in the conference that the CP had overlooked the mass work ever since the autumn harvest uprisings, that it had not expected the quick collapse of T'ang Sheng-chih, and that therefore it was caught unprepared when T'ang fell. Accordingly, the CY recommended the punishment of all the CP leaders who were responsible for these mistakes.[75]

Incidentally, the former members of the Standing Committee of the Hupeh Provincial Committee complained that the party leadership and the Special Committee had adopted a wrong procedure in the case against them.[76]

Of particular interest was the opinion of a peasant representative who declared that "the rural struggle calls for uprisings anyway, even though the enemy is not going to fall". This opinion was well received.[77]

In great tension and confusion the conference finally passed a resolution recommending disciplinary action against all those who were found guilty of the political mistakes made. The charges against Lo I-nung and his Yangtse Bureau centered on the latter's Recent Political Resolution of October 29 and its subsequent letter to the Hupeh Provincial Committee. As noted previously, both the statements were considered to have produced a deterrent effect on the insurrectionary orientation of the Provincial Committee. The Provincial Committee, in turn, was accused of frequent changes of

---

[74] "Report of Comrade I-nung to the Enlarged Conference of the Hupeh Provincial Committee", December 12, 1927, op. cit, sections 3, 5; "Report of the Standing Committee of the Hupeh Provincial Committee to the Enlarged Conference of the Hupeh Provincial Committee", December 12, 1927, op. cit., section 7 (1) (4); for Politburo-prescribed pre-conditions of urban insurrection, see "Resolution on the Current Situation and the Tasks of the Party", section 8, *Central Correspondence*, No. 13, November 30, 1927.

[75] "Resolutuon of the CY Hupeh Provincial Committee", December 10, 1927, *Central Political Correspondence*, No. 20, April 12, 1928.

[76] "Report of the Three Comrades, Ch'en Ch'iao-nien, Jen Hsu and Huang Wu-i, to the Central Politburo", December 31, 1927, op. cit.

[77] "Comprehensive Answers of Comrades Ch'en Ch'iao-nien, Jen Hsu and Huang Wu-i to the Hupeh Question", January 10, 1928, section 4, *Central Political Correspondence*, No. 20, April 12, 1928.

attitude toward insurrection, at first favoring insurrection, then rejecting it and finally becoming a little positive but confused. Specifically, the conference made the following recommendations to the central party leadership:

1. Lo I-nung, secretary of the Yangtse Bureau, should be dismissed as a member of the Central Committee.

2. Ch'en Ch'iao-nien, secretary of the Provincial Committee, should be dismissed as a member of the Central Committee.

3. Among the members of the Standing Committee of the Hupeh Provincial Committee, Wang Tse-chiai, Lin Yu-nan, and Jen Hsu should be dismissed as members of the Provincial Committee and each given a severe warning, while Huang Wu-i should be given a severe warning only.

4. Liu Ch'ang-chun, representative of the CY, should be given a severe warning. In addition, the CY leadership should be requested to punish him.

5. Tsao Hsiang-hua, secretary of the second district at Hankow, should be given a warning (for his responsibility for the abortive attack on Yu-I Street).[78]

It is interesting to note that the punishment of Liu Ch'ang-chun was originally not included in the recommendations made by the CY Provincial Committee to the conference. The conference made this decision apparently because it wanted to show impartiality.

The conference elected a new provincial committee with Ch'en Ch'iao-nien, Jen Hsu, Huang Wu-i, Kuo Liang and Yu Mou-huai as members of the Standing Committee. But the central party leadership was dissatisfied wih the election. It ordered a re-election in two months.[79]

When the conference was over, about a third of the participants charged that the conference was dominated by factional struggles

---

[78] "Resolution of the Enlarged Conference of the Hupeh Provincial Committee Criticizing the Policy of the Yangtse Bureau and the Provincial Committee", n.d., presumably December 15, 1927, *Central Political Correspondence*, No. 20, April 12, 1928.

[79] "Central's Letter to the Hupeh Comrades", January 1, 1928, op. cit. section 3; "Letter from the Hupeh Special Committee to the Central (No. 2)", op. cit., section 4.

in which the members of the Special Committee, particularly Ho Ch'ang, were biased against the former provincial committee and the Yangtse Bureau. They requested the party leadership to correct the misconduct of the Special Committee.[80]

5. Politburo Verdict

Lo I-nung, who was forced to leave Hankow on December 13, arrived at Shanghai on the 16th. Embittered and infuriated, he called at the central office of the Chinese Communist Party the next day with the complaint that he had been illegally expelled from Wuhan and deprived of his right to attend the enlarged provincial party conference there. He tendered his resignation from all party posts and looked for an opportunity to go to Russia to study. He requested a fair and just settlement of his case.[81]

The party leadership was surprised at the mistreatment of Lo I-nung, as reported by him. It hastened to write to the Special Committee on December 18 saying that it was not fair to exclude Lo I-nung and, as he had learned from hearsay, two other leading comrades from the party conference of Hupeh. The conference could not afford to hear one side of the case and ignore the other. Consequently, the members of the Special Committee and of the presidium of the Hupeh party conference were ordered to bring all documentary materials to Shanghai immediately after the conference so that the party leadership would be able to settle the dispute directly.[82]

In addition, Lo I-nung submitted a memorandum to the party leadership on December 21. As he put it in Communist jargon, the central question in the Hupeh dispute was whether at the time of T'ang Sheng-chih's fall it was necessary to stage an immediate armed insurrection for the seizure of political power or to launch an extensive struggle of the worker and peasant masses so as to

---

80 "Report of the Nine Comrades, Kuan Hsüeh-san, Chang Chi-ch'u, *et al*, on the Enlarged Conference of the Hupeh Provincial Committee", n.d., presumably late December 1927, *Central Political Correspondence*, No. 20, April 12, 1928.

81 "Comrade I-nung's Answer to the Hupeh Question", December 21, [1927], *Central Political Correspondence*, No. 20, April 12, 1928.

82 "Central's Letter to the Hupeh Special Committee", December 18, [1927], *Central Political Correspondence*, No. 20, April 12, 1928.

positively create an armed insurrection for the seizure of political power. To put it in plain language, the question was a choice between the immediate staging of an insurrection and the creation of conditions for an insurrection. As before, he admitted that he had not expected the quick collapse of T'ang Sheng-chih. But he pointed out that this was not the main point. The main point, he said, was the inadequacy of the subjective strength available for an armed insurrection at the moment: The party organization was loose and incapable of leading the masses. The workers had not progressed from their daily struggle to a general struggle. The technical preparation for an armed insurrection was almost nil. The peasant uprisings had not yet developed into the stage of setting up local independent areas, nor had they spread to all parts of the province. Under such circumstances, said Lo I-nung, it was evidently impossible to stage a general insurrection. That was why he urged the creation of conditions for an insurrection rather than the launching of an immediate insurrection as suggested by the CY. He admitted that he was very cautious about insurrection which was a most serious thing, indeed. He objected to playing with it. He also frowned upon the idea of using insurrection as a slogan to encourage the comrades at a time when the party had no intention of staging an insurrection at all.[83]

Meanwhile, Lo I-nung, who was in charge of the Hupeh party from July 15 to October 10, when he was appointed chief of the Yangtse Bureau, gave an interesting account of the Communist weaknesses in Hupeh following the KMT-CCP split in July. He said that at least nine out of ten Communist cadres had fled under KMT pressure and that many of them even informed against their own comrades. All the labor unions collapsed after August 2, when the CCP engineered a general strike at Wuhan against the KMT. The peasant movement came to a stop with the dissolution of the peasant associations in the province. Since practically all the party workers in the various countries had escaped without authorization, all contacts with them were cut. There were only 3,000 Communists at Wuhan by the time of the August 2 strike and no more than 2,000 immediately thereafter. This figure was further cut down to 1,269 by September 10 when Su Chao-cheng,

---

[83] "Central's Letter to the Hupeh Comrades", January 1, 1928, op. cit., section 1.

director of the department of labor of the CCP, took personal charge of the labor movement in Wuhan. It was revealed that the Communists by and large did not understand the meaning of struggle, much less secret work, by the time of the KMT-CCP split. They did not feel the necessity of secrecy until August 20 when overwhelming KMT pressure was being brought to bear against them. But later they had gone to the other extreme. They chose to hide, as it were, from the view of the provincial committee which could rarely get in touch with them. The provincial committee itself was also terribly understaffed. It was disclosed that August 2 was a sort of turning point in Communist labor policy in Wuhan. While the labor movement centered on political strikes before that date, it was relegated to economic struggles after it. Needless to say, armed insurrection was out of the question.[84]

In additon, Ch'en Ch'iao-nien and two other members of the Standing Committee of the Hupeh Provincial Committee also made a written report to the party leadership. Like Lo I-nung, they admitted their mistake in judging the timing of T'ang Sheng-chih's fall, a mistake which was, however, shared by the party leadership. They also admitted their mistake in using the term "insurrection" in slogans to improve the morale of the comrades. But apart from these two mistakes, they believed that they were perfectly right. They thought that it was impossible to stage an insurrection either at the beginning of the retreat of T'ang Sheng-chih's forces at Wuhu in southeastern Anhui or at the time of his fall at Wuhan, since none of the conditions of an insurrection were then present: Rural bases had yet to be established. The labor movement was weak. The party itself did not have the strength to direct an organized revolt. In these circumstances, they believed that they had no alternative but to follow the normal party line: (1) To direct the labor movement in the city from scattered struggles to a general strike; and (2) to endeavor to create base areas in the countryside. In this way, they stated, they had made constant efforts to launch a general insurrection in the province.[85]

Ch'en Ch'iao-nien and his two colleagues declared that the CY

84 Ibid., section 2.
85 "Central Politburo's Resolution on the Hupeh Intraparty Question", January 3, 1928, op. cit., section 1; "Resolution of the CY Hupeh Provincial Committee", December 10, 1927, op. cit., section 7.

concept of insurrection was basically wrong. They branded the CY with adventurism, which meant insurrection under all conditions. In addition, they pointed out that the main weaknesses of the CY were found in the rural districts where practically no CY organization and work had ever been seen.   The members of the CY Provincial Committee did not appear in the villages during the autumn harvest uprisings. They were simply not familiar with the conditions of the rural struggle. To make matters worse, they branded guerrilla warfare as a device to shun insurrection.[86]

It was not surprising that Ch'en Ch'iao-nien and company attacked the Special Committee, too. They complained that the Special Committee was actually not so much interested in studying the question of insurrection as in finding fault with the CP in Hupeh.   Accordingly, they requested the party leadership to straighten out this unfortunate situation.[87]

The above two statements by Lo I-nung and the Ch'en Ch'iao-nien group were important additions to the documents which the members of the Special Committee and those of the presidium of the Hupeh party conference had brought to Shanghai. On the basis of these documentary materials and the interviews with the CY and CP leaders from Hupeh, the Central Politburo met twice to discuss the Hupeh question around the turn of the year.[88]

On New Year's Day the party leadership addressed a letter to all comrades in Hupeh. It began by declaring that the central issue of the Hupeh dispute was the strategy and tactics of insurrection. It refuted the CY ideas of (1) launching an uprising at Wuhan at the very beginning of T'ang Sheng-chih's defeat at Wuhu in southeastern Anhui, and (2) using the term "insurrection" in slogans without the intention of carrying it out in practice. Lo I-nung was, therefore, lauded for having stopped these ideas. It was stated that it was right to make preparations for an uprising in the event of T'ang Sheng-chih's fall at Wuhan while it was wrong to decide beforehand that an uprising must be staged at the

---

86 "Resolution of the CY Hupeh Provincial Committee", December 10, 1927, op. cit., section 7.

87 Ibid.; "Central Politburo's Resolution on the Hupeh Intraparty Question", January 3, 1928, op. cit., section 4.

88 "Letter from the Hupeh Special Committee to the Central (No. 2)", op. cit., preamble.

time of his fall and that a soviet was to be set up even for a few days. It was also considered wrong to advocate an uprising when T'ang Sheng-chih actually quit Wuhan, because the conditions for an uprising were still far from adequate. It was pointed out that since Wuhan, unlike small towns and county seats, was an industrial and communications center on the upper Yangtse, an abortive insurrection there would unfavorably affect the cause of workers' and peasants' insurrections in Hupeh and other provinces. Wuhan could not afford to serve as a place to train the masses for insurrection regardless of its success or failure.[89]

After all had been said and done, the party leadership rendered its verdict on the case in dispute. On January 3, 1928, the Central Politburo adopted a resolution on this case to the following effect:

1. The Yangtse Bureau was on record opposed to immediate insurrection, but not to insurrection itself. This attitude was correct. There were a number of conditions of an insurrection, such as the collapse of rulers, the revolutionary high tide of workers and peasants, the strength of the party, the discontent of soldiers and urban inhabitants, and the technical preparation and organization. The collapse of rulers alone was not adequate to justify an insurrection.

When the war between Wuhan and Nanking broke out late in October, the Yangtse Bureau should, on the one hand, point out the rise of the revolutionary wave which would make a general insurrection in Hunan and Hupeh possible and, on the other, urge the party branches in the two provinces to take positive steps to create conditions for that insurrection. These conditions consisted mainly of the expansion of daily work into a general political struggle in the city and the development of guerrilla warfare and base areas in the countryside. As to when a general insurrection could be staged, this would depend on the degree of the preparation of these conditions.

Accordingly, the Yangtse Bureau's Recent Political Resolution of October 29 was on the whole right.

The Yangtse Bureau's mistake lay in the fact that it did not

---

[89] "Central's Letter to the Hupeh Comrades", January 1, 1928, op. cit., section 1.

expect T'ang Sheng-chih to quit so fast. In consequence, it did not give Hunan and Hupeh positive guidance to meet this particular situation. Moreover, the Bureau saw its way clear in its Recent Political Resolution to create a new big tide of revolution in preparation for a general insurrection to seize political power. But it caused confusion by adding that the present time was by no means the time for continuing a general insurrection. Of course, this sort of mistake made by the Yangtse Bureau—political miscalculation and inadequate guidance—was not an ordinary mistake, but it did not amount to a crime.

2. The Standing Committee of the Hupeh Provincial Committee vacillated and procrastinated in the course of T'ang Sheng-chih's retreat. During October 27-29, it showed the trend toward an immediate insurrection, as can be seen from its "Resolution on the Current Urgent Struggle" adopted on October 26. It used the term "insurrection" in slogans to raise the morale of the comrades, and some of its members maintained that the formation of a soviet even for a very short time would be meaningful. This trend of events was brought to an end by Lo I-nung. Then, from October 30 to November 9, the Standing Committee abandoned or at any rate relaxed its effort at a general insurrection under the plea of the Yangtse Bureau's Recent Political Resolution which, as described previously, was actually, on the whole, right. Finally, when T'ang Sheng-chih began to quit Wuhan on November 9, the Standing Committee turned again to the left. It decided to take immediate action culminating in a general strike, thus showing the spirit of a general insurrection.

Thus, during the period of T'ang Sheng-chih's retreat, the Standing Committee of the Hupeh Provincial Committee changed its mind several times. This was the result of vacillation in political policy. As a matter of disciplinary punishment, therefore, the members of the Standing Committee of the Hupeh Provincial Committee who had been responsible for the vacillation were removed from the provincial committee.

3. The CY Provincial Committee of Hupeh was on record as supporting the "Resolution on the Current Urgent Struggle" of October 26, which, as described previously, showed the trend

toward an immediate insurrection. Though the CY contended that it did not advocate an immediate insurrection but a general insurrection at the time of the retreat of T'ang Sheng-chih's troops, the Central Politburo decided that it was not correct to advocate a general insurrection at the time of the retreat of T'ang Sheng-chih's troops and that the CY did show the trend toward an "immediate insurrection". In addition, it was pointed out, the record of the Yangtse Bureau showed that the CY representative, Liu Ch'ang-chun, was wrong in suggesting that immediate insurrections be staged at Shanghai and Canton.

Also, the Central Politburo rejected the CY's charge that the work of the Hupeh Provincial Committee had been opportunistic in nature following the August 7 Conference. It suggested that the CY Central Committee repudiate this charge since this charge was not only improper but also harmful to the CY-CP relationship in Hupeh.

4. As regards the Special Committee, the party leadership pointed out that it did not carry out its mission in Hupeh satisfactorily. Its work had these shortcomings: First, as the committee did not make a careful study of the materials on the Hupeh dispute, it did not grasp the issues, much less answer them. It followed that the conclusions reached by the party conference were not correct. Second, practically all the time of the conference was spent on discussion of the CY-CP dispute and reorganization of the provincial committee. Political problems and party work lying ahead in Hupeh were left untouched while the resolutions on the November session of the Central Politburo were discussed inadequately. Third, it was wrong to exclude Lo I-nung from the Hupeh party conference and force him to return to Shanghai. It was also wrong to deny the former members of the Standing Committee of the Hupeh Provincial Committee the right to vote in the conference.

Since the Special Committee had made various mistakes like the above, the Central Politburo took this opportunity to criticize and correct them.[90]

---

[90] "Central Politburo's Resolution on the Hupeh Intraparty Question", January 3, 1928, op. cit.

To the above verdict of the party leadership on the Hupeh dispute, the CY leadership reacted promptly. As it was, the underlying cause of the Hupeh dispute was the power struggle between the CY and the CP. This intraparty conflict had plagued the CY-CP relations from the central to local levels. On January 4, 1928, the CY leadership wrote to the CP leadership commenting on the latter's verdict on the Hupeh dispute in the following terms:

1. The CY leadership was in general agreement with the party leadership's comments on the political and policy decisions of the Yangtse Bureau and the Hupeh Provincial Committee. But it was pointed out that it was right to suggest the idea around October 26 that preparations should be made to stage an insurrection at the time of T'ang Sheng-chih's fall. (Of course, it was added in parentheses, the question of whether it would be possible to stage the insurrection at the time of T'ang's fall would depend upon whether the conditions prepared for it were adequate.)

2. But the CY leadership was in disagreement with the punishments meted out by the party leadership to the several agencies and individuals held responsible for the dispute. It was suggested that the Yangtse Bureau be punished for misjudging the timing of T'ang's fall and for lacking positive guidance of work for Hunan and Hupeh and that the Special Committee be given a severe warning. In addition, the CY leadership supported the recommendations of the Hupeh party conference for punishment of the individual local leaders involved in the case.[91]

As can be seen from the above CY comment, despite their disagreement on the question of punishment which was more or less a matter of politics, the CY leadership did agree with the party leadership in recognizing the vital fact that the armed insurrection had its conditions and that whether it could be successfully staged at a given time and place would depend upon whether those conditions were adequately fulfilled.

A month later, in February 1928, Pavel Mif, a staunch Stalinist in the Comintern, declared in the Ninth Plenum of the ECCI that

---

[91] "CY Central's Letter Regarding the Party Central's Handling of the Hupeh Question", January 4, [1928], *Central Political Correspondence*, No. 20, April 12, 1928.

the CY had disobeyed the leadership of the party in many places in China and that many a CY cadre had developed the dangerous thought that no insurrection in China would be untimely.[92]

92 Pavel Mif, *The Chinese Revolution*, Chinese version, Moscow and Leningrad, Foreign Workers Publishing House, 1933, p. 214.

CHAPTER V

THE CANTON COMMUNE

1. The Origins

Following the Politburo enlarged session of November the party leadership looked for opportunities to unleash and organize insurrections. Hunan and Hupeh again became targets but insurrections did not materialize there.[1] However, the developments in Kwangtung followed a dramatic course, culminating in the Canton rising of December 11-13, 1927.

Ch'ü Ch'iu-pai disclosed that a few days after the Politburo enlarged session, November 17, a general insurrection plan for Kwangtung province emerged from a discussion in Shanghai between the central leadership and Chang T'ai-lei, secretary of the Kwangtung Provincial Committee.[2] According to Teng Chung-hsia, a top-ranking Communist leader, the party leadership expected an imminent clash between the two militarists, Chang Fa-k'uei and Li Chi-shen, in Kwangtung. The party issued instructions to the Kwangtung Provincial Committee on November 17 to the effect that the only hope of the workers and peasants in Kwangtung was to take advantage of the clash to expand insurrections in town and countryside, instigate soldiers to mutiny and rebellion, and quickly combine the individual insurrections into a general insurrection in order to seize power and establish soviets in the whole province. He revealed that the party issued additional instructions to the Kwangtung Provincial Committee as a specific program of action. The central idea of the program was to unleash widespread peasant insurrection in the countryside which would be coupled with worker

---

[1] "Central's Working Plan", adopted in November 1927, section 2 (A) (1), *Central Political Correspondence*, No. 14, n. d.; "Letter to Hunan and Hupeh", November 15, [1927], *Central Political Correspondence*, No. 14, n. d.

[2] Ch'ü Ch'iu-pai, *The Chinese Revolution and the Communist Party*, 1928, pp. 143-144.

insurrections in county seats and a general political strike in Canton. Military mutinies were to be encouraged. The island of Hainan was to be made an independent regime. Peasant uprisings were to spread in all directions and those in the neighborhood of Canton were to converge toward that city. The revolutionary army in Hai-lu-feng was to draw up a plan to enlist the peasant masses as volunteers in an attempt to attack Huichow with the ultimate objective of capturing Canton. When this plan for Hai-lu-feng was put into practice, it was stressed, the revolutionary army was to call upon the peasants to kill village bosses and gentry and redistribute land in order to expand the land revolution.[3]

But the Canton rising, as it finally broke out over December 11-13, did not follow the course outlined by Teng Chung-hsia. Shortly after the Swatow defeat at the beginning of October, the Kwangtung Provincial Committee foresaw an impending showdown between Chang Fa-k'uei and Li Chi-shen in Kwangtung and concentrated Communist forces in a bid for power.[4]   The showdown came on November 17. Li Chi-shen, who had controlled Canton over a year, left on November 16 for a conference in Shanghai, and within twelve hours after his departure Canton fell into Chang Fa-k'uei's hands. During the ensuing weeks Chang had to denude the city of troops in order to withstand the advance of Li's forces, which were attempting a comeback. That gave the Communists an opportunity to strike.[5]

On November 26 the Kwangtung Provincial Committee met to discuss the new situation in the province. A resolution was adopted in favor of an insurrection. A five-man Revolutionary Military Council was created with Chang T'ai-lei as chairman and Yeh T'ing

---

3 [Teng] Chung-hsia, "The Canton Uprising and the CCP Tasks", section 1, printed in Lozovsky, et al, The Canton Commune, Chinese version, Proletarian Bookstore, 1930, pp. 37-65.

4 "Chang Kuo-t'ao's Report", October 9, 1927, paragraph 5, Central Correspondence, No. 7, October 30, 1927.

5 Article of Frederick W. Hinke, American Vice-Consul at Canton, embodied as enclosure No. 4 in American Consul J. D. Huston's Report on the Peasants, Workers and Soldiers Revolt of December 11-13, 1927, at Canton, China, dated December 30, 1927, hereinafter cited as Huston Report; "The Significance and Lessons of the Canton Uprising", a resolution of the Central Politburo, section 2, January 3, 1928; A. Neuberg, L'Insurrection Armée, Paris: Bureau d'Editions, 1931, p. 106.

as commander-in-chief.[6]   Teng Chung-hsia reported that the
instructions from the party leadership on insurrections in Kwangtung
were discussed and accepted at this meeting.[7]   This may have
been true.   But from that time on there was no more indication of
any further role of the party leadership in the subsequent developments in Canton.

Steps were soon taken to organise the Red Guard with a total
of some 2,000 members, including workers from the various trades.
In addition, the cadet regiment which had come from Wuhan under
the command of Yeh Chien-ying consisted of about 1,000 troops
infiltrated extensively by Communists.[8]

On December 7 the Kwangtung Provincial Committee called
another meeting at which an immediate insurrection was decided
upon.   A soviet of 15 deputies was created, of whom nine were
listed as workers, three as peasants and three as soldiers.[9]   However,
as the Kwangtung Provincial Committee subsequently admitted,
none of them was really a worker or peasant—they were all
intellectuals.[10]   The Comintern charged that the soviet was not
elected.[11]

The revolt at Canton was originally scheduled for December
13.   On the 9th Chang Fa-k'uei received a telegram from his
political leader Wang Ching-wei at Shanghai, telling him to disarm
the cadet regiment in anticipation of the Communist conspiracy.
The man entrusted with the task of disarming the cadet regiment
arrived in Canton on December 10.   Under such circumstances,

---

[6] A. Neuberg, *L'Insurrection Armée*, op. cit., pp. 110, 111, 116; "The
   Significance and Lessons of the Canton Uprising", January 3, 1928, op.
   cit., sections 3, 4, 5; [Teng] Chung-hsia, "The Canton Uprising and the
   CCP Tactics", section 2, printed in *The Canton Commune*, op. cit., pp. 37-65.

[7] [Teng] Chung-hsia, op. cit., section 2.

[8] Ibid.; for Yeh Chien-ying as commander of the cadet regiment, see Jerome
   Ch'en, *Mao and the Chinese Revolution*, London: Oxford University Press,
   1965, p. 136.

[9] Huang Ping, "The Canton Uprising and its Preparations", section 5,
   printed in *The Canton Commune*, Chinese version, op. cit., pp. 67-69; and
   in *Rate-China*, Moskau-Leningrad, 1934, pp. 139-165.

[10] "Resolution on the Canton Uprising", adopted by the Kwangtung Provincial
   Committee, January 1-5, 1928, sections 4(1), 5(4) (5), available in Huston
   Collection, Hoover Institution.

[11] "Resolution on the Chinese Question", adopted by the Ninth Plenum of
   the ECCI, February 25, 1928, section 10.

the Communists felt compelled to advance the date of the revolt to December 11, two days ahead of schedule.[12]

The Canton rising started on December 11 at 3.30 a.m. Both the cadet regiment and the Red Guard acted about the same time. In a matter of 15 hours the whole city except a few strongly protected points fell under Communist control.[13]

Not having been informed of the Canton conspiracy in advance, the party leadership at Shanghai was surprised to learn of the uprising from newspaper reports. In a letter to former party chief Ch'en Tu-hsiu, the party leadership declared shortly after December 13:

> The original plan was to unleash a large-scale uprising of the peasant masses with a view to solving their economic problems——especially their land problem. Judging from newspaper reports, however, this uprising at Canton probably had resulted from the pressure of the enemy (Wang Ching-wei's telegram of December 9)——forcing us to take action at this early date. For it had not yet been possible to hold a general meeting of the peasant unions and unleash peasant uprisings in the surrounding countryside.[14]

Thus, the Canton events took place without the previous knowledge of the party leadership. This was confirmed by Heinz Neumann, a minor Comintern agent at Canton at the time,[15] and by the Ninth Plenum of the ECCI held in February 1928.[16] There was no basis for the subsequent claim that the party leadership endorsed or knew about the Canton rising beforehand and that what it did not know was merely the timing.[17] The eruption of the rising out of all relation with the peasant movement in the outlying districts was obviously in disagreement with the party line.

---

12 Huang Ping, op. cit., section 5; A. Neuberg, op. cit., pp. 114-115.

13 A. Neuberg, op. cit., pp. 116-117; Chao Yü (Ch'en Shao-yü), "A Factual Account of the Canton Uprising", November 1, 1928, section 111(A), printed in *The Canton Commune*, op. cit., 101-198.

14 "Reply to Comrade Tu-hsiu", No. 2, n. d., around the middle of December 1927, *Central Political Correspondence*, No. 14, n. d.

15 A. Neuberg, op. cit. p. 124.

16 "Resolution on the Chinese Question", adopted by the Ninth Plenum of the ECCI on February 25, 1928, section 10.

17 "Central's Letter to Hupeh Comrades," January 1, 1928, section 1, *Central Political Correspondence*, No. 20, April 12, 1928; "The Significance and Lessons of the Canton Uprising", January 3, 1928, section 4, op. cit.; [Teng] Chung-hsia, op. cit., section 1.

2. The Canton Soviet

At the start of the revolt, the Canton Soviet (Council of the Deputies of the Workers, Peasants and Soldiers) was proclaimed with Su Chao-cheng as chairman. Since he was on a party mission in Wuhan, Chang T'ai-lei was acting for him before his arrival. Chang was concurrently commissar of the army and navy. Yeh T'ing was the commander-in-chief of the Red Army. Huang P'ing was in charge of both interior and foreign affairs. P'eng P'ai had charge of land. The other upstarts were Chou Wen-yung as commissar of labor, Ch'en Yü as commissar of justice, Ho Lai as commissar of economics, Yang Yin as commissar for suppression of counterrevolutionaries, Hsü Kuang-ying as chief of staff, and Yun Tai-ying as secretary general.[18]   In addition, Chou Wen-yung was concurrently commander of the Red Guard while Huang P'ing was secretary of the CCP Canton branch.[19]

It is clear that the central figure in the above list was Chang T'ai-lei who, as mentioned previously, was also chairman of the Revolutionary Military Council and secretary of the CCP Kwangtung Provincial Committee. Both Chinese and Comintern sources cite him as the inspirer and organiser of the Canton rising.[20]   But he was killed in action on the 12th, the second day of the revolt. Thereafter, commander-in-chief Yeh T'ing, who had led the military operations at Nanchang and Swatow and who had arrived in Canton from Hong Kong only six hours before the start of the revolt, became the actual leader.[21] But he could not do the impossible. Fighting against heavy odds, he and his fellow rebels were forced to retreat from the city on the 13th. The Canton Soviet existed for approximately two and a half days.[22]

---

[18] *The Red Flag Extra,* December 11, 1927; *Huston Report,* p. 16.

[19] "Resolution on the Canton Uprising", adopted by the Kwangtung Provincial Committee, January 1-5, 1928, section 6.

[20] [Ch'ü] Ch'iu-pai, "In Memory of Comrade Chang T'ai-lei", *Bolshevik,* No. 12, pp. 385-386; N. Fokin, "In Memory of the Organiser of the Canton Rising—Comrade Chang T'ai-lei", *Communist International,* March 15, 1928, pp. 155-156.

[21] Chao Yü, op, cit., section III, B, 4; A. Neuberg, pp. 120, 103.

[22] A. Neuberg, op. cit., p. 119; Lozowsky, "The Lessons of the Canton Rising", printed in *The Canton Commune,* op. cit., pp. 1-14.

At the beginning of the revolt, the Canton Soviet announced its political program based largely on the resolutions of the Politburo enlarged session of November. The major items which transcended the scope of those resolutions were confiscation of all land and expropriation of the property of all capitalists. Obviously these items were diametrically opposed to the Comintern line. The text of the pertinent part of the political program is as follows:

> The Canton Soviet asks all peasants in Kwangtung to rise up strongly forthwith and confiscate all land, exterminate landlords and rich peasants, to pay neither rent nor taxes, to repay no loans and to destroy all title-deeds and promissory notes, and to organise a village soviet government. . . . .

> The Canton Soviet asks all soldiers and revolutionary officers to bring their arms and join the Red Army, seizing and killing all soldiers and officers who oppose the revolution, and setting up a revolutionary soldiers committee. All those soldiers who receive [Chinese currency] $12.00 per month should receive $20.00 per month.

> With a view to helping the Canton laborers, the Canton Soviet publishes the following regulations:

> 1. An eight-hour working day will be enforced in all factories!
> 2. Increase all laborers' pay!
> 3. Use the government resources to support the livelihood of the unemployed!
> 4. Support and increase the original rights and privileges of the Hong Kong strikers!
> 5. Confiscate the rich hotels and give them to the workers to live in!
> 6. Let all banks, railways, mines, factories and steamers come under the control of the state!
> 7. Confiscate the property of all capitalists and landlords!

> With a view to helping the sufferers amongst the people in the city, the Soviet has decided to wipe all loans, to stop the payment of rent by poor people.[23]

Contrary to general expectations, the party and its mass work in Canton were very weak at the time. During the revolt, according

---

[23] "Soviet Administration's Message to the People", December 11, 1927, enclosure No. 2, in *Huston Report.*

to the Kwangtung Provincial Committee, the party organization
had virtually lost its functions. All the comrades, it was stated,
acted at will and it was impossible to order them about, much less
to lead the masses.[24]   It was even impossible to call a meeting of
the secretaries of the party cells.[25]   Moreover, there was no unified
military command and the fighting plans and military operations
were all too confusing.[26]

The rebels set free former political prisoners.[27]   They appealed
to workers for support.[28]   But they failed to win over the masses.
They failed, for instance, to get an adequate number of people for
two mass meetings on the 11th and 12th, and consequently they
had to call a meeting of over 300 representatives drafted from the
people, instead.[29]

The Canton rising was organised in such a hurry that it was not
preceded by a general strike which was ordinarily a prerequisite of
a Communist insurrection in order to rouse the masses to action.
It can not be too often reiterated that the revolt had little mass
support.   Said Yeh T'ing, who had charge of the insurrection after
the death of Chang T'ai-lei:

> The masses took no part in the insurrection. All shops were
> closed and the employees showed no desire to support us. Most
> of the soldiers we disarmed dispersed in the city. The insurrection
> was not linked to the difficulties of the railway workers. The
> reactionaries could still use the Canton-Hankow line. The workers
> of the power plant cut off the light, and we had to work in the
> dark. The workers of Canton and Hong Kong as well as the
> sailors did not dare join the combatants. The river sailors placed
> themselves shamefully at the service of the Whites. The railway
> workers and the Hong Kong and Canton-Hankow line transmitted
> the telegrams of the enemy and transported their soldiers. The
> peasants did not help us by destroying the tracts, and did not try

---

24 "Resolution on the Canton Uprising", adopted by the Kwangtung Provincial Committee, January 1-5, 1928, section 4(7).

25 [Teng] Chung-hsia, op. cit., section III, A, 8.

26 "Resolution on the Canton Uprising", adopted by the Kwangtung Provincial Committee, January 1-5, 1928, section 5(8).

27 Chao Yü, op. cit. section III, (A), (2).

28 *Huston Report*, pp. 17-18.

29 [Teng] Chung-hsia, op. cit. section III, A, 8.

to prevent the enemy from attacking Canton. The workers of Hong Kong did not display the least sympathy for the insurrection.[30]

But Yeh T'ing himself was also to blame, according to Heinz Neumann. The leadership of the rising, Neumann charged, was extremely weak. Yeh T'ing did not arrive in Canton until six hours before the start of the revolt. Consequently, he was not able to make a close study of the situation. Although Yeh was a professional military man with the rank of general, Neumann complained that he did not have sufficient military training, nor any experience of proletarian insurrection in a city.[31]

Eye-witness accounts say that the coup was for the most part a looting and incendiary expedition. It was a terrible shock to the world.[32] During and immediately following the revolt there were wholesale killings and executions, involving many innocent people. The Kwangtung Provincial Committee estimated that more than 200 Communists and over 2,000 Red Guards and Red Army men (so-called workers and peasants) were killed, while no more than 100 deaths were reported on the enemy side.[33]

In a resolution on political discipline by the reorganised Kwangtung Provincial Committee at the beginning of 1928, all the one-time commissars of the Canton Soviet were punished in varying degrees except for the obscure commissar of economics and two absentees. Yeh T'ing, for instance, was placed on probation as a party member for six months. Huang P'ing was removed from the local party leadership since he had failed to draw up a specific plan for retreat with the result that responsible comrades did not even receive orders to pull out when they were forced to do so.[34]

---

[30] "Yeh T'ing's Report on the Canton Insurrection", as cited in M. N. Roy, *Revolution and Counterrevolution in China*, Calcutta, 1946, p. 558; cf. A. Neuberg, pp. 125-126.

[31] A. Neuberg, op. cit., p. 120.

[32] *Huston Report*, pp. 20-21.

[33] "Resolution on the Canton Uprising", adopted by the Kwangtung Provincial Committee, January 1-5, 1928, section 3, 5(6) (10).

[34] "Resolution on the Canton Uprising", adopted by the Kwangtung Provincial Committee, January 1-5, 1928, section 6.

A number of causes for the quick collapse of the Canton Soviet were subsequently given as lessons for the Communists: First, few peasants took part in the rising; the peasants in the outlying districts did not respond at all. The so-called workers in Canton were mostly backward handicraftsmen and the labor union was not cooperative. Second, the KMT troops on hand were five to six times as strong as the Communist forces. Third, there was no general strike before the rising. Fourth, the Red Guard was hurriedly organised and poorly trained, with virtually no arms. Fifth, the Communist forces were scattered over separate parts of the city rather than concentrating their attack on the main enemy base, the island of Honan. Consequently, they had to shift from offensive to defensive when the enemy counter-attacked. Sixth, it was charged that British, Japanese and American marines landed at Canton to stand in the way of the rebels.[35]

The remarkable thing was that the Communists did not concede defeat immediately after the Canton debacle. Upon learning of the Canton events from newspaper reports in Moscow, Lominadze declared that the rising marked only the beginning of a new stage of the Chinese revolution.[36] He testified that Chinese Communist policy after Canton was to organise an armed insurrection on as large a scale as possible.[37] The Chinese Communists on their part regarded the abortive Canton rising as only a temporary setback.[38] Ch'ü Ch'iu-pai made clear that a strong under-current of insurrection existed in China after the Canton events and that putschism prevailed in many parts of the country. Some

35 "The Significance and Lessons of the Canton Uprising", adopted by the Central Politburo, January 3, 1928; "Resolution on the Canton Uprising", adopted by the Kwangtung Provincial Committee, January 1-5, 1928; V. Lominadze, "The Anniversary of the Canton Rising", Communist International, Vol. VI, No. 5; A. Neuberg, L'Insurrection Armée, Paris, 1931, chapter on "The Insurrection of Canton"; articles by Lozovsky, Wei To, Chung Hsia, Huang Ping, Chao Yü and Lominadze in The Canton Commune, 1930; M. N. Roy, "Imperialism and Counterrevolution in China", Inprecor. Vol. 7, No. 72, December 22, 1927.

36 V. Lominadze, "Historical Significance of the Canton Rising", Communist International, German edition, December 28, 1927, pp. 2540-48, English edition, January 15, 1928, pp. 31-34.

37 V. Lominadze, "The Anniversary of the Canton Rising", Communist International, Vol. VI, No. 5, p. 137.

38 "Draft Resolution on the Current Tasks and Working Principles", adopted by the Kwangtung Provincial Committee, January 1-5, 1928; Ch'ü Ch'iu-pai, The Chinese Revolution and the Communist Party, 1928, pp. 147, 148.

provinces, according to him, had even been "divided into insurrection areas", while others had "set the dates for insurrections".[39]
According to a subsequent account of the Mao regime, this putschist
line of the post-Canton period did not cease to function in many
places in China until the first weeks of 1928. It was basically
brought to an end by April of that year.[40]

3. Repercussions in Moscow

It is well known that the Russians were involved in the Canton
incident. Having recaptured Canton, the KMT Kwangtung Provincial Committee declared on December 22 that the revolt was
largely due to the machinations of the Red Russians and that over
ten Russians were found among those killed during the fighting.[41]
The Russian Consul, who had been expelled from Canton, stated
on arriving in Hong Kong on December 30 that all people in his
consulate including himself were made prisoners on the evening
of the 13th and that five Russians and six Chinese, including Vice-
Consul Hassis and Secretary Valcooloff, were taken out and shot
the next morning on the charge that they had taken part in the
street fighting.[42]   According to American Consul J. C. Huston,
Vice-Consul Hassis and four other Russians together with several
Chinese were shot in front of the Bureau of Public Safety which
had been used as the seat of the short-lived soviet government.[43]

Moreover, a large number of documents were found during the
raid on the Russian Consulate.[44]   One of them, which was unsigned,
struck the American Consul in charge at Canton as being in Moscow's

[39] Ch'ü Ch'iu-pai, *The Chinese Revolution and the Communist Party*, p. 145.

[40] "Resolution on Some Historical Problems", April 20, 1945, section 3,
printed in Mao's *Selected Works, IV*, Peking: Foreign Languages Press,
1961, pp. 171-218.

[41] "A dispatch from Chu Chao-hsin, Commissioner of Foreign Affairs for
Canton, to J. C. Huston, American Consul in Charge at Canton", December
22, 1927, embodied in the *Huston Report* as enclosure No. 6.

[42] "Interview with the Soviet Consul", embodied in the *Huston Report* as
enclosure 7.

[43] *Huston Report*, pp. 36-38.   So far as Huston could find out, the names of
the Russians killed or executed in Canton were Hassis, Antonoff, Mackinoff,
Gogol, Tzeigeloff, Kornivaloff, Zawichi, Kroval, Lyboff and Tzeplitzsky:
see *Huston Report*, pp. 24, 36-38.

[44] "A Dispatch from Chu Chao-hsin to J. C. Huston", December 22, 1927,
op. cit.; "Interview with the Russian Consul", December 30, 1927, op. cit.

most ingenuous style.[45] This document was apparently a copy of the insurrection plan for Kwangtung province drafted on the basis of the policy line of the party leadership. It spoke of an armed rising, or rather a peasant rising, in Kwangtung province in contrast with a general strike in Canton. The Canton rising, as it finally occurred independently of the peasant uprising program of Kwangtung province, could not possibly have been the product of the unsigned document.

However, the mere fact that the Russian Consulate at Canton possessed the unsigned document in question indicated that it knew about the Communist conspiracy in Kwangtung province. For some time the Russian Consulate had been suspected of providing shelter to Chinese Communist underground workers.[46] It was not surprising that it was also suspected of having organised the Canton revolt. In consequence, the Nationalist government ordered the closure of the Russian Consulates and trade missions in areas under its jurisdiction over a Russian protest.[47]

Was the Canton rising cleared with Moscow in advance? Lominadze was present as the Comintern representative at the August 7 Conference and apparently also at the November Politburo enlarged session. But by the time of the Canton insurrection he was already back in Moscow, attending the 15th Congress of the CPSU (Communist Party of the Soviet Union) held during December 2-29.[48] He told the Congress prior to the Canton rising that the Chinese Communist Party was faced, in Kwangtung and a number of other provinces, with the problems of the struggle for power and the organisation of armed insurrection. He said that the CCP was fighting under the general slogan of soviets and that it resolved to found soviets only in such places where there was a guarantee of their permanency. He pointed out that soviets already existed in five districts in Kwangtung province

---

45 *Huston Report*, pp. 29-31.

46 Wang Ching-wei's telegrams as printed in Lei Hsiao-ch'en, *Thirty Years of Turmoil in China*, Vol. 1, pp. 119-120.

47 M. N. Roy, "Imperialism and Counterrevolution in China," *Inprecor.*, Vol. 7, No. 72, December 22, 1927, pp. 1632-33; "Declaration of the Soviet Government on Recent Events in China", December 22, 1927, *Inprecor.*, Vol. 7, No. 7, p. 1664.

48 *Inprecor.*, Vol. 8, No. 1, January 5, 1928, pp. 23, 28; B. N. Ponomaryov, *History of the Communist Party of the Soviet Union*, 2nd edition, Moscow: Foreign Languages Publishing House, n.d., p. 414.

and that one would probably hear of great revolutionary action in that province before long.[49] His report in question was clearly concerned with a broad insurrection program starting from the rural districts but not an independent urban rising like the Canton Commune. If he had expected an immediate independent insurrection at Canton, he did not make this clear. As a matter of fact, he learned of the Canton news from bourgeois press reports.[50] He testified that the date of the rising was forced on the Communists by the objective conditions.[51]

The earliest Comintern reaction to the Canton rising came in the form of a Comintern statement on December 15. That statement contained no indication that the Comintern had ordered the insurrection. On the contrary, it learned about the fall of Red Canton and its consequences from bourgeois telegraphic reports.[52] The Comintern president Bukharin, who fully agreed with Lominadze's prognosis of the Chinese situation as reported to the 15th Congress of the CPSU,[53] also learned about the Canton insurrection, according to one source, from the wires published in the newspapers.[54]

Heinz Neumann, a 26-year-old German Comintern agent, was on the spot during the Canton insurrection.[55] According to Mrs. Neumann, who was not yet married to Heinz Neumann in 1927 and was not present at the Canton rising, Neumann did not arrive in China until after the Swatow debacle at the beginning of October, disguised as an Austrian businessman named Gruber. As she points out, the financial support of the Canton revolt was provided by funds he had brought from Shanghai.[56] That might

---

[49] *Inprecor.*, Vol. 3, No. 1, January 5, 1928, p. 24.

[50] A. Lominadze, "Historical Significance of the Canton Rising", *Communist International*, German edition, December 28, 1927, p. 2541, English edition, January 15, 1928, p. 31.

[51] V. Lominadze, "The Anniversary of the Canton Rising", *Communist International*, Vol. VI, No. 5, pp. 139, 140.

[52] *Inprecor.*, Vol. 7, No. 72, December 22, 1927, p. 1633.

[53] *Inprecor.*, Vol. 8, No. 1, January 5, 1928, p. 34.

[54] Ypsilon, *Pattern for World Revolutions*, Chicago, New York: Ziff-Davis, 1947, p. 181.

[55] Margarete Buber Neumann, *Von Potsdam Nach Moskau*, 1957, Deutsche Verlags-Anstalt GmbH, Stuttgart, pp. 178-193; M. N. Roy, *Revolution and Counterrevolution in China*, Calcutta, 1946, pp. 558-559.

[56] Margarete Buber Neumann, op. cit., pp. 178-181.

be true, since the relief funds for the Communist refugees following the Swatow debacle were apparently also appropriated from funds provided by Comintern agents.[57] But this does not mean that the Canton rising was ordered by Neumann, much less by Moscow. Different sources give different accounts of Neumann's mission to China. Mrs. Neumann, who tries to put the blame for the Canton debacle on Stalin, asserts that her husband was ordered by Stalin to prepare or unleash an insurrection at Canton.[58] By contrast, Ypsilon states that Neumann received no mandate from the Comintern to start an armed insurrection.[59]

Whatever the inside story, the new situation in Kwangtung following the clash between Chang Fa-k'uei and Li Chi-shen on November 17 could not have been expected by Stalin when Neumann was despatched to China. It would follow that Neumann had to report back to Moscow on the new situation and that he also had to seek instructions from Moscow when he was faced with the threat of an insurrection at Canton. According to Mrs. Neumann, he did report the new situation to Moscow. As to the crucial question of whether an insurrection should be staged in Canton, Stalin was quoted by Mrs. Neumann as answering in a telegram: "Act in such a way as you can take responsibility for it" (Handeln Sie so, wie Sie es verantworten können).[60] It would seem that even if this telegram were true, it could not possibly mean that Stalin ordered the staging of the Canton insurrection. Rather, it seems to mean that there should be no "playing" with insurrection in Canton. Judging from his strategy of retreating to the countryside to build up agrarian and military strength before an eventual clash with the enemy in the city following the April 12 coup at Shanghai, Stalin could not possibly have ordered the staging of the Canton insurrection without first preparing the peasants in sufficient strength to encircle the city from the countryside. Nor could Moscow have ordered the creation of a soviet regime like the Canton Commune which, as described previously, stood for expropriation of the property of all capitalists.

---

[57] "Letter to the Kwangtung Provincial Committee", October 12, section 5, *Central Correspondence*, No. 7, October 30, 1927.

[58] Margarete Buber Neumann, pp. 178, 181.

[59] Ypsilon, op. cit., p. 180.

[60] Margarete Buber Neumann, op. cit., p. 184.

Almost three years later, on August 26, 1930, Trotsky accused Stalin's emissaries of utilizing the Canton insurrection to cover up the purge of the Trotskyte opposition in the 15th Congress of the CPSU. Without implicating Stalin himself, Trotsky declared:

> On August 7, 1927, the special conference of the Chinese Communist Party condemned, according to previous instructions from Moscow, the opportunist policy of its leadership, that is, its whole past, and decided to prepare for an armed insurrection. Stalin's special emissaries had the task of preparing an insurrection in Canton timed for the 15th Congress of the Communist Party of the Soviet Union, in order to cover up the physical extermination of the Russian opposition with the political triumph of the Stalinist tactic in China.[61]

The short-lived Canton Commune left behind a whole host of questions of revolutionary theory and practice for the Stalinist leadership to tackle, questions which were made all the more serious by complications with the Trotskyte opposition. To facilitate the work of the Ninth Plenum of the ECCI, held February 9-25, 1928, a special conference on the Chinese question was held on the eve of the plenum. The question of the Chinese revolution was discussed at length in this conference. The debate centered around the subjects of imperialism, class regroupings, and permanent revolution with Lominadze and Pavel Mif, a staunch Stalinist at the time, representing the two opposite sides.

Lominadze maintained that there was little or no possibility of compromise between imperialism and the Chinese revolution. He believed that China would either become a colony or have to undergo a revolution, and that there was no middle way. By contrast, Mif held that there was a possibility of compromise between imperialism and the Chinese revolution, however small that possibility might be.

According to Lominadze, the fact that the national bourgeoisie broke away from the revolution and joined the counterrevolutionary camp did not add to the strength of the reactionary side but rather accelerated its collapse. He argued that in politics as distinguished from mathematics, the addition of a new element to the combination of reactionary classes did not necessarily mean the increase of

---

[61] Leon Trotsky, *Problems of the Chinese Revolution*, New York: Pioneer Publishers, 1932, p. 291.

strength on the part of the reaction. By contrast, Mif contended that the desertion of the national bourgeoisie did add to the strength of the counterrevolution and that Marxists could not afford to disregard the principles of mathematics. Since Lominadze refused to recognise the Chinese bourgeoisie as a political force, Mif stated, he belittled the difficulty of the Chinese revolution.

For years the term "permanent revolution" had been associated with Trotskyism. This term was used by the Ch'ü Ch'iu-pai leadership in the Politburo enlarged session of November 1927 and by Lominadze again in the special conference of the ECCI on the Chinese question in February 1928. This was indeed a most serious thing. According to Mif, Lenin had advanced the theory of the transformation of revolution from the bourgeois-democratic stage to the socialist stage, and the first stage should be completed when the door to the second stage was opened. But Lominadze rejected this Leninist theory when he maintained that the Chinese revolution had gone beyond the scope of the bourgeois-democratic stage and that it partook of the nature of a socialist revolution. He was quoted as declaring that "we can no longer call this revolution a bourgeois-democratic revolution" and that "the Chinese revolution has now no more bourgeois-democratic character". Mif pointed out that the Comintern had prescribed the present stage of the Chinese revolution as the bourgeois-democratic revolution with a tendency to grow into a socialist revolution. The main slogans of the bourgeois-democratic revolution were: remove the yoke of imperialism, confiscate the land of landlords, enforce the eight-hour working day, and create the soviets.[62]

With the benefit of the preliminary discussion in the Chinese conference, the Ninth Plenum of the ECCI proceeded without much difficulty. It was not surprising that Lominadze was completely subdued in the plenum. The item of immediate practical urgency on the agenda of the plenum was, of course, discussion of the putschist wave of the post-Canton days which, if not checked, would have condemned the Chinese Communists to hopeless adventures and complete breakup, as Lominadze subsequently admitted. The plenum rejected the CCP policy of the post-Canton period as erroneous and put a stop to the general slogan of an

---

[62] Pavel Mif, *The Chinese Revolution*, Chinese version, pp. 184-205.

immediate insurrection in China. Instead, it introduced a slogan of organizing the masses and preparing them for another revolutionary upsurge.[63]   The plenum set itself against putschism among the working class, against unprepared and unorganized insurrections in the city and countryside, and against playing with insurrection. To play with insurrection, it was stressed, was a sure way to lose the revolution.[64]

Contrary to his original description of the Canton Commune as marking the beginning of a new stage of the Chinese revolution, Lominadze had now come to realize that the Ninth Plenum was right in evaluating the Canton rising as a rear-guard struggle marking the end of the first Chinese revolutionary wave. After Canton, he admitted, the period of rise was replaced by a period, and even a prolonged period, of depression.[65]   Along these lines Lominadze confessed at the Sixth Comintern Congress held in the summer of 1928:

> I must openly declare that, prior to the Ninth Plenum I made a serious mistake, which I want to mention.   My mistake consisted in that I did not look upon the Canton uprising as a rear-guard action, did not consider it to be the concluding engagement which wound up a whole period of the revolution, but that I held it to be the beginning of a new upsurge of the Chinese revolution.   Events have disproved this position, events have shown that the Canton uprising was the last link in a whole chain of revolutionary struggles which had mounted particularly high in the middle of 1927, and slowly declining, had ended with a last mighty flare-up in the Canton uprising.   After the Canton uprising the depression set in.[66]

With regard to the nature of the Chinese revolution, the Ninth Plenum of the ECCI reviewed the question of bourgeois-democratic revolution in relation to socialist revolution.   This question, in turn, was intimately associated with the question of permanent revolution.   On the one hand, Stalin maintained that a revolution would not progress along an unbroken ascending line, but move

---

[63] V. Lominadze, "The Anniversary of the Canton Rising", *Communist International*, Vol. VI, No. 5, p. 137.

[64] "Resolution on the Chinese Question", adopted by the Ninth Plenum of the ECCI, February 25, 1928, section 7.

[65] *Communist International*, Vol. VI, No. 5, p. 137

[66] *Inprecor.*, Vol. 8, No. 53, August 23, 1928, p. 933.

always in zigzags, advancing in some areas and retreating in others.[67] On the other, Trotsky stood for the permanent revolution which was reputed to mean that the revolution developed unbroken along a rising line, going on from victory to victory. This sort of permanent revolution was exactly what had happened in China in late 1927. In addition, it was charged, the CCP had raised slogans that went beyond the bounds of bourgeois-democratic revolution. The revolution of a semi-colonial country, it was stated, was basically an agrarian revolution along with national liberation, taking the political form of democratic dictatorship of workers and peasants. Although it might be necessary, it was said, to confiscate the large enterprises to paralyse the opposition of the bourgeoisie, this should not mean the leaping over of a large stage of the bourgeois-democratic development. It was pointed out that the revolution developed unequally rather than in a direct revolutionary situation throughout the country.[68]

In consequence, the Ninth Plenum of the ECCI reaffirmed the Comintern's China policy and denounced Lominadze who, as the Comintern representative to China, had deviated from that policy. It should be noted that Lominadze's deviation lay in the sphere of proletarian revolution but not peasant revolution. The resolution on the Chinese question adopted by the Ninth Plenum on February 25, 1928 said:

> The present period of the Chinese revolution is a period of bourgeois-democratic revolution, which has not been completed either from an economic point of view (the agrarian revolution and the abolition of feudal relations), nor from the point of view of the national struggle against imperialism (the unification of China and its national independence), nor from the point of view of the class character of the government (dictatorship of the proletariat and the peasantry). The characterization given to the present phase of the Chinese revolution as a revolution which has already gone over into a socialist revolution is wrong. Equally wrong is the characterization given to it as a "permanent" revolution (the position of the ECCI representative). The tendency of skipping over the bourgeois democratic phase of the revolution coupled with the simultaneous appraisal of the revolution as a "permanent" revolution, is a mistake similar to that made by

---

67 Stalin, "Talk With Students of Sun Yat-sen University", Stalin's *Works*, Vol. 9, Moscow, Foreign Languages Publishing House, 1954, p. 265

68 *Communist International*, April 15, 1928, p. 195.

Trotsky in 1905. That mistake is particularly harmful, as such a formulation is excluded also by the profound national peculiarity of the Chinese revolution as a semi-colonial revolution.[69]

In addition, the Ninth Plenum of the ECCI approached the Canton Commune from the soviet point of view. It paid tribute to the heroism of the Chinese proletariat in its attempt to set up a soviet at Canton. This was only natural in view of the fact that the soviet was the political system of the Chinese Communist movement at the time. However, when it came to the evaluation of the Canton Commune from the standpoint of an armed insurrection, the Ninth Plenum blamed the local Communist leaders for committing a whole series of blunders which, taken together, would make the Canton insurrection look like anything but an insurrection in the Communist sense of the word. Among the local Communist leaders under attack was a certain Comrade N, whom observers have generally identified as Heinz Neumann. The resolution said:

> The Canton insurrection, having been a heroic attempt of the proletariat to organize a Soviet government in China, and having played an enormous role in the development of the workers' and peasants' revolution, has, nevertheless, revealed a whole series of blunders made by the leaders:—insufficient preliminary work among the workers and peasants, and among the enemy forces; a wrong appraisal to the working class members of the yellow unions; inadequate preparation of the Party organization and the Young Communist League for the insurrection; complete ignorance of the national party centre of the Canton events; weakness in the political mobilization of the masses (absence of broad political strikes, absence of an elected Soviet in Canton as an organ of insurrection), for which the direct leaders who are politically responsible to the C. I. (Comrade N and others) are partly to blame. Despite all these blunders, the Canton insurrection must be considered an example of greatest heroism of the Chinese workers, who have now the right to claim their historical role as leaders of the great Chinese revolution.[70]

This series of blunders provided the basis of all subsequent discussions of the lessons learned from the Canton rising. That the ECCI held Neumann only partly responsible for the Canton events suggested that he was not the principal organiser of the coup.

---

[69] *Inprecor.*, Vol. 8, No. 16, March 15, 1928, p. 321.
[70] Ibid., p. 322.

After the Ninth Plenum of the ECCI, the Canton uprising continued to be the subject of discussion. The main point at issue was whether the insurrection was staged with the support of the masses. If not, it was then a putsch which was taboo under Communism.

Naturally, Trotsky availed himself of the opportunity to attack the Stalinist leadership. He was quoted as saying that "the Canton rising was a putsch or adventure organised by the Comintern",[71] and that it was "a putsch, a consciously hopeless adventure, previously condemned to a cruel smash owing to the very fact that the revolution in China had clearly been on the ebb long before the Canton events".[72]

Interestingly, the position of Trotsky was shared by some people within the Comintern. In the Sixth Comintern Congress held in the summer of 1928 a certain Comrade Reuberg was quoted as saying: "The military and organizational-technical mistakes made by leaders of this uprising were unquestionably also of considerable influence on the results of the Canton struggle, but nevertheless, as compared with objective causes they had but subordinate and not decisive importance". Lominadze pointed out that Reuberg said everything except the word "putsch".[73]

In the Sixth Comintern Congress, Neumann dealt at some length with the question of "growing over" from the bourgeois-democratic revolution to the proletarian-socialist revolution and expressed the opinion that it would be a Trotskyte mistake to say that the bourgeois-democratic stage of the revolution in China had been passed. He spoke very briefly of the Canton rising. Echoing the Sixth Comintern Congress he stated that "it has become banality that the Canton uprising is no putsch". He supported Canton as the first soviet power in China.[74]

Reuberg, whom Lominadze also attacked under the name of Reyberg after the Sixth Comintern Congress,[75] might or might not be the same person as A. Neuberg, pseudonym of Neumann

[71] *Inprecor.*, Vol. 8, No. 53, April 23, 1928, p. 933.
[72] *Communist International*, Vol. VI, No. 5, p. 138.
[73] *Inprecor.*, Vol. 8, No. 53, August 23, 1928, p. 933.
[74] *Inprecor.*, Vol. 8, No. 76, October 30, 1928, p. 1420.
[75] V. Lominadze, "The Anniversary of the Canton Rising", *Communist International*, Vol. VI, No. 5, p. 142.

who published his book *L'Insurrection Armée* in Paris in 1931.
This book has a chapter entitled "The Insurrection of Canton"
which M. N. Roy identified as Neumann's report to the Comintern.[76]
Roy cited some passages of this report in English translation,[77]
which agree with the French original of the corresponding passages
of Neumann's book.[78]   The interesting thing is that the basic
ideas of Neumann's account of the Canton events in his book were
roughly the same as those of Reuberg which were cited above as
the target of attack by Lominadze.   Neumann says:

> Despite the considerable negative effects of the tactical errors
> we have mentioned, they were in our opinion not the essential
> causes of the defeat.   The principal and decisive causes must
> be sought in another area: The general situation in China and
> the power relationships in Kwangtung province were not favorable
> to the insurrection.[79]

Regarding the city of Canton in particular, Neumann states:

> The great majority of the proletariat and the petit-bourgeoisie
> did not give sufficient support to the new power.   The railway
> workers, the municipal workers, the sailors of Hongkong, and
> others did not stop work.   The petit-bourgeoisie, for the most
> part, adopted a waiting attitude.   At the moment of the insur-
> rection, there was no important revolutionary movement among
> the peasants adjacent to Canton.   The peasants were completely
> isolated; no aid could be expected from them.[80]

Neumann concludes:

> The insurrection of Canton has demonstrated to the Chinese
> workers that an armed insurrection can only succeed in the
> circumstances where it is carefully prepared, where no gross
> military and political errors are made, and where the proletarian
> masses in general, as well as the soldiers of the militarist armies,
> are drawn into the movement.[81]

In contrast, Lominadze who, as noted previously, had apparently
objected to the idea of an immediate uprising in Shanghai and

---

[76] M. N. Roy, *Revolution and Counterrevolution in China*, Calcutta, 1946,
p. 559.
[77] Ibid.
[78] A. Neuberg, op. cit., pp. 111, 113.
[79] Ibid.
[80] M. N. Roy, *Revolution and Counterrevolution in China*, Calcutta, 1946,
p. 559; cf. A. Neuberg, p. 132.
[81] A. Neuberg, p. 128.

Hankow prior to the November session of the Politburo defended
the insurrection of Canton after its outbreak in December.   On
learning of the insurrection from newspaper reports in Moscow, he
declared that it was justified by both objective and subjective
conditions and that therefore it was not a putsch.[82]   In the Sixth
Comintern Congress he continued to defend the Canton rising.   He
said that it would be a distortion of the Comintern line to object
to the Canton rising on the ground that the period of depression
had already begun before it.[83]   On the first anniversary of the
Canton rising he declared that the errors of the leaders of the
revolt did not lie in the fundamental line but in military and
organizational matters.[84]

Amidst the confusion of all these ideas the Sixth Comintern
Congress rendered its verdict on the Canton Commune.   First of
all, it had to refute Trotsky's charge that the rising was a putsch.
In so doing, it logically could not emphasize the blunders of the
leaders of the revolt.   Second, it reaffirmed the insurrection as a
rear-guard battle, thereby rejecting the post-Canton putschist line.
Third, it defended the uprising as a soviet symbol.   The resolution
of the Sixth Comintern Congress said:

> The Congress considers the attempt to look upon the Canton
> uprising as a putsch to be absolutely wrong.   The Canton uprising,
> which was a heroic rear-guard battle of the Chinese proletariat
> in the period of the Chinese revolution which lies behind us,
> remains, despite the grave mistakes of the leadership, the banner
> of the new, soviet stage of the revolution.[85]

Whatever its evaluation of the Canton events, the Comintern was
faced with the hard reality in China that while the peasant movement
in some provinces was still going on, the labor movement had
suffered a terrible setback.[86]   Accordingly, the Comintern took
the position that whereas the Chinese Communists should continue
to lead spontaneous peasant uprisings, the slogan of armed insur-

---

[82] A. Lominadze, "Historical Significance of the Canton Rising", *Communist
International*, German edition, December 28, 1927, pp. 2540-48, English
edition, January 15, 1928, pp. 31-34.

[83] *Inprecor.*, Vol. 8, No. 53, August 23, 1928, p. 933.

[84] *Communist International*, Vol. VI, No. 5, p. 140.

[85] *Inprecor.*, Vol. 8, No. 53, August 23, 1928, p. 933; A. Neuberg, p. 103.

[86] "Resolution on the Chinese Question", adopted by the Ninth Plenum of
the ECCI, February 25, 1928, section 4.

rection should be only a propaganda slogan on a national scale for the moment. Lominadze reported to the Sixth Comintern Congress:

> The Ninth Plenum, and subsequently the Theses proposed to the Sixth World Congress, put this question absolutely correctly; that the slogan for the armed uprising can now be formulated only as a propagandist slogan and only in those districts where there is a spontaneous peasant movement, that the Communists must put themselves at the head of these peasant uprisings, in order to consolidate and strengthen themselves there. On the whole, however, the slogan of the armed uprising is for the present only a propagandist slogan for the Communist Party of China.[87]

---

[87] *Inprecor.*, Vol. 8, No. 53, August 23, 1928, p. 933.

CONCLUSION

The short space of the last five months of 1927 was a turning point in the history of the Chinese Communist movement. It represented the Comintern's policy shift from the city to the country-side in China though the Chinese Communists could not cut off their emotional ties with the city overnight. It marked the beginning of the land revolution in China despite the fact that the Chinese Communists did not know how to make a land revolution at the time. With Moscow as the center of international Communism, a whole host of issues and ideas arose in regard to the revolution in China and, for that matter, the whole underdeveloped world. For convenience in discussion, such issues and ideas may be summed up in two categories, namely, the nature of the revolution and the strategy of the armed insurrection. Certainly, the former determined the latter.

Let us begin with the nature of the revolution. Perhaps the most important result of the 1927 events was the reaffirmation of the bourgeois-democratic character of the Communist movement in China as a semi-colonial country. This can be seen from the verdict of the Ninth ECCI Plenum to the effect that the present period of the Chinese revolution was a bourgeois-democratic revolution, that it was wrong to characterize it as having already gone over into a socialist revolution, and that the tendency to skip over the bourgeois-democratic phase and call the revolution a "permanent revolution" was a mistake which should not be made in view of the national speculiarity of the Chinese revolution as a semi-colonial revolution. It will be recalled that Lenin divided revolution into two stages, namely, the bourgeois-democratic stage and the socialist stage, and that he decided that every national liberation movement could only be a bourgeois-democratic movement—that is to say, it could not be a socialist revolution.

What is, then, a socialist revolution as distinguished from a bourgeois-democratic revolution in the colonial and semi-colonial world, as prescribed by Lenin and supplemented by Stalin?

In the first place, a socialist revolution is directed against capitalism while a bourgeois-democratic revolution is directed against feudalism and imperialism. Since the bourgeois-democratic revolution is not anti-capitalist, its urban policy is necessarily mild. The Chinese Communist urban policy was no more than a trade union movement marked by the eight-hour working day throughout the bourgeois-democratic period.

Second, a socialist revolution is a one-class dictatorship, that is, proletarian dictatorship. In contrast, a bourgeois-democratic revolution is a multi-class dictatorship, at least a dictatorship of workers and peasants. Where the dictatorship is exercised by more than one class, it is called democratic—such as the democratic dictatorship of workers and peasants with the support of the petty bourgeoisie or its lower echelon in the Chinese revolution in late 1927. In the earlier period of the national united front in China, the coalition of revolutionary classes consisted of the workers, peasants, the petty bourgeoisie and the national bourgeoisie. The Seventh ECCI Plenum reduced the Chinese coalition to workers, peasants and the petty bourgeoisie to the exclusion of the majority of the capitalist bourgeoisie. The national bourgeoisie as a whole was regarded as having broken away from the revolution as a result of the Communist purge in the Nanking-Shanghai area in April 1927.

Third, private property is abolished in a socialist revolution, while it is protected in a bourgeois-democratic revolution. Of course, the land of a landlord must be confiscated in a bourgeois-democratic revolution. The landlord class can be divided into large, middle and small landlords to be treated differently. That the land of the landlord was not confiscated in the period of the national united front in China was apparently due to both the objection of the Ch'en Tu-hsiu leadership and the priority given by Moscow to the forging of a united front against imperialism. In addition, to show a socialist trend, the Seventh ECCI Plenum provided for confiscation of large enterprises having the character of foreign concessions. This qualification of the "character of foreign concessions" was dropped by the time of the Ninth ECCI Plenum. In short, the large enterprises can be expropriated in a bourgeois-democratic revolution.

The one thing which distinguished the bourgeois-democratic

revolution in China from that in Russia was the bourgeoisie. Since Russia was an imperialist country, her bourgeoisie was always counterrevolutionary and was therefore the target of attack in the bourgeois-democratic revolution. But the Chinese bourgeoisie was different. Since China was an oppressed country, her bourgeoisie was anti-imperialist and was actually leading the national liberation movement in the initial stage. Accordingly, the Comintern policy was to support the Chinese bourgeoisie in an anti-imperialist united front on a temporary basis. As the Chinese proletariat grew in strength and became an independent political force after the strike wave of 1925, it gradually seized the revolutionary leadership from the bourgeoisie which was breaking away from the revolution. The proletarian leadership of the revolution was necessary because it ensured the transition of the bourgeois-democratic revolution to the socialist revolution, thereby making the bourgeois-democratic revolution a part of the world revolution carried on by the Communist-led proletariat.

Moreover, the question of the bourgeoisie divided the Chinese bourgeois-democratic revolution into two phases or types. The first was the national united front in which the Comintern primarily supported the bourgeoisie. The second was the land revolution in which the Comintern supported the peasantry. Indeed, the peasantry is so important in a dependent country that Stalin made clear that the national question was, in essence, a peasant question. Stalin even thought that the Chinese bourgeois-democratic revolution should properly be considered to begin with the arrival of the troops of the Northern Expedition in the Yangtse valley in late 1926 when a mighty peasant upheaval started.

Of course, the peasant struggle must be waged under the proletarian leadership. The labor struggle, on its part, must not develop to the extent of a proletarian revolution in the bourgeois-democratic stage.

It would be impossible to exaggerate the importance of reaffirming the bourgeois-democratic character of the Chinese revolution in the wake of the 1927 events. It foreshadowed the subsequent development of the bourgeois-democratic movement in the Kiangsi and Yenan periods—the former as a period of the land revolution and the latter as a period of the national united front. To the knowledge of this writer, there is as yet no fuller account of the question of the bourgeois-democratic revolution than Mao's treatise *On New Democracy* written in January 1940. He borrowed almost all the basic ideas on this subject from Lenin and Stalin for the Chinese setting and only changed the term "bourgeois democracy" to "new democracy".* Echoing Lenin and Stalin, Mao pointed out that the bourgeois-democratic revolution is a revolutionary pattern not only for China but for all colonial and semi-colonial countries and that the basic principles of the bourgeois-democratic revolution are the same with only minor differences to suit the peculiar conditions of the individual countries. Accordingly, it cannot be too often reiterated that the Communist movement in the colonial and semi-colonial world can only be a bourgeois-democratic revolution and that the socialist revolution cannot be carried on there until the completion of the anti-feudal and anti-imperialist tasks.

So much for the nature of the Communist movement in China as a semi-colonial country. Let us now discuss the strategy of the armed insurrection as worked out by Stalin following the Communist purge at Shanghai on April 12, 1927. This insurrectionary strategy of Stalin consisted of three steps, namely, (1) avoiding an immediate clash with the enemy in the city, (2) carrying on military and agrarian work in the countryside and demoralizing the enemy's rear and front, and (3) tackling the problem of the city eventually. For the purpose of carrying out this insurrectionary strategy, needless to say, the specific tactics were to be worked out by the Communists in China. The three steps of Stalin's insurrectionary strategy may be outlined below.

In the first place, as the Chinese Communists were then too weak to be able to resist their enemy in the city, Stalin's policy was to discourage urban insurrections which stood little chance of success. Thus, as described previously, the Stalin-Bukharin leadership rejected the suggestion of the Trotsky-Zinoviev Opposition to launch an armed insurrection at Shanghai to retaliate the KMT coup of April 12. Later, in late July, Moscow counseled

---

* Mao confirmed the change of this term in his treatise, *The Chinese Revolution and the Chinese Communist Party*, written in December 1939, Mao's *Selected Works*, Chinese edition, Vol. 2, Peking, People's Publishing House, 1956, p. 646; English edition, Vol. 3, New York, International Publishers, 1954, p. 100.

caution when it learned of the CCP plan for an insurrection at Nanchang. Likewise, Mao was told to place emphasis on work in the countryside when he asked the party leadership for two regiments of troops to attack Changsha at the end of August. The proposed insurrections in Changsha and Wuhan were not covered by the Insurrection Plan for Hunan and Hupeh which was drawn up by the party leadership under the supervision of Lominadze for the autumn harvest uprisings. While the Nanchang rebels rejoiced over their victory in Swatow and thought of setting up a political regime there in late September, they were ordered to abandon the city to work in the countryside. The party leadership supported the position of the local party cadres against a proposed rising in Wuhan at the time of Tang Sheng-chih's fall in November. In reply to the question of whether an uprising should be launched in Canton, Stalin was said to have sent a telegram to Neumann saying: "Act in such a way as you can take responsibility for it". Three years later, in 1930, Li Li-san was denounced by Moscow for his capture of Changsha as the first step on the way to Wuhan.

Second, the armed insurrection in the countryside took the form of the autumn harvest uprisings in 1927. The most important thing the Chinese Communists learned from those uprisings was the mass line. When Mao asked for two regiments of troops to attack Changsha, he was told that the peasant masses should be the main force of insurrection while the troops should be the auxiliary force. This principle was reaffirmed in the Insurrection Plan for Hunan and Hupeh. Obviously the party leadership expected too much of the peasant masses who were then not yet well organized. Equally naive was the party policy to use the county seats as the starting points of insurrection. The county seats were the best protected towns in the countryside and were impossible to take without military attack.

It was not surprising that the insurrectionary tactics were revised when the Central Politburo met in November to review them after the failure of the autumn harvest uprisings. As decided by the Politburo, the armed insurrection was to start with guerrilla tactics in the countryside taking particular care to avoid attacks on county seats. It may be recalled that guerrilla tactics, though adopted in Hupeh as early as July, did not become the main form of struggle until after the *Pravda* article of September 30 supported the peasant guerrilla movement in China. Now the Politburo prescribed guerrilla tactics as the main form of struggle. Ch'ü Ch'iu-pai pointed out that there were two requisites to guerrilla warfare: (1) armed struggle of the masses, and (2) creation of territorial bases. Guerrilla warfare without the support of the masses, he said, was bound to fail. Likewise, it had no hope of success if it failed to lead to the creation and expansion of territorial bases which were the main objective of the Communist effort in the countryside.

Third, the urban insurrection was the last step on the Communist program of action, as can be seen from Ch'ü Ch'iu-pai's testimony that the peasant struggle must proceed from guerrilla tactics to the creation of territorial bases and finally to the capture of cities. The purpose of urban insurrection was to seize political power but not to carry out socialism which was banned in the bourgeois-democratic stage. Since urban centers were ordinarily political centers, whoever controlled them controlled political power. When an adequate number of counties rose in arms, the question of insurrection in the provincial capital would naturally arise. The urban insurrection was the key to the success of the revolution when uprisings erupted in various parts of the countryside. The Politburo set forth four pre-conditions of an urban insurrection: (1) revolutionary zeal of the workers, (2) likely collapse of the ruling class, (3) sympathy of the urban dwellers, and (4) technical preparation and organization of the rising. The workers must proceed from the economic to political struggles. Normally an urban insurrection should be preceded by a political strike.

The nature of the Chinese revolution and the strategy of the armed insurrection were the two major questions which confronted all parties concerned in the Chinese Communist movement in late 1927——the Stalin leadership, the Trotsky Opposition, the Comintern agents in China, and the Chinese Communists. Lenin's ideas, supplemented by Stalin, determined the bourgeois-democratic character of the Chinese revolution. Staltn's cool thinking was responsible for the fairly elaborate system of insurrectionary strategy and tactics worked out by the Ch'u Ch'iu-pai leadership under the supervision of Lominadze. Trotsky and his associates, on their part, were at variance with the Stalin leadership in almost all important respects. For example, they objected to collaboration with the bourgeoisie, denied the existence of the feudal exploitation in rural China, thereby opposing the agrarian revolution, and advocated immediate urban insurrection.

In China, Roy was at loggerheads with Borodin while Lominadze disagreed with them both. Neumann, on his part, was also at odds with Lominadze. As the Comintern representative, Lominadze played a key role in Chinese affairs in late 1927. He was of the opinion that there was little or no chance of compromising with imperialism, that the departure of the bourgeoisie from the revolution did not mean the increase of the strength of the counterrevolution, and that the Chinese revolution was a permanent revolution and would go over immediately into the socialist revolution. His personal opinion was all the more important in view of the fact that Comintern directives usually consisted of only the guiding principles of revolution, leaving details and operational procedures to be worked out on the spot.

From the very beginning the Chinese Communists were oriented toward socialism rather than bourgeois democracy, toward urban centers rather than the countryside. The First Congress of the CCP adopted a socialist program. The Second Congress accepted the idea of bourgeois democracy but failed to adopt an agrarian revolutionary program and excluded the bourgeoisie from the democratic united front proper. The Third Congress rejected the Comintern instruction regarding agrarian revolution. The Fourth Congress excluded the stage of agrarian revolution from its political program. The Fifth Congress failed to provide a thorough solution to the land problem.

When it came to the turbulent months of late 1927, the socialist and urban trend was even more marked than before. The August 7 Conference proclaimed that the bourgeois-democratic revolution could and should grow into the socialist revolution immediately and without interruption. This developed into the well-known socialist deviation of the November session of the Politburo which marked the beginning of the putschist line lasting until early 1928. There was no evidence of disagreement between Lominadze and the Ch'ü Ch'iu-pai leadership in the latter months of 1927.

The local Communists in the various provinces acted mostly on their own, either because of the urgency of local emergencies or out of ignorance of the Communist revolutionary art. With very few exceptions like Lo I-nung in Wuhan, they were all in favor of independent urban insurrection such as Mao Tse-tung in Changsha, Chou En-lai, Li Li-san, *et al* in Nanchang and Swatow, and Chang T'ai-lei in Canton. They were generally more radical than the party leadership which, in turn, was more radical than Moscow in the latter months of 1927.

Of particular interest was the position of Mao Tse-tung on the Chinese Communist movement in 1927 and before. He testified that he became a Marxist in 1920. In other words, he had not become a Leninist by then. That was certainly true and it was true not only of himself but also of almost all other Chinese Communists at the time. It was understandable that he shared responsibility for the socialist program of the First Congress of the CCP. His underestimation of the strength of the peasantry at the time reflected the apathy of the Third Congress toward the Comintern instruction regarding agrarian revolution. Like almost all other Communists in China, he was engaged in organizing students and workers but not peasants in the first few years. It was not until 1925 that he began to organize the peasants in Hunan. In other words, not until then did he begin to follow the important Leninist tenet regarding the peasantry, a Leninist tenet which was best reflected in his *Hunan Report*. But this does not mean that Mao had already become a Leninist apostle of the peasant revolution at that time. He was still inconsistent and noncommittal and had not yet developed a clear and definite ideology regarding the Chinese revolution. On balance, he was inclined more nearly toward socialism than bourgeois democracy, more toward the city than the countryside. This can be seen from the fact that he looked upon the industrial proletariat as the main revolutionary force shortly before the *Hunan Report* and restrained the peasant movement after it. When he was sent to Hunan to organize the autumn harvest uprisings, he took the position that China had already reached her 1917 and was no longer in her 1905. Besides, he asked for two regiments of troops to attack Changsha rather than organizing the peasant masses in the countryside.

Mao admitted that he did not have any experience of the land struggle before the winter of 1927-28. But he was anxious to learn the Soviet ideology and experience and apply them to the Chinese situation. From the Comintern experiment of agrarian revolution in China in late 1927 he learned a whole host of revolutionary ideas and strategies such as the practical meaning of the bourgeois-democratic revolution, the peasant masses rather than the troops as the main insurrectionary force, guerrilla tactics, rural base areas, and encircling the city with the countryside. Armed with such revolutionary ideas and strategies, coupled with his extraordinary ability of execution, Mao was gradually becoming the most successful leader in the Chinese Communist movement.

CHRONOLOGY

July 1920—July 1927

July—August 1920 Second Comintern Congress under Lenin's guidance decides to support the national liberation movement in the East to further world revolution and, to that end, support the native bourgeoisie in the short run and the peasantry in the long run. Lenin maintains that the national liberation movement can only be a bourgeois-democratic movement as distinguished from a socialist movement.

July 1921 CCP founded.

Late 1921—early 1922 First Congress of Toilers of the Far East calls upon the participant countries to carry on a democratic revolution.

Around mid-1922 CCP Second Congress adopts the program of a united front of democratic revolution.

November—December 1922 Fourth Comintern Congress reaffirms that the Communist movement in the East must be based on the peasants.

January 1923 Comintern instructs the Chinese Communists to join the KMT.

May 1923 Comintern sends the CCP a program of agrarian revolution which is, however, not accepted by the CCP Third Congress the following month. Comintern itself gives priority to a national united front in China.

Comintern labor policy in China is throughout a trade union movement marked by the eight-hour working day.

January 1924 KMT-CCP collaboration formally inaugurated.

June—September 1925 Political strikes in Shanghai and Hong Kong. As a result, the proletariat is gradually seizing revolutionary leadership from the bourgeoisie.

January 1926 Mao, like Ch'en Tu-hsiu in July 1923, stands for organization of the peasants.

February 1926 Mao maintains that the industrial proletariat is the main force of revolution.

February—March 1926 The Sixth ECCI Plenum objects to both *right-wing liquidationism* which sacrifices proletarian independence to the national movement and *extreme left moods* which favor skipping over the democratic stage, forgetting the most important and decisive factor of all—the peasantry.

Late summer and fall of 1926 As the Northern Expedition reaches the Yangtse valley, Stalin regards the mighty upheaval of the peasants as the actual start of the bourgeois-democratic revolution in China.

November 30, 1926 The Seventh ECCI Plenum adopts a resolution on the Chinese question, proclaiming that the agrarian question is the central question of the Chinese revolution and that the revolutionary classes are the proletariat, the peasantry and the petty bourgeoisie, excluding the majority of the capitalist bourgeoisie.

January—March 1927   Mao is sent to investigate the peasant movement in five counties in Hunan in January with the result that he drafts his report in February and submits it to the party leadership in March. Borrowing his ideas from Lenin, he divides the peasantry into three classes, namely, rich peasants, middle peasants and poor peasants, and regards the poor peasants as the revolutionary vanguard in the democratic revolution.

April 1927   Mao stands for "political" confiscation (except in Hunan) and defines land confiscation to be a mere refusal to pay land rent.

April 12, 1927   KMT's expulsion of Communists starts in the Shanghai-Nanking area.

After April 12, 1927   Stalin rejects the suggestion of the Trotsky group to launch an armed insurrection in Shanghai to retaliate the KMT coup of April 12. He orders the Chinese Communists to withdraw to the countryside to build up military and agrarian strength and, after that, to tackle the problem of Shanghai eventually.

April 27—May 9, 1927   CCP Fifth Congress convenes in Hankow, advocating confiscation of the land of large landlords.

May 1927   Mao is appointed director of the National Peasant Association under the Wuhan regime.

May 8—30, 1927   Eighth ECCI Plenum decides among other things: (1) the Chinese national bourgeoisie as a whole has broken away from the revolution; (2) a revolutionary democratic dictatorship of the proletariat and the peasantry is proclaimed for China; (3) the armed insurrection in a large city is discouraged; (4) peasants are to take direct action to seize land from below; and (5) a reliable Communist army should be built up.

June 1, 1927   Roy shows Wang Ching-wei a Comintern telegram received in late May, urging: (1) land seizure from below, (2) reorganizing the KMT, (3) arming 20,000 Communists and 50,000 workers, and (4) organizing a military tribunal to punish anti-Communist officers.

June 15, 1927   CCP rejects the above Comintern telegram as impractical.

June 28, 1927   Borodin and Chou En-lai agree to disarm the labor pickets in Wuhan.

Early July 1927   Comintern lashes at CCP rejection of its instructions and calls upon the Chinese Communists to fight opportunism of their party leadership. Borodin tells Ch'en Tu-hsiu to step down from party leadership.

July 13, 1927   Communists withdraw from the Wuhan government by order of the Comintern.

July 15, 1927   Ch'en Tu-hsiu tenders resignation from party leadership. Communists expelled by the KMT at Wuhan.

July 19, 1927   Li Li-san, T'an P'ing-shan, *et al*, meet in Kiukiang and recommend a revolt at Nanchang.

July 20 or 21, 1927   Chou En-lai as CCP minister of military affairs approves the recommendation for a Nanchang revolt with the ultimate objective of establishing a revolutionary base in eastern Kwangtung in hopes of securing Russian aid. In the name of the Central Standing Committee he and Chang Kuo-t'ao decide to launch the Nanchang revolt.

July 22, 1927 Chou En-lai arrives in Nanchang and creates the Front Committee to direct the projected revolt.

July 23, 1927 Lominadze arrives in Hankow. As Chou En-lai wires from Nanchang to request Russian military advisers and financial aid, Chang Kuo-t'ao refers the request to Lominadze who, in turn, seeks instructions from Moscow.

July 26, 1927 Lominadze receives a reply from Moscow saying that no funds are available for the Nanchang revolt and that Russian advisers must not participate in it. Comintern declares that if the revolt has no hope of success, it would be better not to launch it.

July 27, 1927 Chang Kuo-t'ao arrives in Kiukiang with the above Comintern message, but he is told that it is already too late to change the insurrectionary plan.

Toward end of July 1927 Autumn harvest uprisings decided upon. Preliminary work of insurrection starts in Hupeh.

July 30, 1927 Chang Kuo-t'ao arrives in Nanchang, and the Front Committee meets to discuss the Comintern message without result.

July 31, 1927 The Front Committee decides to start the Nanchang revolt on August 1.

August 1927—February 1928

August 1, 1927 Nanchang revolt occurs.

August 5, 1927 Rebels withdraw from Nanchang.

August 7, 1927 August 7 Emergency Conference convenes, setting up Ch'ü Ch'iu-pai in party leadership, accepting the China policy of the ECCI Eighth Plenum as the basic party line, and adopting armed insurrection as the operational program.

August 9, 1927 Moscow authorizes formation of soviets in China.

August 13, 1927 *Pravda* expresses misgivings concerning Nanchang revolt.

August 16, 1927 Communists in southern Hupeh ask for troops to help in insurrection but are told to use the peasants rather than troops as the main force.

August 18, 1927 Mao calls a meeting of the Hunan Provincial Committee to discuss the autumn harvest uprising for which he has been sent to Hunan.

August 20, 1927 Mao sponsors a letter from the Hunan Provincial Committee to the party leadership, saying that China has long reached her 1917, that soviets should be created at once, and that all land should be confiscated. Also, it is probably in this letter that he requests two regiments of troops to attack Changsha on August 31.

August 23, 1927 In reply to Mao and his group, the party leadership endorses the idea of using Changsha as a starting point of insurrection, but points out two mistakes: (1) inadequate peasant work and overstress of military force would result in military adventure; and (2) with attention focused on Changsha, outlying districts are neglected.

Shortly after August 23, 1927 Insurrection Plan for Hunan and Hupeh formulated.

August 30, 1927 Mao and his group reject the position of the party leadership as embodied in its letter of August 23.

September 5, 1927 Party leadership insists on its position as against the Mao group.

September 8, 1927 Autumn harvest uprisings start in both southern Hupeh and eastern Hunan.

September 8—12, 1927 Insurrectionists score one victory after another in eastern Hunan.

September 15, 1927 Hunan Provincial Committee calls off its plan to launch an uprising in Changsha next day.

September 16, 1927 Comrade Ma writes to the Hunan Provincial Committee, urging them to start the proposed Changsha uprising anyway. Meanwhile, he reports the Hunan situation to the party leadership with the request that the Hunan Provincial Committee be censured and reorganized and that a member of the Central Committee be despatched to Hunan to inspect work on the spot.

September 17, 1927 Comrade Ma urges Hunan Communists to carry on insurrection and not to retreat.

September 19, 1927 Party leadership decides to set up soviets.

It sends Comrade Jen to inspect work in Hunan, but without success.

September 24, 1927 Nanchang rebels reach Swatow with plans to set up a political regime there.

September 26, 1927 Chang T'ai-lei arrives in Swatow with party instructions to tell the Nanchang rebels to (1) use the soviet flag, (2) abandon Swatow and move the troops to join the peasants in the countryside, and (3) let Chang Kuo-t'ao and Li Li-san go to Shanghai.

September 30, 1927 *Pravda* publishes a leading article saying that the Chinese Communists have begun to shift their revolutionary base from city to countryside, using guerrilla tactics, peasant risings and the revolutionary army as the methods of struggle.

October 1, 1927 Nanchang rebels quit Swatow.

October 4, 1927 With their troops smashed near Swatow, almost all the rebel leaders leave for Hong Kong by way of Chiatzukang or thereabout.

Early October 1927 Mao takes about 1,000 men to retreat from eastern Hunan to Chingkangshan, while Chu Teh takes several hundred troops to retreat from the northern flank of Swatow to southern Kiangsi.

October 12, 1927 Party leadership gives orders that the survivors of the rebel troops in the Swatow area should retreat to Hunan and eventually to mountains by way of southern Kiangsi and that top rebel leaders should gather in Shanghai.

October 24, 1927 In reviewing the Nanchang-Swatow events, the party leadership declares that the defeat was merely a military one and would not change the course of the revolution.

Late October 1927 In reviewing the uprisings in Hunan and Hupeh, the party leadership attributes the failure to the mistakes made by the local Communist leaders.

October 26, 1927 Hupeh Provincial Committee advocates an uprising in Wuhan and local independent regimes in the countryside in case the warlord Tang Sheng-chih is defeated by Nanking troops in an emerging civil strife.

October 28, 1927 Lo I-nung, secretary of the Yangtse Bureau, warns against immediate insurrection in Hupeh.

October 29, 1927 Yangtse Bureau adopts the Recent Political Resolution advocating preparation for a general insurrection to seize political power rather than staging an immediate general insurrection.

October 30, 1927 Hupeh Provincial Committee accepts the Yangtse Bureau's Recent Political Resolution.

November 9—10, 1927 Central Politburo meets in enlarged session in Shanghai, working out an elaborate system of insurrectionary tactics including guerrilla warfare and territorial bases, but showing marked socialist deviations culminating in permanent revolution.

November 14, 1927 Central Politburo metes out disciplinary punishment for most of the important party agencies and individual leaders in the four provinces designated for autumn harvest uprisings. Mao Tse-tung, T'an P'ing-shan and Chang Kuo-t'ao are among those punished.

November 17, 1927 A general insurrection plan for Kwangtung province emerges.

November 26, 1927 Kwangtung Provincial Committee decides to launch an uprising in Canton following the military vacuum created by the dislodgment of Li Chi-shen from the city on November 17.

December 3, 1927 CY representatives file a complaint to the party leadership against the opportunistic mistakes made by Lo I-nung and the Hupeh Provincial Committee during Tang Sheng-chih's defeat on November 9-12.

December 5, 1927 Special Committee for Hupeh appointed to settle the CY-CP dispute.

December 7, 1927 Kwangtung Provincial Committee decides to launch an immediate insurrection.

December 11, 1927 Canton insurrection occurs.

December 13, 1927 Insurrectionists withdraw from Canton.

December 14—15, 1927 Hupeh provincial party conference resolves to punish Lo I-nung and members of the Hupeh Provincial Committee.

Mid-December 1927 — early 1928 A putschist wave prevails in many parts of China.

January 1, 1928 Party leadership addresses a letter to Hupeh comrades, denouncing CY's ideas of (1) launching an uprising at Wuhan at the time of Tang Sheng-chih's defeat, and (2) using the term "insurrection" in slogans without intention to carry it out.

January 3, 1928   Central Politburo passes verdict on the Hupeh dispute: (1) Yangtse Bureau was on the whole right, (2) Hupeh Provincial Committee was vacillating, (3) CY's Hupeh Provincial Committee was wrong in favoring immediate or general insurrection, and (4) Special Committee was wrong in judgement.

Early February 1928   ECCI sponsors a special conference on the Chinese question.

February 25, 1928   ECCI Ninth Plenum adopts a resolution on the Chinese question, denouncing Lominadze, Neumann and the Canton insurrection, but lauding proletarian heroism in attempting to create a soviet at Canton. In addition, the resolution outlines the future course of the Chinese revolution.

BIBLIOGRAPHY

Armed Insurrection, (武裝暴動 Wu-chuang pao-tung), published by Kung-hsüeh-she, n. p., 1929, bearing no author's name, with an introduction by Chao Yü (Ch'en Shao-yü).

Blueprint for World Conquest, as outlined by the Communist International, with an introduction by William H. Chamberlain, Washington, Chicago, Human Events, Inc., 1946.

Boersner, Demetrio, *The Bolsheviks and the National and Colonial Question 1917-1928*, Geneva, E. Droz, 1957.

Bolshevik (布爾塞維克 Pu-erh-se-wei-k'e), organ of the CCP leadership, issued in Shanghai, ten scattered issues from October 1927 to February 1928 are available in the Library of Congress, namely, No. 1 (October 24, 1927), No. 2 (October 31), No. 5 (November 21), No. 6 (November 28), No. 10 (December 19), No. 11 (December 26), No. 12 (date?), No. 14 (January 16, 1928), No. 15 (date?), No. 17 (February 13), No. 18 (February 20, 1928).

Brandt, Conrad, Benjamin Schwartz, and John K. Fairbank, *A Documentary History of Chinese Communism*, Cambridge, Harvard University Press, 1952.

Bukharin, N., "An Abrupt Turn in the Chinese Revolution", printed in *International Press Correspondence*, Vol. 7, Nos. 41, 42, July 14, 21, 1927.

..............................., "The Results of the Plenary Session of the ECCI", report given at the plenum of the Moscow Committee of the CPSU, June 4, 1927, *International Press Correspondence*, Vol. 7, No. 39, July 7, 1927.

Canton Commune, The, (廣州公社 Kuang-chou kung-she), a collection of six Chinese articles on the Canton Commune by Lozovsky, Wei To (Ch'ü Ch'iu-pai), [Teng] Chung-hsia, Huang P'ing, Chao Yü (Ch'en Shao-yü) and Lominadze, Shanghai, Proletarian Bookstore, 1930.

Carr, Edward Hallett, *The Bolshevik Revolution 1917-1923*, 3 Vols., London, New York, The Macmillan Company, 1950-1953.

Central Correspondence, (中央通訊 Chung-yang tung-hsin), a periodical issued irregularly by the CCP leadership for intraparty circulation, n. p., probably at Hankow in August-September 1927 and then at Shanghai until July 1928. Beginning with No. 14, some time in December 1927, it was re-named *Central Political Correspondence*, (中央政治通訊 Chung-yang cheng-ch'ih tung hsin). Thirteen issues are now available, namely, No. 2 (August 23, 1927), No. 3 (August 30), No. 4 (September 12), No. 5 (September 20), No. 6 (September 30), No. 7 (October 30), No. 11 (n. d., some time in November), No. 13 (November 30), No. 14 (n. d., some time in December), No. 16 (n. d., probably in January 1928), No. 20 (April 12, 1928), No. 22, (n. d.), No. 30 (July 3, 1928). All these issues are on file in the Bureau of Investigation, Taipei, Republic of China, except No. 11 which is available in the Kansai University Institute of Oriental and Occidental Studies, Osaka, Japan.

"Central Politburo's Resolution on the Hupeh Intraparty Question", (中央政治局 關於湖北黨內問題的決議 Chung-yang cheng-ch'ih-chü kuan-yü hu-peh tang-nei wen-t'i ti chüeh-i), January 3, 1928, *Central Political Correspondence*, No. 20, April 12, 1928.

"Central's Circular" (No. 13), [中央通告 (第十三號) Chung-yang tung-kao (ti shih-san hao)], October 24, [1927], *Central Correspondence*, No. 7, October 30, 1927.

"Central's Circular" (No. 16), [中央通告 (第十六號) Chung-yang tung-kao (ti shih-liu hao)], November 18, [1927], *Central Correspondence*, No. 13, November 30, 1927.

"Central's Letter to Comrade I-nung, Inspector for Hunan and Hupeh, and the Hupeh Provincial Committee", (中央致两湖巡視員亦農同志及湖北省委的信 Chung-yang chih liang-hu hsün-shih-yüan i-nung tung-chih chi hup-eh sheng-wei ti hsin), December 5, [1927], *Central Political Correspondence*, No. 20, April 12, 1928.

"Central's Letter to Hupeh Comrades", (中央告湖北同志書 Chung-yang kao hu-peh tung-chih shu), January 1, 1928, *Central Political Correspondence*, No. 20, April 12, 1928.

"Central's Letter to the Hupeh Special Committee", (中央致湖北特委信 Chung-yang chih hu-peh t'e-wei hsin), December 18, [1927], *Central Political Correspondence*, No. 20, April 12, 1928.

"Central's Letter to the Three Provincial Committees of Hunan, Hupeh and Kiangsi", (中央致湘鄂贛三省委信 Chung-yang chih hsiang-o-kan san sheng-wei hsin), March 10, [1928], *Central Political Correspondence*, No. 30, July 3, 1928.

"Central's Reply", (中央覆函 Chung-yang fu-han), *Central Correspondence*, No. 13, November 30, 1927.

"Central's Working Plan", (中央工作計劃 Chung-yang kung-tso chi-hua), November 1927, *Central Political Correspondence*, No. 14, n. d.

Chang Kuo-t'ao (張國燾), "My Memoirs", (我的囘憶 Wo-ti hui-i), *Ming Pao Monthly*, Nos. 7-8, July-August 1966, Nos. 23-28, November 1967-April 1968, Hong Kong.

"Chang Kuo-t'ao's Report", (張國燾報告 Chang-kuo-t'ao pao-kao), October 9, [1927], *Central Correspondence*, No. 7, October 30, 1927.

"Chang T'ai-lei's Report", (張太雷報告 Chang-t'ai-lei pao-kao), made before the joint meeting of the South Bureau and the Kwangtung Provincial Committee, October 15, [1927], *Central Correspondence*, No. 7, October 30, 1927.

Chao Yü (韶玉) [陳紹禹 Ch'en Shao-yü], "A Factual Account of the Canton Uprising", (廣東暴動紀實 Kuang-tung pao-tung chi-shih), November 1, 1928, printed in *The Canton Commune*, pp. 101-198.

Ch'en, Jerome, *Mao and the Chinese Revolution*, London, Oxford University Press, 1965.

"Ch'en Kung's Report", (陳恭報告 Ch'en-kung pao-kao), October 18, [1927], *Central Correspondence*, No. 7, October 30, 1927.

Ch'en Kung-po, *The Communist Movement in China*, edited by C. Martin Wilbur, reproduced for private distribution by the East Asian Institute of Columbia University, September 1960.

Ch'en Po-ta (陳伯達), *Stalin and the Chinese Revolution*, (斯大林和中國革命 Sze-ta-lin han chung-kuo ko-ming), Peking, People's Publishing House, 1952.

[Ch'en] Tu-hsiu (獨秀), "For What Are We Struggling at Present?" (我們現在爲什麼鬥爭? Wo-men hsien-tsai wei shih-mo tou-cheng), *Guide Weekly*, No. 172, September 25, 1926, pp. 1752-1754.

Ch'en Tu-hsiu (陳獨秀), "Letter to All Comrades of the Party", (告全黨同志書 Kao chüan-tang t'ung-chih shu), Decmeber 10, 1929, available as an independent document.

.........................., "The Question of the Chinese Peasantry", (中國農民問題 Chung-kuo nung-min wen-t'i), *Vanguard* (Chien-feng), No. 1, July 1, 1923.

.........................., "Telegram to the Comintern at the Instructions of the Politburo", June 15, 1927, as printed in *M. N. Roy's Mission to China*, pp. 338-340.

Chiang Yung-ching (蔣永敬), *Borodin and the Wuhan Regime*, (鮑羅廷與武漢政權 Pao-lo-t'ing yü wu-han cheng-ch'üan), Taipei, Commercial Press, 1963.

Chinese Peasantry, The, (中國農民 Chung-kuo nung-min), a monthly magazine sponsored by the KMT Ministry of the Peasantry, No. 1, January 1, 1926, No. 2, February 1, 1926.

"Chinese Soviet Regime and Socialism, The", (中國蘇維埃政權與社會主義 Chung-kuo su-wei-ai cheng-ch'üan yü she-hui chu-i), *Bolshevik*, No. 14, January 16, 1928.

"Chou I-ch'un's Report", (周逸群報告 Chou-i-ch'ün pao-kao), *Central Correspondence*, No. 7, October 30, 1927.

[Ch'ü] Ch'iu-pai (秋白), "In Memory of Comrade Chang T'ai-lei", (悼張太雷同志 Tao chang-t'ai-lei tung-chih), *Bolshevik*, No. 12, n.d., probably January 2, 1928.

.........................., "The Peasant Regime and Land Revolution", (農民政權與土地革命 Nung-min cheng-ch'üan yü t'u-ti ko-ming), May 14, 1927, *Guide Weekly*, No. 195, May 8 [sic], 1927, pp. 2120-2124.

.........................., "The Question of Armed Insurrection", (武裝暴動的問題 Wu-chuang pao-tung ti wen-t'i), December 10, 1927, printed in *Bolshevik*, No. 10, December 19, 1927.

.........................., "The Question of Responsibility for the Failure of the Revolution", (革命失敗之責任問題 Ko-ming shih-pai chih tse-jen wen-t'i), *Guide Weekly*, No. 200, July 8, 1927, pp. 2201-2203.

.........................., "What Kind of Revolution is the Chinese Revolution?" (中國革命是什麼樣的革命 Chung-kuo ko-ming shih shih-mo-yang ti ko-ming), November 16, 1927, printed in *Bolshevik*, No. 5, November 21, 1927.

Ch'ü Ch'iu-pai (瞿秋白), *The Chinese Revolution and the Communist Party*, (中國革命與共產黨 Chung-kuo ko-ming yü kung-ch'an-tang), 1928, n. p.

.........................., "Superfluous Words", (多餘的話 To-yü ti hua), May 22, 1935, printed in Szu-ma Lu (司馬璐), *The Biography of Ch'ü Ch'iu-pai*, (瞿秋白傳 Ch'ü-ch'iu-pai chuan), Hong Kong, Tzu-lien Publishing House, 1962.

[Teng] Chung-hsia (中夏), "The Canton Uprising and the CCP Tasks", (廣州暴動與中國共產黨的策略 Kuang-chou pao-tung yü chung-kuo kung-ch'an-tang ti ts'e-lüeh), printed in *The Canton Commune*, pp. 37-65.

"Comprehensive Answers of Comrades Ch'en Ch'iao-nien, Jen Hsu and Huang Wu-i to the Hupeh Question", (陳喬年任旭黃五一同志對於湖北問題之總答辯 Ch'en-ch'ao-nien jen-hsu huang-wu-i tung-chih tui-yü hu-peh wen-t'i ti tsung-ta-pien), January 10, 1928, *Central Political Correspondence*, No. 20, April 12, 1928.

"Comrade I-nung's Answer to the Hupeh Question", (亦農同志對於湖北問題的答辯 I-nung tung-chih tui-yü hu-peh wen-t'i ti ta-pien), December 21, [1927], *Central Political Correspondence*, No. 20, April 12, 1928.

"Comrade Kuo-t'ao's Letter to the Enlarged Session", (國燾同志致擴大會議函 Kuo-t'ao tung-chih chih k'uo-ta hui-i han), November 8, [1927], *Central Correspondence*, No. 13, November 30, 1927.

"Comrade Ma's Letter to the Hunan Provincial Committee", (馬同志致湖南省 委的信 Ma tung-chih chih hu-nan sheng-wei ti hsin), September 16, 1927, *Central Correspondence*, No. 6, September 30, 1927.

"Comrade Ma's Letter to the Hunan Provincial Committee", (馬同志致湖南省 委的信 Ma tung-chih chih hu-nan sheng-wei ti hsin), September 17, 1927, *Central Correspondence*, No. 6, September 30, 1927.

"CY Central's Letter Regarding the Party Central's Handling of the Hupeh Question", (CY 中央對於黨中央處理湖北問題的來信 CY chun-yang tui-yü tang chung-yang ch'u-li hu-peh wen-t'i ti lai-hsin), January 4, [1928], *Central Political Correspondence*, No. 20, April 12, 1928.

"Declaration of the Soviet Government on Recent Events in China", December 22, 1927, *International Press Correspondence*, Vol. 7, No. 7, p. 1664.

Degras, Jane, *The Communist International 1919-1943*, Documents, Vol. 1, 1919-1922, Vol. 2, 1923-1928, Oxford, Oxford University Press, 1956 and 1960.

"A Despatch from Chu Chao-hsin, Commissioner of Foreign Affairs for Canton, to J. C. Huston, American Consul in Charge at Canton", December 22, 1927, embodied in *Huston Report* as enclosure No. 6.

"Draft Party Program of the CCP on the Land Question", (中國共產黨土地問 題黨綱草案Chung-kuo kung-ch'an-tang t'u-ti wen-t'i tang-kang tsao-an), *Bolshevik*, No. 6, November 28, 1927; *Central Correspondence*, No. 13, November 30, 1927.

"Draft Resolution on the Current Tasks and Working Principles", (當前的任務及 工作的方針草案 Tang-ch'ien ti jen-wu chi kung-tso ti fang-chen ts'ao-an), adopted by the Kwangtung Provincial Committee, January 1-5, 1928, in *Huston Collection*.

"ECCI's Directive of Policy to the Third Congress of the Chinese Communist Party", May 1923, reproduced in Xenia J. Eudin and Robert C. North, *Soviet Russia and the East 1920-1927, A Documentary Survey*, Stanford University Press, 1957, pp. 344-346.

Eto, Shinkichi, "Hai-lu-feng—the Frist Chinese Soviet Government", *China Quarterly*, No. 8, October-December 1961, No. 9, January-March 1962.

Eudin, Xenia Joukoff and Robert C. North, *Soviet Russia and the East 1920-1927, A Documentary Survey*, Stanford, Stanford University Press, 1957.

Fokin, N., "In Memory of the Organizer of the Canton Rising—Comrade Chang T'ai-lei", printed in *Communist International*, March 15, 1928.

Fourth Congress of the Communist International, Abridged Report of Meetings Held at Petrograd and Moscow, November 7-December 3, 1922, published by the Communist Party of Great Britain.

From Wuhan to Chingkangshan, (從武漢到井崗山 Ts'ung wu-han tao ching-kang-shan), n. p., n. d., an official documentation on the origins of the Chinese Red Army, prepared probably in the 1950's.

"A Further Statement of the CCP to All the People of the Country on the Canton Uprising", (中國共產黨爲廣州暴動再告全國民衆 Chung-kuo kung-ch'an-tang wei kuang-chou pao-tung tsai kao ch'üan-kuo min-chung), December 17, printed in *Bolshevik*, No. 10, December 19, 1927.

Guide Weekly, The, (嚮導週報 Hsiang-tao chou-pao), CCP organ, a total of 201 issues from September 1922 to July 1927.

Hinke, Frederick W., article on the Canton events, embodied as enclosure No. 4 in *Huston Report*.

Ho Kan-chih (何幹之), *A History of the Modern Chinese Revolution*, (中國現代革命史 Chung-kuo hsien-tai ko-ming-shih), Hong Kong, San-lien Bookstore, 1958.

Hofheinz, Roy, Jr., "The Autumn Harvest Insurrection", London, *China Quarterly*, No. 32, October-December 1967.

Hsia, T. A., "Ch'ü Ch'iu-pai's Autobiographical Writings: The Making and Destruction of a 'Tender-hearted' Communist", London, *China Quarterly*, No. 25, January-March 1966.

Hsiao Tso-liang, "Chinese Communism and the Canton Soviet of 1927", London, *China Quarterly*, No. 30, April-June 1967.

⸻, "The Dispute Over a Wuhan Insurrection in 1927", London, *China Quarterly*, No. 33, January-March 1968.

⸻, *The Land Revolution in China, 1930-1934, A Study of Documents*, Seattle and London, University of Washington Press, 1969.

⸻, *Power Relations Within the Chinese Communist Movement, 1930-1934, A Study of Documents*, Seattle, University of Washington Press, 1961; Vol. 2, *The Chinese Documents*, Seattle and London, University of Washington Press, 1967.

Hsieh Chio-tsai (謝覺哉), "The Accident in Liuyang", (瀏陽遇險 Liu-yang Yü-hsien), *A Single Spark Can Start a Prairie Fire*, (星火燎原 Hsing-huo liao-yuan), Peking, People's Literature Publishing House, 1958, Vol. 1, pp. 145-146.

Huang Ho (黃河), *A Short History of Thirty-five Years of the Chinese Communist Party*, (中國共產黨三十五年簡史 Chung-kuo kung-ch'an-tang san-shih-wu nien chien-shih), Peking, Popular Readings Publishing House, 1957.

Huang P'ing (黃平), "The Canton Uprising and its Preparation", (廣東的暴動及其準備 Kuang-tung ti pao-tung chi ch'i chun-pei), printed in *The Canton Commune*, pp. 67-99, and in *Räte-China*, Moskau-Leningrad, 1934.

Huston Collection, containing some materials on the Canton Commune, Hoover Institution and Library, Stanford University.

J. D. Huston's Report on the Peasants, Workers and Soldiers Revolt of December 11-13, 1927, at Canton, China, dated December 30, 1927, usually cited as *Huston Report* available in the *Huston Collection*.

"Insurrection Plan for Hunan and Hupeh", (兩湖暴動計劃 Liang-hu pao-tung chi-hua), *Central Correspondence*, No. 4, September 12, 1927, and No. 11, n. d., probably late November.

"Interview with the Soviet Consul", embodied in *Huston Report* as enclosure 7.

Kung Ch'u (龔楚), *The Red Army and I*, (我與紅軍 Wo yü hung-chün), Hong Kong, South Wind Publishing Co., 1954.

Lei Hsiao-ch'en (雷嘯岑), *Thirty Years of Turmoil in China*, (三十年動亂中國 San-shih-nien tung-luan chung-kuo), Vol. 1, Hong Kong, The Asia Press, Ltd., 1955.

Lenin, V. I., "The April (1917) Theses", printed in his *Selected Works*, Vol. 24, Moscow, Progress Publishers, 1964.

...., "Preliminary Draft of Theses on the Agrarian Question", prepared for the Second Comintern Congress, printed in his *Selected Works*, Vol. 10, pp. 218-230, New York, International Publishers, 1943.

...., "Preliminary Draft of Theses on the National and Colonial Questions", dated June 5, 1920, submitted to the Second Comintern Congress held July-August 1920, printed in his *Selected Works*, Vol. 10, pp. 231-238.

...., "Report of the Commission on the National and Colonial Questions at the Second Congress of the Communist International", July 26, 1920, printed in his *Selected Works*, Vol. 10, pp. 239-244.

...., "Two Tactics", printed in his *Collected Works*, Vol. 9, Moscow, Foreign Languages Publishing House, 1962.

"Letter of the CCP 'August 7' Conference to All Members of the Party", (中共「八七」會議告全黨黨員書 Chung-kung "pa-ch'i" hui-i kao ch'uan-tang tang-yuan shu), August 7, 1927, *Red Documents*, pp. 93-135.

"Letter from Comrade Lin Chung-tan to the Special Committee for Hupeh", (林仲丹同志致湖北特委信 Lin-chung-tan tung-chih chih hu-peh t'e-wei hsin), December 12, [1927], *Central Political Correspondence*, No. 20, April 12, 1928.

"Letter from Comrade Tu-hsiu" (No. 1), (獨秀同志來信 [1] Tu-hsiu tung-chih lai-hsin [i]), November 12, [1927], *Central Political Correspondence*, No. 14, n. d.

"Letter from Comrade Tu-hsiu" (No. 2), (獨秀同志來信 [2] Tu-hsiu tung-chih lai-hsin [erh]), November 12, [1927], *Central Political Correspondence*, No. 14, n. d.

"Letter from the Hsu-chia-p'eng District Committee to the Special Committee for Hupeh", (徐家棚區委致湖北特委信 Hsu-chia-p'eng ch'ü-wei chih hu-peh t'e-wei hsin), [December] 12, [1927], *Central Political Correspondence*, No. 20, April 12, 1927.

"Letter from Hunan to the Central", (湖南致中央函 Hu-nan chih chung-yang han), August 20, [1927], *Central Correspondence*, No. 3, August 30, 1927.

"Letter from the Hunan Provincial Committee", (湖南省委來信 Hu-nan sheng-wei lai-hsin), August 30, [1927], *Central Correspondence*, No. 5, September 20, 1927.

"Letter from the Hupeh Special Committee to the Central" (No. 1), (湖北特委致中央信[一] Hu-peh t'e-wei chih chung-yang hsin [i]), December 13, [1927], *Central Political Correspondence*, No. 20, April 12, 1928.

"Letter from the Hupeh Special Committee to the Central", (No. 2), (湖北特委致中央信[二] Hu-peh t'e-wei chih chung-yang hsin [erh]), n.d., probably December 15 or 16, 1927, *Central Political Correspondence*, No. 20, April 12, 1928.

"Letter from the Yangtse Bureau to the Hupeh Provincial Committee", (長江局致湖北省委信 Chang-chiang-chü chih hu-peh sheng-wei hsin), October 30 (?), [1927], *Central Political Correspondence*, No. 20, April 12, 1928.

"Letter to Hunan and Hupeh", (致兩湖信 Chih liang-hu hsin), November 15, [1927], *Central Political Correspondence*, No. 14, n. d.

"Letter to the Hunan Provincial Committee", (致湖南省委函 Chih hu-nan sheng-wei han), September 5, [1927], *Central Correspondence*, No. 5, September 20, 1927.

"Letter to the Hunan Provincial Committee", (致湖南省委函 Chih hu-nan sheng-wei han), September 19, [1927], *Central Correspondence*, No. 16, September 30, 1927.

"Letter to the Kwangtung Provincial Committee", (致廣東省委函 Chih kuang-tung sheng-wei han), September 9, [1927], *Central Correspondence*, No. 5, September 20, 1927.

"Letter to the Kwangtung Provincial Committee", (致廣東省委函 Chih kuang-tung sheng-wei han), September 23, [1927], *Central Correspondence*, No. 6, September 30, 1927.

"Letter to the Kwangtung Provincial Committee", (致廣東省委函 Chih kuang-tung sheng-wei han), October 12, [1927], *Central Correspondence*, No. 7, October 30, 1927.

"Letter to the Northern Hupeh Special Committee", (致鄂北特委信 Chih o-peh t'e-wei hsin), September 13, [1927], *Central Correspondence*, No. 5, September 20, 1927.

"Li Li-san's Report", (李立三報告 Li li-san pao-kao), *Central Correspondence*, No. 7, October 30, 1927.

Li Wei (李偉), *Chingkangshan*, (井崗山 Ching-kang-shan), Shanghai, New Knowledge Publishing House, 1956.

Liu Hsien-sheng (劉先勝), "The Armed Workers of Anyüan", (武裝起來的安源工人 Wu-chuang ch'i-lai ti an-yüan kung-jen), *A Single Spark Can Start a Prairie Fire*, (星火燎原 Hsing-huo liao-yüan) Vol. 1. pp. 179-187.

Lo Jung-huan, "Early Days of the Chinese Red Army", printed in *Peking Review*, Vol. 5, No. 31, August 3, 1962.

Lominadze, V., "The Anniversary of the Canton Rising", English version in *Communist International*, Vol. VI, No. 5; Chinese version in *The Canton Commune*, pp. 199-219.

...., "Historical Significance of the Canton Rising", printed in *Communist International*, German edition, December 28, 1927, English edition, January 15, 1928.

Lozovsky (羅佐夫斯基), "The Lessons of the Canton Rising", (廣東暴動的教訓 Kuang-tung pao-tung ti chiao-hsün), printed in *The Canton Commune*, pp. 1-14.

Lü Mo (呂謨), "The Significance of the CCP Central's Recent Enlarged Session", (中國共產黨最近中央擴大會議之意義 Chung-kuo kung-ch'an-tang tsui-chin chung-yang k'uo-ta hui-i chih i-i), *Bolshevik*, No. 11, December 26, 1927.

"Manifesto of the Central Committee of the CCP on the Political Situation", (中國共產黨中央委員會對政局宣言 Chung-kuo kung-ch'an-tang chung-yang wei-yüan-hui tui cheng-chü hsüan-yen), printed in *Guide Weekly*, No. 201, July 18, 1927, pp. 2214-2217.

"Manifesto of the Second Congress of the CCP", (中國共產黨第二次全國代表大會宣言 Chung-kuo kung-ch'an-tang ti-erh-tz'u ch'üan-kuo tai-paio ta-hui hsüan-yen), May 1922, printed in *Red Documents*, reproduced in Wang Chien-min (王健民), *Draft History of the Chinese Communist Party*, (中國共產黨史稿 Chung-kuo kung-ch'an-tang shih-kao), Vol. 1, Taipei, Taiwan, 1965.

Manuilsky, D. Z., "The Importance of the National Problem in the Oppressed Countries", a statement at the Fifth Comintern Congress, June 1, 1924, as printed in Xenia J. Eudin and Robert C. North, *Soviet Russia and the East 1920-1927, A Documentary Survey*, Stanford, Stanford University Press, 1957, pp. 326-328.

Mao Tse-tung (毛澤東), "An Analysis of the Various Chinese Peasant Classes and Their Attitudes Toward the Revolution", (中國農民中各階級的分析及其對於革命的態度 Chung-kuo nung-min chung ko chiai-chi ti fen-hsi chi chi' tui-yü ko-ming ti t'ai-tu), *The Chinese Peasantry*, a monthly magazine, No. 1 January 1, 1926.

..............., "An Analysis of the Various Classes of Chinese Society", (中國社會各階級的分析 Chung-kuo she-hui ko chiai-chi ti fen-hsi), *The Chinese Peasantry*, No. 2, February 1, 1926.

..............., "The Chinese Revolution and the Communist Party", (中國革命與共產黨 Chung-kuo ko-ming yü kung-ch'an-tang), December 1939, printed in Mao's *Selected Works*, Chinese edition, Vol. 2, Peking, People's Publishing House, 1956, pp. 615-650; English edition, Vol. 3, New York, International Publishers Co., Inc., 1955, pp. 72-101.

..............., *Investigations of the Rural Dsstricts*, (農村調查 nung-ts'un t'iao-ch'a), published at Yenan in 1941, reissued by Hsinhua Bookstore, Shantung, 1946.

..............., "The Peking Coup and the Businessmen", (北京政變與商人 Pe-ching cheng-pien yü shang-jen), *Guide Weekly*, combined issue of Nos. 31, 32, July 11, 1923, pp. 233-234.

..............., "Report on the Investigation of the Peasant Movement in Hunan", (湖南農民運動考察報告 Hu-nan nung-min yün-tung k'ao-ch'a pao-kao), February 18, 1927, *Guide Weekly*, No. 191, March 12, 1927, pp. 2061-66; reprinted with some revisions and a long additional closing section (making the revised version almost three times the length of the original) under date of March 1927 in Mao's *Selected Works*, Vol. I, (Chinese eidtion, Peking, 1953, pp. 13-46; English edition, New York, 1954, pp. 21-59).

..............., *Selected Works of Mao Tse-tung*, (毛澤東選集 Mao-tse-tung hsüan-chi), compiled by the Mao Tse-tung Selected Works Publishing Committee, CCP Central Committee, published by the People's Publishing Company, Chinese edition, 3 volumes, Peking, Vol. 1, 1953, Vol. 2, 1956, Vol. 3, 1957; English edition, four volumes, New York, International Publishers, 1954-56.

..............., "Struggle in the Chingkang Mountains", (井崗山的鬥爭 Ching-kang-shan ti tou-cheng), November 25, 1928, in Mao's *Selected Works*, Chinese edition, Vol. 1, pp. 79-80, (Peking, 1953), English edition, Vol. 1, p. 99, (New York, 1954).

..............................., "Talks at the Yenan Forum on Art and Literature", (在延安 文藝座談會上的講話 Tsai yen-an wen-i tso-t'an-hui shang ti chiang-hua), May 1942, as printed in Mao's *Selected Works*, Chinese edition, Vol. 3, Peking, People's Publishing House, 1957, pp. 849-880; English edition, Vol. 4, New York, International Publishers, 1956, pp. 63-93.

McLane, Charles B., *Soviet Policy and the Chinese Communists 1931-1946*, New York, Columbia University Press, 1958.

Miao Ch'u-huang (繆楚黃), *A Short History of the Chinese Communist Party (First Draft)*, (中國共產黨簡要歷史 [初稿] Chung-kuo kung-ch'an-tang chien-yao li-shih [ch'u-kao]), Peking, Hsüeh-hsi-tsa-chih She, 1957.

Mif, Pavel (米夫), *The Chinese Revolution*, (中國革命 Chung-kuo ko-ming), Chinese version, Moscow and Leningrad, Foreign Workers' Publishing House, 1933.

..............................., *Heroic China—Fifteen Years of the Communist Party* of *China*, New York, Workers Library Publishers, 1937; Chinese version entitled 英勇奮鬥的十五年 (Ying-yung fen-tou ti shih-wu nien), 1936.

Neuberg, A., *L'Insurrection Armée*, Paris, Bureau d'Editions, 1931.

Neumann, "Statement at the Sixth Congress of the Communist International 1928", printed in *International Press Correspondence*, Vol. 8 No. 76, pp. 1416-1420.

Neumann, Margarete Buber, *Von Potsdam Nach Moskau*, Stuttgart, Deutsche Verlags-Anstalt Gmbh, 1957.

North, Robert C. and Xenia J. Endin, *M. N. Roy's Mission to China: The Communist-Kuomintang Split of 1927*, Berkeley, University of California Press, 1963.

"Political Report of the Hupeh Provincial Committee", (湖北省委政治報告 Hu-peh sheng-wei cheng-ch'ih pao-kao), September 10, [1927], *Central Correspondenec*, No. 5, September 20, 1927.

Politicus, "We And the East", dated 1923, printed in Eudin and North, pp. 194-196.

Ponomaryov, B. N., *History of the Communist Party of the Soviet Union*, 2nd edition, Moscow, Foreign Languages Publishing House, n. d.

Räte-China, documents on the Chinese revolution, published by Verlagsgenossenschaft Auslandischer Arbeiter in der Udssr, Moskau-Leningrad, 1934. Also published in Russian as Johanson i Tabue, *Soviety v Kitae*, translated from German, Partiinoe Izdatyel'stve, Moskau, 1934.

Red Documents, (紅色文獻 Hung-se wen-hsien), containing basic CCP documents of 1922-28 and key Comintern directives from November 1926 to July 1931, printed and issued by Chiai-fang-she, February 1938.

"Red Flag Extra, The", (紅旗號外 Hung-chi hao-wai), December 11, 1927, in *Huston Collection*.

"Reply to Comrade Tu-hsiu's Letter" (No. 1), (覆獨秀同志函 [一] Fu tu-hsiu tung-chih han [i]), from the Central Standing Committee, December 9, [1927], *Central Political Correspondence*, No. 14, n.d.

"Reply to Comrade Tu-hsiu" (No. 2), (覆獨秀同志信 [二] Fu tu-hsiu tung-chih hsin [erh]), n. d., about mid-December, 1927, *Central Political Correspondence* No. 14, n. d.

"Reply to Hunan, A", (覆湖南函 Fu hu-nan han), August 23, [1927], *Central Correspondence*, No. 3, August 30, 1927.

"Report from Comrade Ma in Hunan", (湖南馬同志報告 Hu-nan ma-tung-chih pao-kao), September 16, 1927, *Central Correspondence*, No. 6, September 30, 1927.

"Report of Comrade Huang Chih-kuang from Southern Hupeh", (鄂南黃赤光同志的報告 O-nan huang-chih-kuang tung-chih ti pao-kao), December 15, [1927], *Central Political Correspondence*, No. 20, April 12, 1928.

"Report of Comrade I-nung to the Enlarged Conference of the Hupeh Provincial Committee", (亦農同志對於湖北省委擴大會的報告 I-nung tung-chih tui-yü hu-peh sheng-wei k'uo-ta-hui ti pao-kao), December 12, [1927], *Central Political Correspondence*, No. 20, April 12, 1928.

"Report of the CY Hupeh Provincial Committee to the Special Committee", (湖北 CY 省委致特委報告 Hu-peh CY sheng-wei chih t'e-wei pao-kao), n. d., received December 12, 1927, *Central Political Correspondence*, No. 20, April 12, 1928.

"Report of the Kiangsi Provincial Committee", (江西省委報告 chiang-hsi sheng-wei pao-kao), December 12, [1927], *Central Political Correspondence*, No. 16, n. d.

"Report of the Nine Comrades, Kuan Hsüeh-san, Chang Chi-ch'u, *et al*, On the Enlarged Conference of the Hupeh Provincial Committee", (關學參張計儲等九同志關於湖北省委擴大會議的報告 Kuan-hsüeh-san chang-chi-ch'u teng chiu tung-chih kuan-yü hu-peh sheng-wei k'uo-ta hui-i ti pao-kao), n. d., probably late 1927, *Central Political Correspondence*, No. 20, April 12, 1928.

"Report of the Standing Committee of the Hupeh Provincial Committee to the Enlarged Conference of the Hupeh Provincial Committee", (湖北省委常委向湖北省委擴大會的報告 Hu-peh sheng-wei ch'ang-wei hsiang hu-peh sheng-wei k'uo-ta-hui ti pao-kao), December 12, 1927, *Central Political Correspondence*, No. 20, April 12, 1928.

"Report of the Three Comrades, Ch'en Ch'iao-nien, Jen Hsu and Huang Wu-i, to the Central Politburo", (陳喬年任旭黃五一三同志向中央政治局的報告 Ch'en-ch'iao-nien jen-hsu huang-wu-i san tung-chih hsiang chung-yang cheng-ch'ih-chü ti pao-kao), December 31, [1927], *Central Political Correspondence*, No. 20, April 12, 1928.

"Report on the Autumn Harvest Uprising in Hupeh", (湖北農民暴動經過之報告 Hu-peh nung-min pao-tung ching-kuo chih pao-kao), prepared by the Hupeh Provincial Committee toward the end of October 1927, printed with many errors in mimeography in *Central Correspondence*, No. 11, n. d., probably late November 1927, made legible in Chinese and translated into Japanese along with the English title in 1961 by Taicho Mikami, Tadao Ishikawa and Minoru Shabata of the Kansai University Institute of Oriental and Occidental Studies, Osaka, Japan.

"Report on the Hupeh Question by the Hupeh CY Representatives, Liu Ch'ang-chun and Han Kuang-han", (湖北 CY 代表劉昌群韓光漢對於湖北問題的報告 Hu-peh CY tai-p'iao liu-ch'ang-chun han-kuan-han tui-yü hu-peh wen-t'i ti pao-kao), December 13 [?], 1927, *Central Political Correspondence*, No. 20, April 12, 1928.

"Report on the Organization in Hunan", (湖南組織報告 Hu-nan tsu-chih pao-kao), for May-August (1927), prepared by the Hunan Provincial Committee, September 5, [1927], *Central Correspondence,* No. 6, September 30, 1927.

"Report on the Recent Political Situation, A" (最近政治狀況報告 Tsui-chin cheng-ch'ih chuang-k'uang pao-kao), *Central Correspondence,* No. 7, October 30, 1927.

"Resolution of the CY Hupeh Provincial Committee", (湖北 CY 省委決議案 Hu-peh CY sheng-wei chüeh-i-an), December 10, 1927, *Central Political Correspondence,* No. 20, April 12, 1928.

"Resolution of the ECCI on the Expected Attitude of the Chinese Communist Party Toward the Kuomintang", January 12, 1923, as printed in Eudin and North, pp. 343-344.

"Resolution of the ECCI on the Present Situation of the Chinese Revolution", printed in *International Press Correspondence,* Vol. 7, No. 44, July 28, 1927; dated July 14, 1927 in Jane Degras, *The Communist International 1919-1943,* Documents, Vol. 2.

"Resolution of the Enlarged Conference of the Hupeh Provincial Commeeitt Criticizing the Policy of the Yangtse Bureau and the Provincial Committee", (湖北省委擴大會議批評長江局和省委政策決議案 Hu-peh sheng-wei k'uo-ta hui-i p'i-p'ing chang-chiang-chü han sheng-wei cheng-ts'e chüeh-i-an), n. d., probably December 15, 1927, *Central Political Correspondence,* No. 20, April 12, 1928.

"Resolution of the Hanyang County Committee Criticizing the Work of the Provincial Committee", (漢陽縣委對於省委工作的批評及決議 Han-yang hsien-wei tui-yü sheng-wei kung-tso ti p'i-p'ing chi chüeh-i), n. d., *Central Political Correspondence,* No. 20, April 12, 1928.

"Resolution of the Joint Conference of Hankow's 1st, 2nd, and 3rd Districts", (漢口一二三區聯席會議議決案 Han-kuo i-erh-san ch'ü lien-hsi hui-i i-chüeh-an), December 11, [1927], *Central Political Correspondence,* No. 20, April 12, 1928.

"Resolution of the Joint Plenum of the C.C. and the C.C.C. After Hearing Comrade Bukharin's Report of August 9, 1927", printed in *International Press Correspondence,* Vol. 7, No. 48, August 18, 1927.

"Resolution of the Wuch'ang Municipal Committee", (武昌市委決議 Wu-ch'ang shih-wei chüeh-i), December 12, [1927], *Central Political Correspondence,* No. 20, April 12, 1928.

"Resolution on the Canton Uprising", (廣州暴動決議案 Kuang-chou pao-tung chüeh-i-an), adopted by the Kwangtung Provincial Committee, January 1-5, 1928, available in *Huston Collection.*

"Resolution on the Chinese Question", adopted by the Sixth Enlarged Plenum of the ECCI, February-March 1926, *International Press Correspondence,* Vol. 6, No. 40, pp. 648-649.

"Resolution on the Chinese Question", adopted by the Seventh Plenum of the ECCI, toward the end of November 1926, Chinese version in *Red Documents,* pp. 245-66, English version, with a different date given by the editors, in Robert C. North and Xenia J. Eudin, *M. N. Roy's Mission to China,* 1963, pp. 131-145.

"Resolution on the Chinese Question", adopted by the Eighth Plenum of the ECCI, May 1927, Chinese version in *Red Documents*, pp. 267-88, English version in *International Press Correspondence*, Vol. 7, No. 35, June 16, 1927, pp. 733-41.

"Resolution on the Chinese Question", adopted by the Ninth Plenum of the ECCI, February 25, 1928, Chinese version in *Red Documents*, pp. 289-96, English version in *International Press Correspondence*, Vol. 8, No. 16, March 15, 1928, pp. 321-23.

"Resolution on the Current Situation in China and the Tasks of the Party", (中國現狀與黨的任務決議案 Chung-kuo hsien-chuang yü tang ti jen-wu chüeh-i an), *Bolshevik*, No. 6, November 28, 1927; *Central Correspondence*, No. 13, November 30, 1927.

"Resolution on the Current Urgent Struggle", (目前緊急爭鬥決議案 Mu-chien chin-chi cheng-tou chüeh-i an), October 26, 1927, embodied in the "Report of the Standing Committee of the Hupeh Provincial Committee to the Enlarged Conference of the Hupeh Provincial Committee", December 12, 1927 *Central Political Correspondence*, No. 20, April 12, 1928.

"Resolution on the Important Tasks in the Recent Organizational Question", (最近組織問題的重要任務議決案 Tsui-chin tsu-chih wen-ti ti chung-yao jen-wu i-chüeh an), November 14, [1927], *Central Correspondence*, No. 13, November 30, 1927.

"Resolution on Political Discipline", (政治紀律決議案 Cheng-ch'ih chi-lü chüeh-i-an), November 14, [1927], *Central Correspondence*, No. 13, November 30, 1927.

"Resolution on the Political Tasks and Tactics of the CCP", (中國共產黨的政治任務與策略的決議案 Chung-kuo kung-ch'an-tang ti cheng-ch'ih jen-wu yü ts'e-lüeh ti chüeh-i-an), n. d., probably around mid-August, 1927, *Central Correspondence*, No. 2, August 23, 1927.

"Resolution on the Present-day Labor Movement", (最近職工運動的決議案 Tsui-chin chih-kung yün-tung ti chüeh-i-an), adopted by the August 7 Conference, *Cental Correspondence*, No. 2, August 23, 1927.

"Resolution on the Present-day Peasant Struggle", (最近農民鬥爭的議決案 Tsui-chin nung-min tou-cheng ti i-chüeh an), adopted by the August 7 Conference, *Central Correspondence*, No. 2, August 23, 1927.

"Resolution on the Questions of the 'Left-wing Kuomintang' and the Soviet Slogan", (關於「左派國民黨」及蘇維埃口號問題議決案 Kuan-yü "tso-p'ai kuo-min-tang" chi su-wei-ai kuo-hao wen-ti chüeh-i an), adopted by the Provisional Central Politburo, September 19, [1927], *Central Correspondence*, No. 6, September 30, 1927.

"Resolution on the Question of the Organization of the Party", (黨的組織問題議決案 Tang ti tsu-chih wen-t'i i-chüeh-an), adopted by the August 7 Conference, *Central Correspondence*, No. 2, August 23, 1927.

"Resolution on Some Historical Problems", (關於若干歷史問題的決議 Kuan-yü jo-kan li-shih wen-t'i ti chüeh-i), adopted by the Seventh Enlarged Plenary Session of the CCP Sixth Central Committee, April 20, 1945; reprinted in Tso-liang Hsiao, *Power Relations Within the Chinese Communist Movement 1930-1934*, Vol. II, *The Chinese Documents*, pp. 786-803, Seattle and London, University of Washington Press, 1967.

Roy, M. N., "For a Better Understanding of the National Movements in Colonial and Semi-colonial Countries", a statement at the Fifth Comintern Congress, June 1, 1924, as printed in Eudin and North, pp. 328-330.

............................, "Imperialism and Counterrevolution in China", printed in *International Press Correspondence*, Vol. 7, No. 72, December 22, 1927.

............................, "The National Revolution and Socialism", a speech at the CCP Fifth Congress, as printed in *M. N. Roy's Mission to China*, pp. 231-33.

............................, "Revolution and Counterrevolution in China", printed in *International Press Correspondence*, Vol. 7, No. 42, July 21, 1927, p. 926; *Guide Weekly*, No. 127, June 8, 1927, pp. 2155-2157; *M. N. Roy's Mission to China*, pp. 310-313.

............................, *Revolution and Counterrevolution in China*, Calcutta, Renaissance Publishers, 1946.

............................, "Supplementary Theses on the National and Colonial Questions", submitted to the Second Comintern Congress held in July-August 1920, reproduced in *Blueprint for World Conquest*, as outlined by the Communist International, Washington, Chicago, Human Events, Inc., 1946, pp. 126-131.

M. N. Roy's Memoirs, Bombay, Allied Publishers Private Ltd., 1964.

Safarov, "The Interrelation Between the National Revolutionary Movement and the Revolutionary Proletarian Movement", a statement at the Tenth Session of the First Congress of the Toilers of the Far East, January 27, 1922, as printed in Eudin and North, pp. 227-228.

Schram, Sturat R., "On the Nature of Mao Tse-tung's 'Deviation' in 1927", printed in *China Quarterly*, No. 18, April-June 1964.

............................, *The Political Thought of Mao Tse-tung*, New York, Washington, London, Frederick A. Praeger, Inc., 1963, fifth printing, 1967.

"Second Congress of the Communist International, The" as Reported and Interpreted by the Official Newspapers of Soviet Russia, Petrograd-Moscow, July 19-August 7, 1920, Washington, Government Printing Office, 1920.

"Significance and Lessons of the Canton Uprising, The" (廣州暴動之意義與敎訓 Kuang-chou pao-tung chih i-i yü chiao-hsün), a resolution adopted by the Central Politburo, January 3, 1928, printed as an appendix to Ch'ü Ch'iu-pai, *The Chinese Revolution and the Communist Party*, 1928.

Snow, Edgar, *Red Star Over China*, copyright, 1938, 1944, by Random House, Inc.; First Black Cat Edition, New York, Grover Press, Inc., 1961.

"Soviet Administration's Message to the People", December 11, 1927, available in *Huston Report* as enclosure No. 2.

Stalin, Joseph, "Concerning the National Question in Yugoslavia", Stalin's *Works*, VII, Moscow, Foreign Languages Publishing House, 1954, pp. 69-76.

............................, "The International Situation", a speech before the Soviet C.P., August 1, 1927, printed in *Communist International*, October 15, 1927, and in extract form in Stalin, *Marxism and the National and Colonial Question*, New York, International Publishers, n. d.; and in Eudin and North, *Soviet Russia and the East 1920-1927*, pp. 377-380.

..............................., *Marxism and the National and Colonial Question*, New York, International Publishers, n. d., an English translation from a Russian edition of 1934.

..............................., "The Prospects of the Revolution in China", a speech delivered at the Chinese Commission of the Seventh Plenum of the ECCI, November 30, 1926, Stalin's *Works*, IX, pp. 373-391; *International Press Correspondence*, Vol. 6, No. 90, December 23, 1926, pp. 1581-1584; Eudin and North, pp. 350-356.

..............................., "Questions of the Chinese Revolution: Theses for Propagandists, Approved by the CC, CPSU (B)", Stalin's *Works*, IX, pp. 224-234.

..............................., "The Revolution in China and the Tasks of the Comintern", a speech delivered at the Tenth Sitting of the Eighth Plenum of the ECCI, May 24, 1927, Stalin's *Works*, IX, pp. 288-318; cf. Eduin and North, p. 369.

..............................., "Talk With Students of the Sun Yat-sen University", May 13, 1927, Stalin's *Works*, IX, pp. 243-273.

T'an P'ing-shan and Su Chao-cheng (譚平山蘇兆徵), "Letter of Resignation", (辭職書 Tz'u-chih-shu), dated July 1927, printed in *Guide Weekly*, No. 201, July 18, 1927, pp. 2219-2221.

"Theses of the Fourth Congress of the Communist International on the Eastern Problem", adopted in November-December 1922, reproduced in Xenia J. Eudin and Robert C. North, *Soviet Russia and the East 1920-1927*, pp. 231-237.

"Theses on the Peasant Question", adopted by the Enlarged ECCI Meeting, April 1925, *International Press Correspondence*, Vol. 5, No. 47, June 4, 1925.

"Theses on the Trade Union Movement in the Colonial and Semi-colonial Countries", adopted by the Sixth Enlarged Session of the ECCI, February 17—March 15, 1926, as printed in Eudin and North, p. 325.

T'ieh Hsin (鐵心), "Mao Tse-tung Became a Bandit in Chingkangshan", (毛澤東落草井崗山 Mao-tse-tung lo-ts'ao ching-kang-shan), printed in *Modern Historical Materials*, (現代史料 hsien-tai shih-liao), Vol. 3, pp. 232-253.

Trotsky, Leon, *Problems of the Chinese Revolution*, New York, Pioneer Publishers, 1932, 2nd edition 1962.

..............................., *The Stalin School of Falsification*, New York, Pioneer Publishers, 1937.

Ts'ai Ho-sen (蔡和森), "A History of Opportunism", (機會主義史 Chi-hui chu-i shih), September 1927, printed in Li Min-hun (黎民魂), *Red Archives*, (赤色檔案 Ch'ih-se tang-an), July 1928.

Vanguard, (前鋒 Chien-feng), a monthly magazine, No. 1, July 1, 1923.

Wang Chien-min (王健民), *Draft History of the Chinese Communist Party*, (中國共產黨史稿 Chung-kuo Kung-Ch'an-tang Shih-Kao), 3 vols., Taipei, Taiwan, 1965.

Wang Ching-wei (汪精衛), "The Story of the Expulsion of the Communists at Wuhan", (武漢分共之經過 Wu-han fen-kung chih ching-kuo), November 5, 1927, printed in Wang's *Selected Works*, Vol. 3, edited by Hsun Ju, Shanghai, Kuangming Bookstore, 1927.

Wang Shih, Wang Ch'iao, Ma Ch'i-ping and Chang Ling (王實，王翹，馬奇兵，章凌), *A Brief History of the Chinese Communist Party*, (中國共產黨歷史簡編 Chung-kuo kung-ch'an-tang li-shih chien-pien), Shanghai, People's Publishing House, 1958.

Wei To (維它) [瞿秋白], "The Canton Uprising and the Chinese Revolution", (廣州暴動與中國革命 Kuang-chou pao-tung yü chung-kuo ko-ming), October 1, 1928, printed in *The Canton Commune*, pp. 15-35.

Whiting, Allen S., *Soviet Policies in China 1917-1924*, New York, Columbia University Press, first pnblirhed 1954, second printing, 1957.

Wilbur, C. Martin, "The Ashes of Defeat", printed in *China Quarterly*, April-June 1964.

Wilbur, C. Martin and Julie Lien-ying How, *Documents on Communism, Nationalism, and Soviet Advisers in China 1918-1927*, New York, Columbia University Press, 1956.

Wittfogel, Karl, *A Short History of Chinese Communism*, an unpublished manuscript, on file in the Far Eastern and Russian Institute of the University of Washington, 1956.

Yang, Li-san (楊立三), "The Garrison Regiment at the Time of the 'August 1' Revolt", (「八一」起義時的警衛團 Pai-i ch'i-i shih ti ching-wei t'uan), printed in *Reminiscences About the Struggle in the Chingkangshan Area*, (回憶井崗山區的鬥爭 Hui-i ching-kang-shan ch'ü ti tou-cheng), Peking, Workers' Publishing House, 1956, pp. 1-3.

"Yangtse Bureau's Recent Political Resolution", (長江局最近政治決議案 Chang-chiang-chü tsui-chin cheng-ch'ih chüeh-i-an), October 29, [1927], *Central Political Correspondence*, No. 20, April 12, 1928.

"Yeh T'ing's Report on the Canton Insurrection", as cited in M. N. Roy, *Revolution and Counterrevolution in China*, Calcutta, Renaissance Publishers, 1946, p. 558.

Ypsilon, *Pattern for World Revolutions*, Chicago, New York, Ziff-Davis, 1947.

GLOSSARY

Anhua 安化
Anyüan 安源
August 7 (Emergency) Conference 八七 (緊急)會議
Autumn Harvest Insurrection (Uprising) 秋收暴動

Bolshevik 布爾塞(什)維克
Bourgeois-democratic revolution 資產階級民主革命
Bureau of Public Safety 公安局

Canton Commune 廣州公社
Canton Soviet 廣州蘇維埃
CCP Politburo 中共政治局
Central Committee 中央委員會，中委
Central Executive Committee 中央執行委員會
Central Standing Committee 中常委
Chaching 渣津
Chang Chao-feng 張兆豐
Chang Fa-k'uei 張發奎
Chang Kuo-t'ao 張國燾
Changhsu 樟樹
Chang T'ai-lei 張太雷
Changte 常德
Chatzukong 甲子港
Ch'en Ch'iao-nien 陳喬年
Chenchou 郴州
Ch'en Tu-hsiu 陳獨秀
Ch'en Yi 陳毅
Ch'en Yü 陳郁
Chiangling 江陵
Chiayü 嘉魚
Chiehyang 揭陽
Chikung 紀功(俄人)
Chinese Communist Party, CCP 中國共產黨
Chinese Revolutionary Committee 中國革命委員會
Chingkangshan 井岡山
Chinhsien 進賢

Ch'iu Kuo-hsien 邱國鮮(邱國軒)
Chou En-lai 周恩來
Chou I-ch'ün 周逸群
Chou Shih-ti 周士第
Chou Wen-yung 周文雍
Ch'ü Ch'iu-pai 瞿秋白
Chuchou 株州
Chunghopu 中伙鋪
Chung Wen-chao 鍾文釗
Chungyang 崇陽
Chu Teh 朱德
Communist Youth International 少共國際
Communist Youth League, CY 共產主義青年團，少共

Democratic United Front 民主聯合陣線

East River 東江
Eleventh Army 第十一軍

Fan Chung-hsiu 樊鐘秀
Fanck 范克(俄人)
Fang Cheng-wu 方振武
Fenghsin 奉新
First Division of the First Army of the Chinese Workers' and Peasants' Revolutionary Army 中國工農革命軍第一軍第一師
Fourth Army 第四軍
Front Committee 前敵委員會，前委
Fuchou 撫州

Hai-feng 海豐
Hai-lu-feng 海陸豐
Hainan 海南
Hankow 漢口
Han Kuang-han 韓光漢
Hanshou 漢壽
Hengshan 衡山
Hengyang 衡陽

Ho Ch'ang 賀昌
Ho Lai 何來
Ho Lung 賀龍
Honan 河南
Hoshengchiao 賀勝橋
Hsia Ming-han 夏明翰
Hsiang Chung-fa 向忠發
Hsianghsiang 湘鄉
Hsiangtan 湘潭
Hsiangyang 襄陽
Hsiangying 湘陰
Hsiang Ying 項英
Hsienning 咸寧
Hsikeng 西坑
Hsingning 興寧
Hsinti 新堤
Hsintien 新店
Hsiushui 修水
Hsu Kuang-ying 徐光英
Hsunwu 尋鄔
Hua Kang 華崗
Huang P'ing 黃平
Huang Wu-i 黃五一
Huayung 華容
Huichang 會昌
Huichow 惠州
Hunan Provincial Committee 湖南省委
Hunan Report 湖南農民運動考察報告
Hupeh Provincial Committee 湖北省委

I-chang 宜昌
I Li-yung 易禮容
Independent Regiment 獨立團
Independent situation 獨立局面
Insurrection Plan for Hunan and Hupeh 兩湖暴動計劃
I-yang 益陽

Jen Hsu 任旭
Jen Pi-shih 任弼時
Jucheng 汝城
Juichin 瑞金

Kanchow 贛州
Keep Time-ism 合拍主義
Kian 吉安
Kiukiang 九江

Kungan 公安
Kuo Liang 郭亮
Kwangtung Provincial Committee 廣東省委

Li Chi-shen 李濟琛
Li Fu 立夫
Liling 醴陵
Li Li-san 李立三
Linchuan 臨川
Lin Piao 林彪
Lin Yu-nan 林育南
Liu Ch'ang-chun 劉昌羣
Liu Pu-i 劉步一
Liusha 流沙
Liuyang 瀏陽
Li Wei-han 李維漢
Local independent areas 割據局面
Lo I-nung 羅亦農
Lo Jung-huan 羅榮桓
Lominadze 羅明納茲
Lu Ch'en 陸沈
Luchikou 陸溪口
Lu Fu-yuan 盧福垣
Luiyang 耒陽
Lushan 廬山
Lu Te-ming 盧德明

Ma Ke-fu 馬克夫(俄人)
Meihsien 梅縣
Mienyang 沔陽
mow 畝

Nanchang revolt (uprising) 南昌暴動
Nanhsien 南縣
Ninghsiang 寧鄉
Ninth Army 第九軍
Northern Hupeh Special Committee 鄂北特委
November Politburo Enlarged Session 十一月政治局擴大會議

Paisha 白沙
Paoching 寶慶(邵陽)
P'eng Kung-ta 彭公達
P'eng P'ai 彭湃
P'eng Shuh-chih 彭述之

Pingchiang 平江
Pingchiang-Liuyang Self-defense Corps 平瀏自衛隊
Pinghsiang-Liling Self-defense Corps 萍瀏自衛隊
Political Security Bureau 政治保衛局
Provisional Central Politburo 臨時中央政治局
Puchi 蒲圻

Red Army 紅軍
Red Spears 紅槍會
Revolutionary Committee of China 中國革命委員會
Revolutionary Military Council 革命軍事委員會

Sanhopa 三河壩
Second Front Army 第二方面軍
Second Guard Regiment 第二警衛團
Shanghang 上坑
Shanpo 山坡
Shihshou 石首
Socialist revolution 社會主義革命
South Bureau 南方局
Southern Hupeh Special Committee 鄂南特委
Special Committee 特委
Standing Committee 常委
Su Chao-cheng 蘇兆徵
Su Hsien-chün 蘇仙俊
Swatow 汕頭

Tangkeng 湯坑
T'ang Sheng-chih 唐生智
T'an P'ing-shan 譚平山
Taoyuan 桃源
Teng Chung-hsia 鄧中夏

Tingchow 汀州
Tingszuchiao 汀泗橋
Ts'ai Ho-sen 蔡和森
Ts'ai T'ing-k'ai 蔡廷楷
Ts'ao Hsiang-hua 曹祥華
Tsaoyang 棗陽
Tungcheng 通城
Tungku 銅鼓
Tungshan 通山
Tutitang 土地堂
Twentieth Army 第二十軍

Wang Ching-wei 汪精衛
Wang Tse-chiai 汪澤楷
Wenchiashih 文家市
Whampoa Military Academy 黃埔軍官學校
Worker-Peasant Red Army 工農紅軍
Wuhu 蕪湖
Wuhua 五華

Yanglouszu 羊樓司
Yang Shen 楊森
Yangtse Bureau 長江局
Yang Yin 楊殷
Yeh Chien-ying 葉劍英
Yeh T'ing 葉梃
Yenan 延安
Yuanling 沅陵
Yuehyang (Yuehchou) 岳陽(岳州)
Yü Fen-nin 余賁民
Yu-I Street 友益街
Yü Mou-huai 余茂懷
Yunghsing 永新
Yung Tai-ying 惲代英
Yü Shai-tu 余洒度

INDEX

Agrarian revolution: and autumn harvest insurrection, 44; and the national revolution, 20, 21-22, 23, 31, 151; Comintern policy on, 12-15, 21, 23, 25, 28-29, 163, 165; CY views on, 32; interpreted by Borodin, 30; opposed by Trotsky, 162;, *Pravda* on, 97; resisted by Ch'en Tu-hsiu, 30, 31, 33, 36; started by August 7 Conference, 39

Agricultural proletariat, 17, 19

Anyüan, 70, 71

Armed insurrection: adopted as party line by August 7 Conference, 39; after Canton rising, 143, 155; principles of, 27, 46, 109-114

August 7 (1927) Conference: changed party leadership, 40-42; on nature of Chinese revolution, 43-45, 163; sponsored by Comintern, 39; started agrarian revolution, 39

Autumn harvest insurrection: as Kremlin-inspired agrarian revolution, 44; decided prior to August 7 Conference, 44; led by Mao in Hunan, 46-53, 58, 59, 60, 61, 68-79, 164; started in Hupeh, 62-67, 79-80

Base areas: 110, 111, 112, 119, 128, 130, 162, 165; also known as local independent areas, 115, 127; and independent situation, 56, 62, 66

Borodin, Michael: conflicted with Roy, 30; favored surrender of Wuhan labor pickets, 34; left for Moscow, 35, 36; resisted agrarian revolution, 30

Bourgeois-democratic revolution: and CCP Second Congress, 12; and national-revolutionary movement, 3-4; as basis of Mao's *Hunan Report*, 22; as feature of revolution in colonial and semi-colonial countries, 157-60; basic in Lenin's theory, 8-9, 162; equivalent to Mao's 'New Democracy', 160; in the Ninth ECCI Plenum, 150-52; viewed by Stalin, 16-17

Bourgeoisie, 1, 2, 3, 5, 6, 9, 11, 15, 17, 107, 109, 159, 162

Bukharin, 33, 39, 146

Cadet regiment, 137, 138

Canton Commune, 135-156, 161

Chaching, 70

Chang Chao-feng, 56, 64, 77, 79

Chang Fa-k'uei: 59, 85-87; and Li Chi-shen, 135-7, 147

Chang Kuo-t'ao: agreed to launching Nanchang revolt, 87; approaching Lominadze, 84; delivered Comintern telegram to Nanchang, 85; disclosed Communist ignorance of making a land revolution, 47; endorsed Nanchang revolt, 83; on First Congress of Toilers of Far East, 11; removed from party leadership, 103; reported to Politburo, 101; told to leave Swatow for Shanghai, 95

Changsha coup of 21 May 1927, 32, 42

Chang T'ai-lei, 35, 40, 95, 97, 102, 105, 136, 137, 139

Ch'en Ch'iao-nien, 105, 125, 128, 129

Ch'en Tu-hsiu: challenged Comintern, 33, 34; downfall of, 29, 35; favored liberal democracy, 31; heard of Canton rising, 138; on Mao's urban orientation, 59; on origin of democratic revolution in China, 10; on peasant problem, 13-14; opposed agrarian revolution, 30, 158; opposed armed insurrection, 114; versus Ch'ü Ch'iu-pai, 41, 102; versus Mao, 32

Ch'en Yi, 98

Ch'en Yü, 139

Chingkangshan, 52, 66, 77

Ch'iu Kou-hsien, 69

Chou En-lai: advised by Lominadze to mobilize masses, 84; advocated establishing base in eastern Kwangtung, 83; as member of five-man Politburo, 35; as secretary of Front Committee, 83; endorsed Nanchang revolt, 82, 164; endorsed surrender of labor pickets in Wuhan, 34, 42; escaping to Hong Kong, 98; expected Comintern aid, 83, 84; led staff corps in Nanchang, 88; ordered raising of soviet flag, 98; put back to Politburo, 105

Chou I-ch'ün, 86

Chou Shih-ti, 81, 87

Chou Wen-yung, 139

Ch'ü Ch'iu-pai: advocated radical agrarian program, 31; agreed with Galen, 82; became party leader, 41; disclosed insurrection plan for Kwangtung, 135; formulated insurrectionary strategy and tactics, 162; in August 7 Conference, 40; joined CCP, 41; learned of Lominadze's arrival, 35; on insurrectionary strategy, 109-11, 161-2; on Mao's insurrectionary tactics, 77; on nature of Chinese revolution, 107, 149; on situation in Wuhan, 30; on urban insurrection, 112, 113, 114

Chuchou, 71, 72

Chung Wen-chao, 69

Chu Teh, 94, 98

Communist International (Comintern): and Canton rising, 145-7, 153-5; and Nanchang revolt, 85-86, 102; conflicted with Ch'en Tu-hsiu, 15, 33-37; Eighth ECCI Plenum and China, 17, 23-26, 27, 28, 42, 43-44, 46, 97; initiated Chinese agrarian revolution, 12-13, 14-15, 18, 25, 28-30, 33; Ninth ECCI Plenum and China, 149, 150, 152, 157; ordered convocation of August 7 Conference, 39; possible aid expected by Nanchang rebels, 83; revolutionary program for the East, 1, 4, 5, 157-9; Seventh ECCI Plenum program for China, 20, 22; stood for KMT-CCP alliance, 15, 16

Communist Youth International, 35, 85 117

Communist Youth League, 32, 40, 115

Comrade Jen, 74

Comrade Li Fu, 109

Comrade Ma, 71-79

Comrade Reuberg: alias Reyberg, 153

Democratic revolution, 8-12, 17, 18, 24, 31, 43, 51, 97, 107, 151. See also Bourgeois-democratic revolution

Democratic United Front, 9, 11-12, 163

East River, 83, 84, 85

Economic confiscation, 23, 112-4

Eight-hour working day, 11, 24, 43, 78, 92, 108, 140, 149, 158

Eleventh Army, 94. See also Yeh T'ing

Encircling city with countryside, 59, 74, 109, 147, 165

Fan Chung-hsiu, 64, 79

Federation of Peasant Unions, 32

Fanck, 85

Fifth Congress of CCP, 14, 25, 30, 32, 163

First Congress of CCP, 11, 18, 163, 164

First Congress of Toilers of the Far East, 10

First Division of the First Army of the Chinese Workers' and Peasants' Revolutionary Army, 69

Fourth Army, 81, 82. See also Chang Fa-k'uei

Front Committee, 83, 86, 87, 89, 92, 102-3

Galen, Vassili Blücher, 82, 85, 86

General Labour Union of Hupeh, 41

Guerrilla Tactics: adopted first in Hupeh, 62, 110, 161; advocated by Pravda, 96, 110, 161; based on masses, 110; became main method of struggle, 110, 161; became party line, 110; explained by Ch'ü Ch'iu-pai, 110-1, 112, 161-62; learned by Mao, 165; led to base areas, 111; proposed for Hupeh, 115, 118-9, 129, 130

Hai-lu-feng, 19, 83, 97, 100, 136

Hankow, 35, 83, 84, 118

Han Kuang-han, 120

Hassis, 144

Hengyang, 50, 51, 55, 68

Ho Ch'ang, 121, 126

Ho lai, 139

Ho Lung, 83-84, 87, 90-91, 94, 98

Hsia Ming-han, 79

Hsiang Chung-fa, 40

Hsiangyang, 64

Hsiang Ying, 40

Hsienning, 66, 67

Hsikeng, 67

Hsintien, 67

Hsiushui, 69, 70

Hsü Kuang-ying, 104, 139

Hua Kang, 74

Huang P'ing, 139, 142

Huang Wui-i, 125

Huichow, 100

Hunan Provincial Committee, 32, 42, 46, 47, 48, 51, 53, 68, 69, 71, 72, 73, 74, 76, 78

Hunan Report, 22, 23, 60, 164

Hupeh Provincial Committee, 47, 64, 65, 115, 116, 121, 131, 132, 133

Huston, J. C., 144

I Li-yung, 79

Imperialism, 2, 5, 9, 11, 16, 24, 26, 66, 115, 127, 148, 149, 160

Independent situation, see Base areas

Insurrection Plan for Hunan and Hupeh, 54-62, 65, 68, 74, 78, 99, 110, 111, 161

Insurrection in Southern Hupeh, 65-67, 72, 77-78, 79-80

Jen Hsu, 105, 125

Jen Pi-shih, 40. *See also* Comrade Jen

Juichin, 91, 92, 94, 103

Keep Time-ism, 77

Kiukiang, 40, 68, 82, 83, 84, 86

KMT Peasant Movement Training Institute, 18

Kuo Liang, 121, 125

Kwangtung Provincial Committee, 46, 104, 135-7, 139, 141, 142

Labor union, 41, 116, 119, 143

Land revolution, see Agrarian revolution

Lenin, 2-9, 18, 22, 149, 157, 164

Li Chi-shen, 135, 136, 147

Liling, 70, 71

Li Li-san, 35, 40, 82, 83, 86, 89, 98, 105, 164

Lin Piao, 98

L'Insurrection Armée, 154

Lin Yu-nan, 125

Liu Ch'ang-chun, 105, 115, 117, 120, 125, 132

Liu Pu-i, 67

Liusha, 98

Liuyang, 55, 70, 71, 76

Li Wei-han, 35, 40, 85, 105

Lo I-nung, 40, 58, 116, 117, 120, 121, 122, 126, 127, 128, 129, 131, 132, 163

Lo Jung-huan, 76

Lominadze: arrived in Hankow, 35; asked instructions regarding Nanchang revolt, 84, 85; confessed at Ninth ECCI Plenum, 150, 151; debated with Mif, 148-9; favored post-Canton insurrection, 143, 149; on Nanchang revolt, 84, 86, 101; on revolution in Kwangtung, 145-6; opposed uprisings in Shanghai and Hankow, 117, 118; present at August 7 Conference and November session of Politburo, 39, 105, 145; responsible for Insurrection Plan for Hunan and Hupeh, 53, 161

Lu Ch'en, 64

Lu Fu-yuan, 40

Lu Te-ming, 68, 69, 70

Manuilsky, D.Z., 5

Mao Tse-tung: accepted priority of peasants over troops, 60; admitted poor discipline of his troops, 70; advocated military attack on Changsha, 48, 58, 77, 160, 161; against fighting from countryside to city, 58, 74; a summing-up of revolutionary experience of, 164-5; at August 7 Conference, 40; attended First and Third CCP Congresses, 9-10, 13; branded as 'Keep Time-ism', 77; captured by KMT militia, 76; classified proletariat, 19; considered industrial proletariat as main revolutionary force, 17, 164; defined land confiscation, 23; directed insurrection in eastern Hunan, 76; disagreed with Yü Shai-tu, 76-77; dismissed from Politburo, 79; favored political confiscation, 23; followed radical peasant policy in Hunan, 47; formulated insurrection plan for Hunan, 48; influenced by Stalin's idea on peasants, 19-20; interested primarily in city, 59; joined by Chu Teh in Chingkangshan, 98; learned encircling city with countryside, 59; lessoned by party leadership, 53; looked down upon workers and peasants, 18; no experience in land struggle before winter of 1927, 47, 48; not interested in peasants until 1925, 18; not of peasant origin, 18; on land problem, 49, 52; on question of soviets, 49; proposed assignment to Szechuan, 47; published his first article on peasants, 19; regarded China as reaching her 1917, 49, 59; regarded poor peasants as revolutionary vanguard, 22; restrained peasant movement, 32-33; retreating to Chingkangshan, 66, 77; sent to launch autumn harvest uprising in Hunan, 46, 48; supported bourgeoisie, 13; underestimated peasant strength, 13, 164; wrote *Hunan Report*, 22-23, 60

Masses, 15, 50, 51, 53, 59, 64, 65, 79, 80, 110, 111, 112, 113, 138, 140, 141, 152, 154, 161, 162, 164

Mif, Pavel: attacked Ch'en Tu-hsiu leadership, 12, 13, 14, 31, 33, 36; criticized CY, 134; debated with Lominadze, 148-9

National bourgeoisie: as temporary ally, 4, 5, 9; deserted revolution, 23, 24, 148, 149, 158; led national liberation movement, 2, 3; not originally included in democratic united front, 12; not subject to expropriation, 43; supported by Comintern, 1, 3, 4

National liberation movement, 2, 3, 4, 5, 9, 10, 19, 20, 21, 22, 102, 157, 158, 159
National Peasant Union, 32, 42
Neuberg, A., see Neumann
Neumann, Heinz, 138, 142, 146, 147, 152, 153, 154
Ninth Army, 92. See also Chu Teh
Ninth Plenum of ECCI, 148, 149, 150, 151, 152, 156, 157
Northern Hupeh Special Committee, 64, 79

Owner-peasant, 49, 50, 52

Paisha, 70
Peasants' soviets, 6, 10, 97
P'eng Kung-ta, 40, 68, 73, 78, 79
P'eng P'ai, 86, 97
P'eng Shuh-chih, 41
Permanent revolution, 43, 106, 148, 149, 150, 151
Pingchiang, 70, 71, 76
Pinghsiang, 70, 71, 72
'Play' with insurrection, 27, 46, 77, 116, 147, 150
Political confiscation, 23, 113
Pravda: on China policy shift, 95-97; on guerrilla tactics, 110, 161; on Nanchang revolt, 87-88; on soviets, 52
Proletarian dictatorship, 17, 18, 107, 108, 158
Proletarian leadership, 16, 17, 40
Proposed Changsha rising, 72, 73, 74
Puchi, 66-67, 78, 79
Putschism, 129, 143-4, 149, 150, 153, 155

Radek, Karl, 15
Red guard, 137-9, 142, 143
Red Spears, 64
Reuberg, 153, 154
Revolutionary Committee of China, 54
Revolutionary Military Council, 136, 139
Reyberg, see Reuberg
Roy, M.N.: and Wuhan regime, 30; attacked Ch'en Tu-hsiu leadership, 30; criticized Mao, 32-33; disagreed with Lenin, 3, 7; identified Neumann's report to Comintern, 154; interpreted Chinese revolution, 20-21; left for Moscow, 36; versus Borodin, 29-30, 163; versus Lominadze, 163

Safarov, 10
Second Congress of CCP, 10, 12, 163
Second Guard Regiment, 65
Seventh Plenum of ECCI, 20, 21, 22, 158
Sixth Plenum of ECCI, 16, 20, 21, 22
Snow, Edgar, 32, 45n, 49n, 70, 76
Socialist revolution: and permanent revolution, 149; and soviets, 108; and urban insurrection, 162, 163; as a stage following bourgeois-democratic revolution, 8, 11, 16, 17, 20, 24, 97, 107, 149, 157, 160; as distinct from bourgeois-democratic revolution, 158; not intended for national liberation movement, 9; not meant for semi-colonial China, 107, 157, 160; preferred by CCP, 10, 163; preferred by Mao, 51, 164
South Bureau, 104
Southern Hupeh Special Committee, 65-68
Soviets: advocated by Comintern, 51-52; advocated by Pravda, 96, 97; as understood by Mao, 49, 51; as viewed by Lenin, 5, 6, 7; as viewed by Roy, 7; created at Canton, 137, 139, 140, 142, 143, 153; defined by CCP Politburo, 108-9; existed in Kwangtung, 145; interpreted by Ch'ü Ch'iu-pai leadership, 50; proposed for Wuhan, 115, 116; suggested by Eighth ECCI Plenum, 97
Special China Conference of Ninth ECCI Plenum, 148-9
Stalin: alleged telegram on Canton rising, 147; at variance with Trotsky, 162; divided bourgeoisie into two kinds, 9; emphasized importance of peasants, 18, 159; failed in utilizing KMT, 29; invented strategy of fighting from countryside to city, 26, 27, 160; not implicated by Trotsky in Canton rising, 148; on Lenin's views of bourgeois-democratic revolution, 8; pointed out two paths for China, 16-17; suggested three stages of Chinese revolution, 20
Su Chao-cheng, 40, 105, 121, 123, 139
Su Hsien-chün, 69
Swatow debacle, 83, 92, 97, 98, 100, 146, 147
T'ang Sheng-chih, 114, 115, 116, 119
T'an P'ing-shan, 41, 82, 83, 84, 88, 89, 95, 98, 103
Teng Chung-hsia, 40, 100, 135, 137, 146

Trotsky: attacked Stalin leadership, 148, 153, 155, 162; opposed cooperation with KMT, 15; went along with Zinoviev, 26, 27, 148, 160
Ts'ai Ho-sen, 40, 42
Ts'ai T'ing-k'ai, 91, 94, 103
Tsao Hsiang-hua, 125
Tungku, 70, 76
Twentieth Army, 83, 94. *See also* Ho Lung

Urban insurrection, 111-3, 123, 160, 162
Urban policy: in the East, 6; in Hunan and Hupeh, 56-59, 60, 113-4; and Nanchang rebels, 88

Valcooloff, 144

Wang Ching-wei, 33, 137
Wang Hsin-ya, 69

Wang Tse-chiai, 125
Wenchiashih, 76, 77

Yang Yin, 139

Yeh Chien-ying, 137

Yeh T'ing: commented on Canton rising, 141-2; fled to Hong Kong, 98; and the Fourth Army, 81; left Nanchang, 90

Ypsilon, 147
Yü Fen-min, 69
Yu-I Street, 119, 120, 125
Yu Mou-huai, 125
Yü Shai-tu, 68, 69, 70, 76, 77
Yung Tai-ying, 86

Zinoviev, 26, 27, 31, 148, 160

INDEX

Tisdale, attacked India, depredation, 199, 157, 158, 112; depredation compared with Gizeh, 115; reflections with Zunyi, 89, 93, 118, 119.

T'ai-Ho, 96, 98, 12.

Peking, 94-95, 94, 102.

Pico Hieronymo, 115.

Tungu, 39.

Tungsten Ssu, 53, 79, 107 and Haslberry.

Titan, suspension, 111, 112, 114, 199, 167.

Tsin, rebellion in Shen to to, 86-89; and Hupeh, 89-90, 64; alliance and the River rebels, 88.

Vanguard, 135.

Wang Chang-shu, 71, 112.

Wang Hsin, 1, 164.

Wang Tao-min, 155.
Wei-hsiang-Ts. 77.

Yang Sin, 155.

Yeh Ch'ien-sun, 117.

Yü, T'ung attacked on Canton city, 141; fled to Hong Kong, 98, 98, 118; found Sun-tsu, 97, 89, Nanking, 38.

Yüan, Hsi, 95, Feng-ming, 80.

Yü Sheng, 119, 160, 125, 155.
Yü Sheng-tu, 89.

Yung Tzu-niu, 155.

Yün, Tai-ming, 140.

Zhdanov, K., 42, 53, 81, 144, 160.